READING DUNCAN READING

CONTEMPORARY NORTH AMERICAN POETRY SERIES

Series Editors Alan Golding, Lynn Keller, and Adalaide Morris

READING
Robert Duncan and the Poetics of Derivation
DUNCAN
edited by Stephen Collis and Graham Lyons
READING

UNIVERSITY OF IOWA PRESS | IOWA CITY

University of Iowa Press, Iowa City 52242

www.uiowapress.org
Printed in the United States of America

Design by April Leidig

The University of Iowa Press is a member of Green Press Initiative and is committed to preserving natural resources.

Printed on acid-free paper

Library of Congress Cataloging-in-Publication Data
Reading Duncan reading: Robert Duncan and the poetics of derivation / edited by Stephen Collis and Graham Lyons.
p. cm—(Contemporary North American poetry series)
Includes bibliographical references and index.
ISBNS 978-1-60938-116-5, 1-60938-116-5 (pbk)
ISBNS 978-1-60938-134-9, 1-60938-134-3 (ebook)
1. Duncan, Robert, 1919–1988—Criticism and interpretation.
I. Collis, Stephen, 1965– II. Lyons, Graham.
PS3507.U629Z848 2012
811'.54—dc23 2012006954

CONTENTS

Permissions ix

INTRODUCTION | STEPHEN COLLIS
The Poetics of Derivation
xi

PART ONE | DUNCAN READING

ONE | SARAH E. EHLERS
Robert Duncan's Miltonic Persuasion:
The Emergence of a Radical Poetic
3

TWO | GEORGE FRAGOPOULOS
Robert Duncan's Derivative Poetics:
Community, the Metaphysicals, and the Nature of War
25

THREE | SIOBHÁN SCARRY
Textual Poetics and the Politics of Reading
in Duncan's "Night Scenes"
45

FOUR | JEFFREY TWITCHELL-WAAS
The Airs of Duncan and Zukofsky
67

FIVE | GRAHAM LYONS
Is the Queendom Enough (without the Queen)?
Poetic Abdication in Robert Duncan and Laura Riding
89

SIX | CLÉMENT OUDART
Reading A/Drift:
Robert Duncan's Use of Foreign Words
107

PART TWO | READING DUNCAN

SEVEN | ROSS HAIR
Derivation or Stealth? Quotation in the Poetry
of Robert Duncan and Ronald Johnson
129

EIGHT | STEPHEN FREDMAN
Symposium of the Whole:
Jerome Rothenberg and the Dream
of "A Poetry of All Poetries"
151

NINE | CATHERINE MARTIN
How the Dead Prey upon Us:
Robert Duncan and Susan Howe
173

TEN | ANDY WEAVER
Divining the Derivers:
Anarchism and the Practice of Derivative Poetics
in Robert Duncan and John Cage
189

ELEVEN | J. P. CRAIG
The Poets' War:
Inflation, Complicity, and the Daimonic
211

TWELVE | PETER O'LEARY
Talking Cosmos:
Robert Duncan and Ronald Johnson
231

Bibliography 253

Contributors 265

Index 267

PERMISSIONS

Material from Robert Duncan's notebooks is copyright © by the Jess Collins Trust and reproduced by permission.

Unpublished material from Ronald Johnson's papers is used here by permission of the Ronald Johnson Literary Estate and the Special Collections, Kenneth Spencer Research Library, University of Kansas Libraries.

All materials by Louis Zukofsky are copyright © Paul Zukofsky and are used here by permission and cannot be reproduced in any manner without the explicit permission of the copyright holder.

An earlier version of Stephen Fredman's essay appeared in *Contextual Practice: Assemblage and the Erotic in Postwar Poetry and Art* (Stanford, CA: Stanford University Press, 2010).

An earlier version of Andy Weaver's essay appeared in *Jacket* 40 (late 2010), http://jacketmagazine.com/40/weaver-duncan-cage.shtml.

INTRODUCTION

The Poetics of Derivation

STEPHEN COLLIS

To begin with the sorts of claims about Duncan's originality or unique contribution that might typically form the foundations of a new collection of essays on a single and in some senses neglected author would be entirely out of place and character here. It is not a question of Duncan's meeting or failing to meet our conventional notions of the artist-genius but, rather, that his work is built around the central *refusal* of genius and originality as such, taking on instead the mantle of "derivative" poet. When Duncan writes, "what I thought slavishly derivative proved to be 'mine,'" he is embracing, not excusing, the status of the derivative—and realizing that "mine" is a category needing considerable qualification, if it is taken to exist as such at all.[1] Statements of this sort proliferate throughout Duncan's oeuvre and are at the core of his readers' understanding of his poetics: "I'm always derivative," he tells George Bowering and Robert Hogg in a 1969 interview. "I derive all my forms, and they come from adoration and falling in love with poets."[2]

Paradoxically, what one winds up arguing for as this poet's *singularity* (if not "uniqueness") is his *plurality*—his "unique" combination of the words of others—the diverse chorus of sources and intertexts he orchestrates into the "chrestomathy" of poem and essay, talk and interview—any instance of his venturing into the field of the word. No other poet has made more out of poetry's self-referentiality and intertextuality than Duncan. No other poet has so openly expressed his admiration for and gratitude toward his predecessors—to the point that Harold Bloom's "anxiety of influence" theory could not be more completely out of place.

In part, much of what is characteristic in Duncan's work derives from his being the sort of poet who *thematizes* poetry itself. In *The Structure of Rime* or *Passages* series Duncan operates at the level of the "master code" of poetry, where "the work of art is itself the field we would render the truth of."[3] A "poetry of all poetries" or "grand collage," Duncan's syncretic poetics is based upon the conviction that "an ideal study of poetry would be concerned with all the kinds of poetries, the ideas men have had of what poetry is, with identifying the species of poetry, varieties of the poem in evolution."[4] Such an evolutionary or "naturalist's" approach to poetry is typical of Duncan—especially, as we shall see, when he is discussing derivation—and whether he is writing a poem or an essay or answering an interviewer's question, Duncan is always at work upon his "ideal study of poetry"—always attempting to descry the "species-being" of his genre.[5]

Duncan's "romantic" tendencies—his embracing of the Shelleyan notion of a "world poem"—have caused some to see his project as in part a bridge built back from modernism to its rejected antecedent, romanticism. This—despite Duncan's own references to himself as "romantic"—is only partially true.[6] The bridge (or *bridges*) Duncan's work fashions via derivation points most importantly back to the postromantic sources of modernism (Whitman and the French symbolists, from Baudelaire to Mallarmé) and to the preromantic (to the Renaissance and the early modern work of Shakespeare and Dante). This collection of essays, while including work on Duncan's modern sources, highlights this pre- and postromantic reach of Duncan's derivation as well as exploring the sort of source Duncan has been to poets who can now be seen to derive in turn from the master-deriver—the bridge his own work forms through the postmodern.

It is the implications of derivation as a field I would like to attempt to render the "truth" of here in this introduction. I will approach derivation along two interwoven paths: as a material condition of the production of poetry and as suggestive of a particular sense of the subject and its relation to language.

WERE WE TO approach Duncan as a "projective" poet—and certainly he noted, on numerous occasions, how Charles Olson's essay "called" him "to order"—then he would be one for whom Olson's first proposition for "composition by field" is most apropos: "(1) the *kinetics* of the thing. A poem is energy transferred from where the poet got it (he will have some several causations), by way of the poem itself to, all the way over to, the reader."[7] Where, one might ask, is the "author" in this transaction? The poem here is a "transference" of "some several causations" where, as it moves "all the way over to the reader," the poet and poem are mere vehicles, mere intermediaries between "source" and "reader." The first step in a "projective" poetics is thus "derivative": a collecting of "some several" sources. And one of the basic implications of a derivative poetics is the peculiar sort of *authorship* it assumes and, thus, the sort of (intellectual) "property" such an author produces. The poet is never single, never individual for Duncan; rather, he or she is "a crowd of one who writes," and the lyric "I" is not "the private property of the writer" but a form "in which all men may participate."[8] Duncan's vision here is characteristically collaborative: poetry is a process poets collaborate (and participate) in rather than originate—and poetry is something larger than any single poet can encompass.

If, as I have argued above, Duncan's most important derivation is his reaching back beyond modernism not only to romanticism but also to preromantic poetries (all the while never losing sight of his position *amongst* modern and postmodern contemporaries), this is characteristically a reaching back to a particular notion of the author not as an *originator* but as a *deriver* of texts who collaborates in the unfolding of the written work over time. As Martha Woodmansee writes in *The Construction of Authorship*, "from the Middle Ages right down through the Renaissance new writing derived its value and authority from its affiliation with the texts that preceded it, its derivation rather than its deviation from prior texts."[9] Derivation, we should keep in mind, is a term familiar to copyright law, where the term appears in section 101 of the US Copyright Act: "A 'derivative work' is a work based upon one or more preexisting works." Our modern sense of copyright, in turn, is "the result of a quite radical reconceptualization of the creative process that culminated less than 200 years ago in the heroic self-presentation of the Romantic poets."[10] Woodmansee and Jaszi take up William Wordsworth —a poet rarely in Duncan's derivative sights—as the cardinal example of the romantic "self-aggrandizing" that has led to the modern conception of the author-originator via a "misrepresentation of a collaborative creative process as a solitary, originary one."[11]

During Wordsworth's lifetime the final enclosure of England's common lands was unfolding, as in a very material sense the *private* was coming to replace the *shared*. In a letter from 1801 the two senses of property—and literary property—can be seen to jostle uncomfortably together. Thus, Wordsworth can refer to poems in the *Lyrical Ballads* as being "written upon subjects, which are the common property of all Poets," while simultaneously noting that other poems in the same collection describe the "domestic life" of "small independent proprietors of land here called statesmen, men of respectable education who daily labour on their own little properties."[12] A more mature Wordsworth, long having given up his early collaborations with Coleridge and his sister, Dorothy, similarly leaves aside the conception of poetry as a "common property," the latter having been completely replaced by a sense of the poet as "independent proprietor" tending his "own little properties" (the Wordsworth, in short, who in the 1830s would argue strenuously for an extension of copyright *in perpetuity* in order to protect "original productions").

Obviously, Duncan's derivative poet has more in common with the Wordsworth of "common property" than the Wordsworth of "independent proprietorship." "The goods of the intellect are communal," he writes in *The H.D. Book*, and flow "from the language itself."[13] Derivation implies a preromantic sense of authorship and intellectual property (only just still discernable in the early Wordsworth). Even Duncan's modernist "fathers," the quotation-drunk Pound and Eliot, saw poetry as a property that could be "stolen" and that needed protection—I am thinking of Eliot's famous quip that "immature poets imitate, mature poets steal," or Pound's description of his and Eliot's return, in the late 1910s, to the formal strictures of the quatrain as the project of "two authors, neither engaged in picking the other's pocket."[14] For the derivative poet, "property" in poems or poetics is revealed as a paradox—as when Duncan refers to Robert Creeley's quatrains as being influenced by Coleridge, H.D., and Zukofsky ("all his own property would be Coleridge, H.D., and Zukofsky").[15] Or it is discredited altogether, as in his comments on "Whitman's line":

> Where the line itself that Whitman adventured in his great experiment at last might be recognized to be not Whitman's personal extravagance and private property but his donation to our new language in poetry must be today. It is only in a new poetry that the transmission of poetry is ever justified, is ever carried forward. Where at last the new force of that line must be recognized in the spiritual transmission of poetic form is in our work, indeed, in the very advancing of sentences ever hearing in their advance the "Whitman" line—eternal now, for it is a common property of the mind.[16]

The issue of derivative authorship that Duncan's practice proposes continues to be of material import in part because, as Peter Jaszi notes, "romantic 'authorship' is alive and well in late twentieth-century American legal culture"—*despite* "the realities of contemporary polyvocal writing practice —which increasingly is collective, corporate, and collaborative."[17] Thus I would argue that Duncan's practice is more current than ever—less romantic than has been assumed, more preromantic, and, paradoxically, more contemporary as technological changes in production and distribution once again reveal literary property to be at its core collective and collaborative.

Duncan's description of the genesis of "Poem Beginning with a Line by Pindar" in "The Truth and Life of Myth" can stand as an example of derivative collaboration—as well as the "several causations" that go into making a poetry that is as much a reading (of others) as it is the writing (of an individual).

> When . . . reading late at night the third line of the first Pythian Ode in the translation by Wade-Gery and Bowra, my mind lost the hold of Pindar's sense and was faced with certain puns, so that the words *light*, *foot*, *hears*, *you*, *brightness*, *begins* moved in a world beyond my reading,

> these were no longer words alone but also powers in a theogony, having resonances in Hesiodic and Orphic cosmogonies where the foot that moves in the dance of the poem appears as the pulse of measures in first things. Immediately, sight of Goya's great canvas, once seen in the Marquis de Cambo's collection in Barcelona, came to me, like a wave, carrying the vision—out of the evocation of the fragment from Pindar and out of Goya's pictorial evocation to add their masterly powers to my own—the living vision, Cupid and Psyche, were there; then the power of a third master, not a master of poetry or of picture but of story-telling, the power of Lucius Apuleius was there too.[18]

From his reading of Pindar, Duncan's meditations are drawn to elements of "Hesiodic and Orphic cosmogonies," then—by sudden association—to Goya's painting *Cupid and Psyche*, then to that myth as told by Apuleius in *The Golden Ass*—and finally to the beginning of Duncan's poem (which will in turn draw upon and respond to Whitman, Charles Olson, and Pound, among others). Here are one poem's "several causations," involving the "collaboration" of numerous authors—something we might describe as a "serial collaboration": "works resulting from successive elaborations of an idea or text by a series of creative workers, occurring perhaps over years or decades."[19] The theme Duncan picks up and elaborates at the beginning of the "Pindar" poem is that of the theophany—the manifestation of a god—a theme that resonates throughout the history of poetry as corresponding with the initiation of poetic speech (the channeling of the muse into the poet's work) and that plays such a crucial role in the Cupid and Psyche myth (Psyche's surprising vision of Cupid by lamplight) and Apuleius's whole story (which involves the secret rituals of an Isis cult and the veiling and unveiling of the goddess's image).

In his discussion of the story in *The H.D. Book*, Duncan reads poetry as a "serial collaboration" into the very fabric of the Cupid and Psyche myth, so that the Palace of Eros (which is discovered by Psyche) "is like the wealth of works the imagination has left that we call our culture."[20] In terms of intellectual property, the works of the past are here seen as a *commons* upon which all future productions depend; they are decidedly not "little properties" held in private by "independent proprietors." As Duncan notes, "the Palace of Eros has another likeness to the world that exists through the arts: '*No single chain, bar, lock or armed guard protected it*,' the story tells us. It lay an open secret for those who discovered it to live in."[21]

Essentially, what I'm arguing for is the *social significance* of intertextuality —the model of sociality the pursuit of a radically derivative practice such as Duncan's projects. If Bloomian anxiety theory, which has to rear its head in any discussion of derivation, is based upon a conception of authors as contesting individual owners of literary property, Duncan's free appropriation of poetic resources is based upon a conception of the author as a collaborator who participates in the working of a common, open field. It is the politics of poetic form—and his consistent aesthetic undercutting of capitalist logic—that Duncan's derivation insistently guides us toward.

We see such a blending of the aesthetics and politics of derivation in a poem such as "Orders: Passages 24." Here Duncan collages material from Dante, the Abbé of Citeaux, T. S. Eliot ("Gerontion"), and Proclus's *Commentaries on Plato's Timaeus*; paraphrases Eliot's famous "Prufrock" refrain (the latter's "In the room the women come and go" echoed by Duncan's "From house to house the armed men go"); and retells the story of Gassire's lute. In the same poem Duncan makes direct reference to his collaborative practice by acknowledging his "debt" to Eliot:

> and now that Eliot is dead, Williams and H.D. dead,
> Ezra alone of my old masters alive,   let me
>   acknowledge Eliot was one of them,   I was
>   one of his,   whose   "History has many
>   cunning passages, contrived corridors"
>
>   comes into the chrestomathy.[22]

Source and derived text are not related hierarchically here but in terms of aesthetic solidarity or *affinity* (a term a number of the essays here will employ): Duncan is "one of" Eliot's, Eliot "one of" Duncan's. It is, perhaps, a version of Eliot's "tradition" model, but Duncan makes it overtly political in several ways: first, because the admission comes in the midst of a poem in the series of Duncan's anti–Vietnam War *Passages*, and second, because in this same poem Duncan outlines the political philosophy, as it were, of his commitment to derivation, which is framed as a critique of private property.

> There is no
> good a man has in his own things except
> it be in the community of every thing;
> no nature he has
> but in his nature hidden in the heart of the living,
> in the great household.[23]

The "good"—however variously defined—is common, part of "the community of everything," and unencloseable as an individually owned "good."

Duncan's discussions of derivation elsewhere suggest a particular conception of the biosocial subject and that subject's relation to *language*. In "The Adventure of Whitman's Line" (from which I have quoted above) Duncan describes the "realm of the arts" as

> a culture, in the sense of a medium in which new life grows. Speech itself, nowhere other than common, every where the source from which we derive our individuality. So I have written and rewrite I am a derivative poet, even as I remember in every individuality that I have derived my being from the human community into which I was born, even as I know my physical body and life-pattern to be derived from the common code and the dance of two strands of that encoding.[24]

Derivation for Duncan is the process through which the individual simultaneously distinguishes itself *from* and signals its ground *in* the common. Such a "being," in the language of ontology, is "singular plural"—a term I take from Jean-Luc Nancy, who argues that a "single being is a contradiction in terms," that "all appearance is co-appearance," and that it is "the 'with' that constitutes being."[25] Duncan, in very similar terms, writes of a "Mankind" whose "Nature is in the wholeness of his species" and that is "made up of a multitude of individualities."[26] We are also not far here from Marx's notion of "species-being": "Man is a species-being . . . because . . . he adopts the species . . . as his object. . . . It is only because he is a species-being that he is a conscious being, i.e., that his own life is an object for him. Only because of that is his activity free activity."[27] Species-being, for Marx, is the process by which the human is able to reflect upon itself as an individual instance of a general category—as, in other words, a singular-plural being. The ground of the self—its "common coding"—is in poetry the shared resources of language, and one's writing is individual only insofar as one is an instance of the general fact of linguistic being. "Language," Marx writes in the *Grundrisse*, "as the product of an individual is an impossibility."[28]

Duncan's reference to the "common [genetic] code" above is typical of his discussions of derivation.

> I'm a development in a language, but I certainly didn't develop the language, so I refer to myself as derivative entirely. And at the same time I am the only place where that derivation can happen, so I don't resemble what I derive from, couldn't possibly because there's only one locality for something going on. Where would the language be? The language is the source of all the possible poetries. It's like asking where the DNA would be if your own local sperm hadn't connected with this local egg.[29]

Conflating the biological, aesthetic, *and* social, Duncan typically marks this insight as both a poetics and a politics. In the introduction to *The Years as Catches* he writes of his sense of "belonging to a larger human life that was foreign to the society into which I had been born, to the American way, to the capitalist ethic with its identification of work with earning a wage and of the work with a saleable commodity. . . . I saw the state and the war as diseases, eternal enemies of man's universal humanity and of the individual volition."[30] The political creed that argues simultaneously both for "individual volition" and "universal humanity" could be called anarcho-communist, but it is, more importantly, for Duncan a matter of the nature of human subjectivity and the derivation of that subjectivity in the shared resources of language.

> It has never seemed to me that the true form of a poem was a convention or an ideal of form, but, as in life, a form having its information in

> the language of our human experience, as our bodies have their information in the life-code of the species, and our spirit in the creative will. The individual poem stirs in our minds, an event in our language, as the individual embryonic cell stirs in the parent body. The beginning of the poem stirs in every area of my consciousness, for the DNA code it will use toward its incarnation is a code of resources my life pattern itself carries.[31]

The individual body is to DNA as the individual poem is to its language (and by extension the individual person to the social community). DNA, like a language, carries historical information regarding its evolution—the mutations it has accrued over the course of time. Language, too, drags its past mutations along with it, which we access, in part, through the study of etymology.

Like Eros's palace, language is open (without "chain, bar, lock or armed guard") to poets as their common inheritance. But it comes—each word—bearing the weight of its past, so that the words we use are never "ours" as such—always multivoiced, polyvocal, singular-plural. Language—in a derivative poetics—exercises a certain degree of autonomy. It is an outside the poet listens to, a determinate *before*, and a *ground*. This is why Duncan so often writes of "obedience"—not to states or party lines or individuals but to words, to language as a shaping DNA of what the poet is. Thus, an individual poet is a "development in a language," but "the language is not ours."[32] The poet's task is to serve, not own, the word.

All this comes to bear on Duncan's consciousness as he writes his various and multiple responses to other poets—and to Poetry itself (conceived as a project of—even coterminous with—Language itself). Derivation, taken to its furthest extreme, leads to the attempt to formulate a "poetry of all poetries"—a "grand collage" or "world poem" all poets collaborate in. "It" is inevitably a poetry in which the lines between reading and writing dissolve: "You too if you have read have written, as my poor mind knows not if it has read or written."[33] Helen Keller, in very different circumstances, writes much the same thing: "I [simply] cannot always distinguish my own thoughts from those I read, because what I read becomes the very substance and texture of my mind."[34]

Such acts of reading-writing and writing-reading form the substance of this collection. The essays in part 1 trace a variety of Duncan's derivations—from Sarah Ehlers's demonstration of how "Duncan's early poetic aspirations are significantly shaped by a Miltonic persuasion," through Siobhán Scarry's unveiling of the many sources (including translation and correspondence) drawn into the palimpsest of a single poem, to Clément Oudart's exploration of Duncan's use of "foreign words" to fashion "a language to which no one is native." Part 2 turns to examinations of those poets who can be seen to in some way derive *from* Duncan—and so in turn reveal other aspects of Duncan's derivative poetics. Whether it is J. P. Craig reading Nathaniel Mackey's use of Duncan's "would-be shaman," Catherine Martin's discussion of Susan Howe's "development of a poetics where the twin concepts of trespass and 'permission' hold comparable sway," or Ross Hair's discussion of Ronald Johnson's "reading to steal," the essays collected here trace paths of affiliation and affinity held up as provocative possibilities in Duncan's own inexhaustible work.

Notes

1. Duncan, "Pages from a Notebook," 401.
2. Duncan, *Robert Duncan: An Interview*, n. pag.
3. Duncan, "The Truth and Life of Myth," 48.
4. Duncan, "Man's Fulfillment in Order and Strife," 111.
5. I am taking the notion of "species-being" from Marx and, in a move Duncan might have been likely to make, reapplying it to poetry. See below.
6. Duncan makes several comments to this effect; see, for instance, "The Truth and Life of Myth," 27.
7. Olson, "Projective Verse," 240. In "An Interview," Duncan notes that "Charles called everything to order with 'Projective Verse'" (515).
8. Duncan, *Letters: Poems 1953–56*, x; Duncan, *The H.D. Book*, 559.
9. Woodmansee, "On the Author Effect," 17.
10. Woodmansee and Jaszi, introduction, 3.
11. Ibid., 4.
12. Robert Duncan to Charles James Fox, January 14, 1801, in Wordsworth, *Letters*, 40–42.
13. Duncan, *The H.D. Book*, 546.
14. Eliot and Pound qtd. in Longenbach, "Mature Poets Steal," 176, 179.
15. Duncan, *Robert Duncan: An Interview*.

16. Duncan, “The Adventure of Whitman’s Line,” 197.
17. Jaszi, “On the Author Effect,” 38.
18. Duncan, *Fictive Certainties*, 17.
19. Jaszi, “On the Author Effect,” 40.
20. Duncan, *The H.D. Book*, 81.
21. Ibid.
22. Duncan, *Bending the Bow*, 78. The quoted lines in this passage are from Eliot’s poem “Gerontion.”
23. Ibid., 79.
24. Duncan, *Fictive Certainties*, 199.
25. Nancy, *Being Singular Plural*, 28–30.
26. Duncan, “Man’s Fulfillment in Order and Strife,” 115.
27. Marx, “Economic and Philosophical Manuscripts of 1844,” 3:275–76.
28. Marx, *Grundrisse*, 490.
29. Duncan, “An Interview,” 537.
30. Duncan, *The Years as Catches*, vii.
31. Duncan, “The Truth and Life of Myth,” 15.
32. Duncan, “Passages 33: Transmissions,” in *Ground Work: Before the War/In the Dark*, 25.
33. Duncan, *Letters: Poems, 1953–56*, xv.
34. Helen Keller qtd. in Woodmansee and Jaszi, introduction, 1.

Part One

DUNCAN READING

CHAPTER ONE

Robert Duncan's Miltonic Persuasion: The Emergence of a Radical Poetic

SARAH E. EHLERS

In his 1942 poem "The Years as Catches," Robert Duncan writes: "I brood upon these lines of Milton, words / where there moves such a tide to feed / my restlessness."[1] The restlessness Duncan refers to is multifarious: during the late 1930s and early 1940s, already feeling alienated because of his homosexuality, Duncan realized (as he writes in his 1966 introduction to *The Years as Catches*) that his "deepest social feelings were irregular too," and he wrestled with his growing abhorrence for the American state and what he bitingly referred to as "the Roosevelt panacea."[2] This manifested in what Duncan retrospectively called "poems of irregularity"—poems that, as his friend Thom Gunn observes, allowed the poet's "merging consciousness, finding its desires out of harmony with those of the society around it," to extend itself into a realm of art "where things are not judged by mere regularity" and "where one in fact aspires to the extraordinary—*The Divine Comedy, King Lear, Ulysses*."[3] Certainly, one could add John Milton's *Paradise Lost* to Gunn's list of "extraordinary" literary works; and further, as I demonstrate in what follows, Duncan's early poetic aspirations are significantly shaped by what Duncan calls a "Miltonic persuasion," by his "brood[ing] upon" the lines of Milton. But Milton does more than fire Duncan's political and poetical imaginations. By making Milton a key figure in his own tradition,

Duncan traces new lines of influence and thus establishes his own unique version of the trajectory of modern and contemporary American poetry.[4]

Gunn's essay catches Duncan on the cusp of his groundbreaking 1944 essay "The Homosexual in Society," and he posits that Duncan's public avowal of his homosexuality ultimately helped to establish him as the "chief originator" for speaking openly about sexuality in American poetry.[5] But more recent readers of Duncan, like Eric Keenaghan, have emphasized Duncan's commitment to a universalism that addresses "homosexual content" in poetry without either "elevating or denigrating" it.[6] Indeed, what a particularized version of Duncan's poetic biography might miss is that "The Homosexual in Society" is as much about the relationship of the individual will to social control and the potential dangers of group membership as it is about heterosexism per se. As Robert J. Bertholf puts it in his essay "Decision at the Apogee: Robert Duncan's Anarchist Critique of Denise Levertov," "the freedom of the individual to act on his own is the paramount assumption of the essay."[7] And, I would add, this is one of the paramount assumptions of Duncan's career: the individual working against—to borrow the very terms Duncan uses in "The Homosexual in Society"—the "overwhelming forces of inhumanity."[8]

But such declarations never come ready-made. During the earliest years of his career Duncan borrows heavily from Milton. It seems that Milton, perhaps more than any of Duncan's diverse influences, provides a persona and a vision that facilitate how Duncan shapes his visions of poetry and self and ultimately prompt the important work of "The Homosexual in Society." A consideration of Duncan's life and work during the 1930s and 1940s reveals how, during a moment of political and creative crisis, Milton offers Duncan an apt model for an individual who stands outside of or in opposition to established institutions, literary or otherwise. Duncan's biographer Ekbert Faas provides a key to this influence, noticing the presence of Milton in poems like "Variations upon Phrases from Milton's *The Reason of Church Government*" and "The Years as Catches." As Faas notes, the theological rhetoric of Milton's prose influenced the style of Duncan's early poems, including their logic and syntax. Such rhetoric, in turn, helped to provide a persona for the young poet. For Duncan, "also impressive in Milton was the revolutionary fervor of the Protestant patriot as well as the poet's final disillusionment."[9] In the 1966 introduction to *The Years as Catches*, Duncan explains that during the early 1940s he was "seeking to find areas of being thru a series of rhetorics," and this search included "ransacking the theological rhetoric of Milton."[10] In Duncan's early poetry he often emulates Milton's poet-activist stance as well as his laureate ambition, and what one finds is that the vision of individual volition the young poet articulates in "The Homosexual in Society" is derived from the discursive space Milton opened within Duncan's burgeoning poetic. Duncan exploits the American tradition of viewing Milton as enabling and empowering.[11] He also provides an alternative to the harsh critiques against Milton that gained so much currency in American poetry and criticism during the twentieth century. Appropriating and esteeming Milton, Duncan offers a subversive, almost Blakean reading of this pervasive seventeenth-century figure in a twentieth-century American context.

MILTON'S INFLUENCE on Duncan is as much a story of Duncan's early personal development, told in memoir and biography, as it is an example of an important strain of his poetry writing, his new and different uses of borrowed rhetorics, figures, and forms. In his critical study/aide-mémoire of the earliest years of Duncan's career, Hamilton Tyler recalls the voraciousness with which Duncan read Milton's work: "Robert and I shared a common fault," Tyler remembers. "If we had read one example of Milton's prose, such as the assigned *Areopagitica*, why not then go on to find out what else he had to say on church and state and then perhaps why."[12] Importantly, understanding how actively Duncan read Milton's prose and poetry offers us more than a historicist reconfiguration of Duncan's own political and poetic development. As Duncan looks back to the seventeenth-century poet, he traces a radical Miltonic tradition that gives shape to his social and political views; but Duncan also makes another radical move within his contemporary literary establishment: refiguring a place for Milton in opposition to the new canon being established by twentieth-century literati like T. S. Eliot and Ezra Pound and then kept in place by fellow descendants of Pound like Charles

Olson.[13] In many ways, this reconfiguration is part of Duncan's effort to reveal a romantic strain in the modern: Milton, an important influence on the romantic poets, now also becomes a parent to the modernist tradition.

The larger artistic community Duncan wrote amidst in the 1930s and 1940s campaigned, almost relentlessly, to dismiss Milton the poet as well as Milton the man, prompting F. R. Leavis to assert in *Revaluation* (1947) that "Milton's dislodgment, in the past decade, after his two centuries of predominance, was effected with remarkably little fuss."[14] While Leavis attributes this "dislodgment" to Eliot's "irresistible argument" regarding Milton's verse, Duncan's primary concern is Pound's (and later Olson's) disavowal of Milton.[15] Duncan of course considers himself part of Pound's tradition. And yet Duncan also uses his "poetic of derivations" to challenge Pound: venerating Milton, Duncan stands with one foot outside the Poundian establishment. Christopher Beach explains in *ABC of Influence: Ezra Pound and the Remaking of American Poetic Tradition* that Duncan's inclusion of Milton in his own canon "is part of a self-conscious polemic against what [Duncan] sees as the restricted lists of acceptable writers maintained by Pound and Olson."[16] Beach adds: "This inclusion is also an attempt to bring Milton's poetry into a camp that Pound would accept—poetry as 'news that stays news.'"[17] Duncan's reclamation of Milton forges a link that forces reconsiderations of both Pound and Milton. In his book Beach quotes from a 1980 interview Duncan gave Jack Cohn and Thomas O'Donnell that is worth quoting in full here:

> I come in heavy over and over again on Milton because Milton was disallowed by Ezra Pound from the main track of poetry, so in general I'm making it impossible for us to read Duncan without both Ezra Pound and Milton. Now, that forces Ezra Pound into a different court and it forces Milton into a different court, but it also forces a whole track of poetry into a different one. It was one Charles Olson would not accept; and Williams attacked Eliot for coming back and putting a memorial on top of him. That's not the way I think of my Milton; my Milton is news, not memorial.[18]

In imperatives reminiscent of Pound's pedagogical prose, Duncan gestures toward two important facets of his Miltonic derivations. On the one hand, including Milton in his own canon provides a new way of understanding Pound's poetics; on the other, rescuing Milton from beneath the memorial wreath resurrects the radical Milton esteemed by poets of the romantic tradition. Such chiastic-like movement is in line with Duncan's own tendency toward poetic variances. In the introduction to *Bending the Bow*, Duncan writes that Hermes "invented the bow and lyre to confound Apollo, god of poetry," and he picks up Heraclitus's observation that "they do not apprehend how being at variance it agrees with itself. . . . There is a connexion at work in both directions."[19] This quotation suggests a characteristic feature of Duncan's poetry and his thought—that is, that Duncan often attempts to account for, and even reconcile, oppositions. Indeed, Duncan's derivative poetics is, at least in part, based on the supposition that such oppositions are generative. As Bertholf suggests in his analysis of the relationship between Duncan and Blake, Duncan "has searched out in conscious maneuvers the texts which immersed him in the continuous contention of universal contraries."[20] It is in this sense that Duncan places Milton at the center of the chiasmus and connections between Milton and Pound. He decides to make Milton part of a "primary experience" of poetry, and he refuses to commemorate the seventeenth-century poet.[21]

As seen above, Duncan borrows from Pound even as he reconceptualizes the Poundian tradition: Duncan alludes to *The ABC of Reading* in order to suggest Milton's import, that Milton is "news that stays news."[22] In the 1966 introduction to *The Years as Catches* Duncan wrote that, during the early 1940s, he found himself "caught up, in the midst of [his] adoration as a reader for Pound's poetics . . . a writer of a Miltonic persuasion."[23] Even though Duncan admires Pound's formal innovativeness, his political tendencies are unsuitable to the sociopolitical views Duncan wants to establish in his own poetry, so he trades a Poundian rhetoric for a Miltonic one.[24] "Pound would not do," Duncan writes, "for, though, he had given voice to Confucian principles of individual order, he had, at the same time, as Kung did, put the State in the place of the communal order or identified the State with the human community."[25] Instead, Duncan prefers Milton, the poet of exile, as he works to establish a poetic that reflects his own view of the human community. At this juncture in Duncan's development, Milton provides an able example for critiquing institutional powers as well as a model for speaking in self-imposed alienation from the state while remaining at one with a human community. As Richard Helgerson explains in his influential *Self-Crowned Laureates*, the shape of Milton's poetic ambition is tied to his alienation from the established church and government. Such alienation, however, never swayed Milton from his ambition to speak with a national voice. "It simply meant that before he could assume his destined role there would have to be a new church and a new government."[26] Helgerson's rubric for understanding Milton's poetic career bears a striking similarity to Duncan's own: in "Rites of Participation" Duncan writes that the poetic imagination must work to "hold its own" in opposition to "the infamy and lies of the new capitalist war state." And he continues: "We too, in a hostile environment, taking our faith and home in our exile, live in a creative crisis."[27]

Might we then view Milton as Duncan's example for "taking faith" in exile? Knowing how Duncan defined Milton—both in tandem with and in opposition to Pound—it is clear that the young Duncan harks back to the seventeenth-century poet in order to form a radical position in the face of harmful or delimiting political and literary establishments. Feeling alienated —or, to use his term, *irregular*—in the midst of social and political unrest, Duncan reflects: "I saw my own personal life as belonging to a larger human life that was foreign to the society in which I had been born," and as he comes to terms with such a position he goes to Milton's work, "searching out there a vision of the individual freedom and the communal commitment of man."[28] Like Milton, Duncan purports to speak to national concerns like government corruption; and also like Milton, Duncan works to find that voice outside of the strictures of state and/or social institutions.

CONSIDERING THAT established poets like Pound were harshly critiquing Milton, it seems a bold move for the young Duncan to imagine and publish a poem called "Variations upon Phrases from Milton's *The Reason of Church Government*."[29] As its title suggests, Duncan's poem is as much inspired by Milton's polemical tract as it is occasioned by a need for revision or alteration of the same. In the poem Milton begins to provide a new derivative location for Duncan—a "court" that redirects the Poundian paradigm. Duncan "ransacks" Milton's canonical prose piece, using Milton as a tool for carving out his own ambitions and ideas: just as the Milton of *The Reason of Church Government* admonishes a system he could not support, the Duncan of "Variations" attempts to write outside of restrictive political, social, and even literary milieus. But again, the project suggested by the poem's title implies an impudence that engages Milton's own.

Of course, to begin with Milton is also to borrow (rhetorically) from Milton. To announce that Milton's political tract is the poem's inspiration demonstrates learnedness or authority, a rhetorical strategy Milton himself employs in *The Reason of Church Government*. The tract begins with Milton drawing from Plato and from the book of Genesis, and the use of classical and biblical references to establish authority is a strategy Milton also uses in the aforementioned *Areopagitica*. Throughout "Variations" Duncan attempts to use what he perceives to be a Miltonic rhetoric and persona in order to create a poetic that critiques what he understands as interrelated social diseases. The historical and biographical contexts surrounding "Variations" illuminate how important the influence of Milton's persona was for Duncan as he attempted to comprehend—and eventually work against—what he abhorred in the American war state and in heterosexist society. "Variations" was written in 1941, the same year Duncan was drafted into the army and subsequently discharged for publicly declaring his homosexuality. Duncan's distaste for the war and the American state was only heightened by his life in the barracks. "I wonder if I sometimes would be happier if I tried to be a martyr," Duncan wrote in a May 1941 letter from his station in Fort Knox, Kentucky. "I think of the draftee who bled himself to death in San Antone. He opened an artery and in the morning they found him lying on his clotted bed. But there is so far no brutality here—everything is sugar coated—but sugar coated shit is still shit."[30] This letter reveals how Duncan's time in the army forced an intense examination of his feeling that the war and state are enemies of man's humanity and the individual volition, and its contemplation of martyrdom seems to suggest a desire for public and powerful modes of expression. As evidenced by "Variations," this is wedded to Duncan's study of Milton, the poet he claims to have looked to as he attempted a poetry that would lend a voice to his social and political views. And here, again, Duncan works against the grain of influential modernist predecessors like Pound and Eliot. While he might concur with both poets' attempts to conjure literary forebears, by integrating Milton's artistic and political lives into his own, Duncan counters Pound's tendency toward antibiographical criticism and Eliot's emphasis on impersonality.

In the introduction to *The Years as Catches* Duncan speaks of the difficulty of "tak[ing] over readily the accepted paradigms and conventions of the Protestant Ethic."[31] Somewhat ironically, though, Milton's fervent Protestantism aids Duncan in his attempt at such a "take over": Milton becomes the figure through which Duncan reconstellates his network of derivations, and he then rewrites Milton's revolutionary spirit in a twentieth-century American context. The young poet works at this in "Variations," as Duncan manipulates the premise and the language of *Reason* to create a moral space that exists outside of his diseased social and political cultures. In the poem this new space is formed around the recurring image of a singular body, and it is mediated by politically and erotically charged imagery and the incorporation of lines from *The Reason of Church Government*. The poem begins:

> Organized, as perfect as an army there
> your body lies. It gleams upon the sweet
> unorganized, the field of dark. It flashes
> in the evening air perfection's battlements
> as naked blade as unsheath'd self. It pierces
> ease of body and makes unquiet soul.
> Now I shall rise, awake as when a trumpet blows,
> and go into the world laid bare;
> for I have seen in her audible harmony
> Virtue who walks in the regular and disciplined
> City of God, known this precision: irregular
> absolute vision sure and persistent
> renders the illusive its full face.[32]

The body in these lines seems to exist on two significant referential planes. Recalling the letter Duncan wrote from Fort Knox, the body is recognizable as the draftee turned martyr who lies on a blood-clotted bed in his army barrack. The image might also be read as a sexualized one, a perfect and naked male body gleaming in the dark. In both readings the body represents a disruptive or interruptive force: it stands out against the "perfect army" as it "gleams upon . . . the field of dark" and "flashes / in the evening air perfection's battlements." As well, it proffers a new kind of organization and discipline, and such an attempt at reordering manifests itself again in "Variations" when Duncan writes that "the body is / God's world in image" and asserts that "love shall be / Truth's order."[33] Here the disruptive body more specifically represents an attempt to reorder the world according to love, and this "love as Truth's order" anticipates the schema for loving that Duncan eventually lays out in "The Homosexual in Society" and that will permeate later major poems like "Poem Beginning with a Line by Pindar" and "The Torso." Further, the love that "shall be Truth's order" resembles Duncan's concept of Eros, which Bertholf explains in "Robert Duncan: Blake's Contemporary Voice": "Duncan takes Eros, the god of love and the first form in the Orphic mysteries, as his guide into the realms of wholeness of primal creation where all things exist in the purity of first appearances."[34]

When Duncan writes in the above-quoted lines that "I shall rise, awake as when a trumpet blows, / and go into the world laid bare," he uses a Miltonic phrase to suggest that the poem's speaker (presumably Duncan himself) is going into the world carrying his own vision. In order to construct such a vision, one that seems to suggest autonomy and self-revelation, Duncan takes Milton's language as his own in order to establish a positive affiliation. The image of God's trumpet blowing is an allusion to Milton's *Reason*, and the first stanza also seems to borrow formally from Milton. This is reiterated in "Variations" through a play with Milton at the level of the idea as well as the levels of the syntactical pattern ("vision sure") and the word ("fals"), as Duncan opens a discursive space where he can begin to carve out the "area of being" that will allow him to pursue his vocation and to oppose "the State and the War," which he saw "as diseases, eternal enemies of man's universal humanity and of the individual volition."[35]

Considering how Duncan consciously used Milton to give voice to his views regarding the war and the state, when Duncan writes in "Variations" that he "see[s] undone the American origins," one recognizes that such insight, as well as the ability to speak it, is shaped by what he construes as a Miltonic pose—a patriot with "revolutionary fervor" and "a persona for surveying the ravages of war while being forced to sit by in idleness."[36] This is apparent in "Variations" as the undoing of American origins dovetails into one of the more explicit appropriations from Milton's *Reason of Church Government.* In the opening of the second book of *Reason*, Milton argues that the "pretious truths" and talents bestowed by God have "such an orient luster as no diamond can equall," and he warns against ornate doctrines that might swallow real truths and "gratify the corrupt desires of men in fleshly doctrines."[37] In "Variations" Duncan takes the figures Milton uses to demonstrate the above—"the great Marchants of this world" who with the "fals glitter of their deceitfull wares . . . abuse the people like poor Indians with beads and glasses"—to express his own anxieties about American origins.[38] Duncan constructs similar images and asserts:

> The Merchants of this World have such
> crackd show for merchandize as needs
> be little more disguised to buy
> each incorruptible Indian's soul.
> The commerce of this world
> does cover, daily does disgrace each jewel
> with counterpart, to buy a continent with axes,
> knives, with beads and color'd cloths, and needs
> call Truth a shameful thing that they
> might so betray & barter with a lie.[39]

Here Duncan uses Miltonic tropes to figure his own opposition to the "American way," which he defines as "a capitalist ethic with its identification of work with earning a wage and of the work with a saleable commodity, and with its ruthless exploitation of human energies for profit."[40] Duncan relates the exchange of work for wages with the exploitation of human labor, what he describes elsewhere as a "mercantile utilitarianism" that exploits "the mind and spirit to keep the rackets going."[41] So in much the same way that the great merchants of Milton's world suggest that glittering commodities are but "deceitfull wares" that threaten the real value of truth, Duncan's merchants become symbols for the corruption inherent in the capitalist ethic—merchandise "buys out" human souls, and whole continents are purchased with weapons and trivialities like beads and colored cloths. "The commerce of this world," which might be read as a capitalist ethic based on the logic of commodity and exchange, "betrays and barters" with deceit, disgracing and shaming the "jewel of Truth." Duncan uses Miltonic rhetoric to construct a poem critiquing a capitalist ethic based on bartering. But Duncan's using Milton's figures as his own also seems to undercut the very logic of the capitalist ethic itself. The materials of the poem, themselves borrowed, are the result of a collaboration with another's materials—a collaboration that is located outside the processes of bartering and borrowing and that refuses to treat texts as commodities.

The language of bartering and borrowing will reappear in another of Duncan's poems from the 1940s, "Among My Friends Love Is a Great Sorrow." This time the terms will be used to express the difficulty of living in a world where love, specifically love between those of the same gender, "is a payment" and a "wage / that one might have for an honest living."[42] For Duncan, surveying and understanding social ills like the capitalist ethic, especially as it manifested in Roosevelt's war economy, are bound to the unease he felt as he struggled to come to terms with his place as a homosexual in a heterosexist society. Eventually, in his 1959 "Reflections" on "The Homosexual in Society," Duncan would draw a correlation between the honoring of homosexual love and the creation of a greater public trust, but before he can confidently and publicly do so, he must confront and work through these ideas on the field of the poem. The time in which Duncan worked on *The Years as Catches* was formative for this aspect of his personal development. Duncan's 1941 discharge from the army constituted an institutionalized outing that he declared made him "an officially certified fag" and that he would retrospectively describe as a "new birth."[43] This "new birth" took on a symbolic meaning when that same year Duncan shed the surname of his adopted parents.[44]

As I have already discerned, one of the overarching aims of Duncan's politics is the realization of an individual volition that involves the disestablishment of affiliative identities. However, before he is able to fully take on such a position—that of the Miltonic poet-activist standing outside of established, institutionalized codes and mores—Duncan must still come to terms with the relationship between his homosexual identity and his social contexts. This involves the construction of a new order outside those of the society and the state—a move that mirrors Milton's own positioning of himself as a poet who would speak to national concerns but would ultimately "acknowledge no patron but God."[45] Somewhat paradoxically, then, Duncan's own crafting of his position as an outsider requires some sort of positive affiliation with Milton's political identity. That is, Duncan needs to affiliate with Milton in order to resist affiliative identities. Like Milton, Duncan registers concern for a national or public good, but he also comes to understand that such opinions must be formed in an imaginative space exiled from existing social and governmental frameworks. In this vein Duncan will borrow from Milton's assertion in *The Reason of Church Government* that discipline and virtue come not from the strictures of man-made governing bodies but from the divine.[46] Though obviously quite different concepts, on the allegorical level Milton's Judeo-Christian God and Duncan's notion of a governing Eros inhabit similar structural positions: both are divine authorities that discount the authority of man-made governing bodies.[47]

IF ONE CONSIDERS "Variations upon Phrases from Milton's *The Reason of Church Government*" in light of "The Years as Catches," Duncan's 1942 poem in which he again specifically references Milton, one sees a significant development in his early poetry—even in the course of one year. The young poet is still searching out an "area of being" vis-à-vis Milton, but the different manner in which Duncan mobilizes and alludes to Milton indicates a newfound patience and thus also a new assuredness. In "Variations" Duncan seems to circumvent the power of Milton's epic poetry by focusing on Milton's political prose. But when Duncan announces in "The Years as Catches" that he "broods upon these lines of Milton," he provides a rich allusion that demonstrates a different confidence as well as a self-conscious alignment with a radical Miltonic tradition. "The Years as Catches," "King

Haydn of Miami Beach," and "An African Elegy" occupy a central location in Duncan's earliest poetry, and he considered these poems to be "part of a major breakthrough that epitomizes an important strain of his later work."[48] Friends like Hamilton Tyler shared this sense of the poems' importance. As Tyler remembers, "The Years as Catches," along with "An African Elegy," seemed to stand "well above his [Duncan's] own earlier work and that of the other younger poets we knew, and would likely find a lasting place in the field of Anglo-American poetry. We were convinced of this even though none was published then and they would not appear in little magazines until several years later."[49] This assertion, coupled with the extent to which the poem addresses and imagines Milton, reemphasizes the importance of the seventeenth-century writer to the early Duncan.

In "The Years as Catches" Duncan overtly allies himself with Milton. The poem begins with a reference to Milton's 1632 sonnet on "the passing of his three-and-twentieth year," an allusion that works to align Duncan's own anxieties with the Milton who, according to the first stanza of "The Years as Catches,"

> past twenty-three, saw that year
> gone from him, stood in the hasting days of his soul's April,
> stood in the weary stretch of Christendom
> impatient for the green, the bud & bloom of manhood.[50]

From this image Duncan asks: "Is this a later hour when we rise?"[51] Such a question aligns with what Milton scholars, like Helgerson, have noticed in Milton's 1632 sonnet. As Helgerson elaborates, "an extraordinary delay marks Milton's progress as a poet," and a significant amount of time passes between Milton announcing his epic ambition in *The Reason of Church Government* and the writing of his epic *Paradise Lost*.[52] In "The Years as Catches" it seems that Duncan is calling on Milton's poetic frustration in order to control and comprehend his own impatience. This Duncan, like Milton also passing his twenty-third year, is restless, anticipating social change as well as the unfolding of his "true nature." But Duncan learns patience through Milton's example. "The Years as Catches," much like "Variations," is a poem about surveying the ravages of war, and the poem is riddled with images of clamor and cacophony. Yet, unlike "Variations," there is a quiet stillness to the restlessness Duncan describes in the poem. Looking to Milton as an ally and an example, Duncan also seems to possess a Miltonic confidence, a knowledge that his "epic" will ultimately be written. Certainly, Duncan would tackle projects of epic proportions later in his career (notably, his ongoing *Passages* sequence), and he would also enter a period of self-imposed delay—the fifteen-year absence from publishing that preceded *Ground Work: Before the War* (1984).

Michael Davidson notes that "Duncan often turned to Milton, Herbert, and the metaphysical poets for a kind of rhetorical diction and blank verse that embodied passional states held in check."[53] And so, even though Eliot admires and promotes the seventeenth-century Metaphysical poets while denying Milton, Duncan formally employs each of them to create the same effect. We see Duncan using this compositional strategy in "Years" as the evenly paced lines that open the poem exemplify Davidson's suggestion—and also show that Duncan looks to Milton, especially, to "check his anticipation" and work toward his poetic goals. This is most palpable in the poem's middle section when the young poet, brooding upon the lines of Milton, also alludes to the seventeenth-century poet in such a way that he announces his place in a radical Miltonic tradition:

> I brood upon these lines of Milton, words
> where there moves such a tide to feed
> my restlessness. Where shall we sometime meet
> in this dark land no longer having
> darkness in us? And bring our tired souls home
> to linger over wine about a fire, to hear
> with equal grace a little Mozart playd
> within the gloom of an Autumnal room, to linger
> over these last rude & somber moments
> come to rest.[54]

Duncan's claim that he "brood[s] upon" Milton's work might be a deliberate allusion to the Holy Spirit "brooding on the vast abyss" in the opening of *Paradise Lost*.[55] Such an allusion is compelling considering that Milton's vision of the Spirit "making pregnant the vast abyss" with his creation comes just before he announces that his poem, with an unprecedented epic grandeur, will attempt to "justify the ways of God to Man"—and just before the poem plunges down into Satan's hell.[56] In "The Truth and Life of Myth," Duncan expresses how he admired the "mythic architecture of *Paradise Lost*," and he specifically references how this part of the poem sweeps from heaven to hell, writing: "The vast theatrical space projected in the opening passages of Milton's *Paradise Lost* is mythic architecture, passing from artifice into a felt dimension, given by the depth of Satan's fall, where again the fictional form operates to move the poet and the reader into an 'other' space in the reality of which actual space fades."[57]

Duncan uses spatial metaphors to describe how the opening of Milton's epic creates a deep and meaningful myth—one that collapses the distinction between the poem's artifice and the poem as a "felt dimension" of reality and thus reveals a universal, or common, experience of history as myth. As I've suggested, this very striving toward commonality or universality guides Duncan's politics and vision in important essays like "The Homosexual in Society." But *Paradise Lost* does more than provide Duncan with a significant example of the relationship between myth and history; it is also a nexus for understanding how he derives from Milton and participates in the life of the seventeenth-century poet's "mythic" work. As Duncan explains in "The Truth and Life of Myth," he considered Milton's mind, like his own, to be a "mythological mind" that conveys the "actual drama or meaning of history, the plot and intention of Reality."[58] Duncan continues:

> In Milton's myth, all of history is a travail, and the Truth of What Is Happening, its What Is, lies only in the second coming, the end of Happening. Christ's life is the immediate historical reality of the Form, or the proclamation of that Form, happening in this poetry of process; and the Second Coming is the Form of Forms from which all Judgment and redemption of events flows. But here again I am speaking of the wholeness of a poem in which all its parts are redeemed as meaning. Creatively, in turn, everything that happens in writing the poem, as it belongs to the poem, must be acknowledged and undertaken as

> meaning. "Think upon the meaning of this act," is the command of the creative will.[59]

The way Duncan positions himself in relation to Milton here is not unlike the way Bertholf reads Duncan's relationship to Blake's poetry and ideas. According to Bertholf, Duncan "regards his poems as part of a larger whole that is still incomplete, in the same way that he regards the body of his work as part of Blake's 'Grand Poem,' existing in the energies of the universal imagination in which all poems participate."[60] Bertholf's explanation demonstrates how Duncan saw in Milton and Blake—and in Dante and Shakespeare—manifestations of an eternal and infinite mind. Duncan writes: "Once the operations of their art began they were transported from the sense of myth as literary element into the immediacy of the poem where reality was mythological."[61]

Duncan discerns a similar quality in Blake, and in the introduction to *The Years as Catches* he recalls that, during his early career, he returned to Blake and to Milton through the "apocalyptic voice of [George] Barker." Emphasizing the importance of both poets to his early development, Duncan continues: "I would return again to Milton and to Blake, . . . searching out there a vision of the individual freedom and the communal commitment of man."[62] And it is Blake, of course, who claimed that Milton was "a true Poet and of the Devil's party without knowing it."[63] Indeed, Duncan seems to establish his place within the radical poet-prophet tradition established by romantic readers of Milton. This tradition relates Milton to the Satan of *Paradise Lost*, taking him as an example of "a daring individualist who took his place outside the circle of conformists."[64] Like the romantics before him, Duncan appropriates Milton to turn apostate and to find a way for surviving—and then writing and acting against—the ravages of war. This is hinted at in the first stanza of "Years" with the allusion to Milton in the question, "Is this a later hour when we rise?" Like Wordsworth's 1802 apostrophe to Milton—"Milton! thou shouldst be living at this hour: / England hath need of thee"—Duncan invokes Milton in a time of crisis.[65]

"The Years as Catches" anticipates Duncan's future ambitions. In the midst of war and confusion, amid the clamor of bells and sirens, and in a century in which "Virtue, / charity and hope avail not," Duncan is sure that he, like Milton before him, is a true poet and that his greatest poetry is being—and has yet to be—written.[66] Milton seems to return throughout such vocational pursuits—as in Duncan's later volume *Roots and Branches* and the aptly titled "Returning to the Rhetoric of an Earlier Mode."

Duncan's reference to the autumnal room where Mozart plays in "The Years as Catches" is a literal one, recalling a time when he was avidly reading through Milton's prose and poetry. This is evidenced by a letter Duncan later wrote to Tyler; it reflects: "Our friendship has always been grounded not only upon good times, the company we've had since the days of *The Years as Catches* in the food and wine, the glow of Mozart and Milton, but it was also, is, grounded in a common view of what humanity might mean."[67] Of course, this particular sentiment is written for Tyler; however, we might also extrapolate it, taking it as a way to position the relationship of Milton's work to Duncan's early poetic project. Considering the two poets in tandem, we find that both figures—in their peculiar and historical contexts—share a desire to find "what humanity might mean"; and, further, both are willing to establish such meanings in exile from harmful or limiting social and political frameworks. Duncan seems to learn such strategies from Milton, and his Miltonic persuasions are largely related to the bold and radical persona he discerns in the seventeenth-century poet. Milton provides a model for positing and fulfilling poetic ambitions as well as for using such ambitions to speak on behalf of a larger human good. Thus, when Duncan asserts in "The Homosexual in Society" that "the forces of inhumanity are overwhelming, but only one's continued opposition can make any other order possible," there is a sense that the strength to forge such an opposition and believe such new orders are possible is derived from the discursive space Milton opens.[68]

As we have seen, Milton provides a significant derivative location for Duncan's early poetry, and his radical project helps Duncan to, as he writes at the close of "The Homosexual in Society," face the "forces of inhumanity" and, through a "continued opposition" to such forces, imagine a way to "break at last the fetters that seem now so unbreakable."[69] Somewhat paradoxically, affiliating himself with Milton teaches Duncan to be an outsider and allows him to disavow harmful social and institutional identities and strictures at the same time that he finds the roots of his individual creative expression. In many ways, for Duncan these artistic affiliations operate outside of the socially constructed identities and group affiliations that he wrote against in "The Homosexual in Society." Duncan's poetics of derivation works according to a different logic. "I'm a locality of what's happening in poetry, as I am personally a locality in the universe," Duncan told Jack Cohn and Thomas O'Donnell in an interview. "At the same time I am the only place where that derivation can happen, so I don't resemble what I derive from. I couldn't possibly because there's only one locality for something going on."[70] While Duncan's derivative poetics—and, indeed, his Miltonic persuasion—is the result of an affiliation with another poet's work, that work is also uniquely appropriated and reimagined according to Duncan's specific locality and his own "area of being" in the social world.

Notes

1. Duncan, *The Years as Catches*, 37.
2. Ibid., vii.
3. Gunn, "Homosexuality," 144–45. Duncan explains how he positions himself in the traditions of Shakespeare, Dante, and Joyce in "The Truth and Life of Myth."
4. In "Robert Duncan: Talent and the Individual Tradition," Michael André Bernstein argues for Duncan's importance in this regard. Bernstein writes that Duncan's artful way of imagining his tradition and, by extension, modern literary history teaches us new ways to understand the modern traditions themselves (182–83). In this vein, Duncan's use of Milton is different from (and, I think, ultimately more remarkable than) other midcentury uses of Milton such as Robert Lowell's. Duncan employs Milton not only for personal ends (i.e., as poetic inspiration or model persona) but also in order to radically revise more deeply ingrained poetic traditions and social contracts.
5. Gunn, "Homosexuality," 160.
6. Keenaghan, "Vulnerable Households," 57.
7. Bertholf, "Decision at the Apogee," 10.
8. Duncan, *A Selected Prose*, 48.
9. Faas, *Young Robert Duncan.*
10. Duncan, *The Years as Catches*, ii.

11. As scholars have explored, nineteenth- and twentieth-century American writers employed Milton's poetry and his political persona for various ends, and Milton was figured to be both a defender of high culture as well as a revolutionary hero. For explorations of productive tensions between these two strains of Miltonic influence, see Van Anglen, *The New England Milton*, and Herron, "Milton and Afro-American Literature."
12. Tyler and Tyler, "In the Beginning," 4.
13. See Beach, *ABC of Influence*. Beach notes that Olson and his critics acknowledge the former's debt to the Pound-Williams tradition, and he concludes that Pound and Williams were "important 'guides'" (110, 134). As I show later, Duncan suggests that Olson endorsed a "track of poetry," espoused by Pound, that disallowed Milton.
14. Leavis, *Revaluation*, 42. Both Eliot and Pound berated Milton's syntactical irregularities and decadent rhetoric. However, both also intimated a dislike for Milton the man. In "A Note on the Verse of John Milton," Eliot asserts that "judging by the ordinary standards of likeableness in human beings, Milton is unsatisfactory" (12). In "Notes on Elizabethan Classicists," Pound criticizes Milton mercilessly, asserting that he is willing to give "honour where it is due" but also admitting "a personal active dislike" (237–38). For an overview of Pound's and Eliot's criticism of Milton, see Sammons, "A Note on the Milton Criticism."
15. The quotes "dislodgment" and "irresistible argument" are from Leavis, *Revaluation*, 42.
16. Beach, *ABC of Influence*, 138.
17. Ibid.
18. Duncan, "An Interview."
19. Duncan, *Bending the Bow*, iv.
20. Bertholf, "Robert Duncan," 92.
21. Duncan, *A Selected Prose*, 3. The reference to a "primary experience" of poetry is from Duncan's essay "Towards an Open Universe."
22. Pound, *The ABC of Reading*, 29.
23. Duncan, *The Years as Catches*, ii.
24. Much later in his career, in the sequence "A Seventeenth Century Suite in Homage to the Metaphysical Genius in English Poetry," collected in *Ground Work: Before the War/In the Dark*, Duncan would again cross Pound's work with a seventeenth-century rhetorical mode.
25. Duncan, *The Years as Catches*, vii.
26. Helgerson, *Self-Crowned Laureates*, 242.
27. Duncan, *A Selected Prose*, 123.

28. Duncan, *The Years as Catches*, vii–viii.
29. Chace gestures toward this in *The Political Identities*, noting that Pound "waged a strenuous campaign" against Milton "not only because of the syntactical irregularities he saw in Milton's poems, but also because Milton's aims rival his own grandeur" (10n).
30. Robert Duncan, personal communication, quoted in Faas, *Young Robert Duncan*, 113.
31. Duncan, *The Years as Catches*, ii.
32. Ibid., 25.
33. Ibid., 26.
34. Bertholf, "Robert Duncan," 93.
35. Duncan, *The Years as Catches*, vii.
36. Ibid., 25; Faas, *Young Robert Duncan*, 125–26.
37. Milton, *Complete Prose Works*, 801–2.
38. Ibid., 802.
39. Duncan, *The Years as Catches*, 25–26.
40. Ibid., vii.
41. Duncan, "Rites of Participation," in *A Selected Prose*, 123.
42. Duncan, *The Years as Catches*, 74.
43. Robert Duncan, personal communication, quoted in Faas, *Young Robert Duncan*, 114.
44. Ibid., 113.
45. Helgerson, *Self-Crowned Laureates*, 277.
46. Milton, *Complete Prose Works*, 753.
47. Interestingly, Duncan's concept of Eros seems to be written in the spirit of Marcuse's subsequent view in *Eros and Civilization* that Eros is an abstract force restrained by capitalism and society.
48. Faas, *Young Robert Duncan*, 126.
49. Tyler and Tyler, "In the Beginning," 4.
50. Duncan, *The Years as Catches*, 36.
51. Ibid.
52. Helgerson, *Self-Crowned Laureates*, 76.
53. Davidson, *Ghostlier Demarcations*, 187.
54. Duncan, *The Years as Catches*, 37–38.
55. Milton, *Paradise Lost*, 4.
56. Ibid.
57. "The Truth and Life of Myth," in Duncan, *Fictive Certainties*, 28–29.
58. Ibid., 46.
59. Ibid.

60. Bertholf, "Robert Duncan," 93.
61. Duncan, "The Truth and Life of Myth," 28.
62. Duncan, *The Years as Catches*, viii.
63. William Blake, "The Marriage of Heaven and Hell," in Blake, *The Complete Poems*, 182.
64. Wittreich, *The Romantics on Milton*, 11.
65. William Wordsworth, "London, 1802," in Wordsworth, *Poetical Works*, 116.
66. Duncan, *The Years as Catches*, 36.
67. Robert Duncan to Hamilton Tyler, quoted in Tyler and Tyler, "In the Beginning," 3.
68. Duncan, *A Selected Prose*, 48.
69. Ibid.
70. Duncan, "An Interview," 537.

CHAPTER TWO

Robert Duncan's Derivative Poetics: Community, the Metaphysicals, and the Nature of War

GEORGE FRAGOPOULOS

The Derivative Poet

For Robert Duncan, poetic tradition is not simply a means to poetry but poetry itself; and use and acknowledgment of tradition through appropriation bring with them a certain degree of "derivativeness." This derivativeness by no means implies a passive acceptance of literary precursors and history. At many points in Duncan's oeuvre it even suggests an intensely antagonistic and confrontational relationship with tradition. As Nathaniel Mackey has pointed out, "Duncan's description of himself as simply a derivative poet is belied by the strikingly contentious character of his relationships to the poets, both present and past, from whom his work is derived. There is very little of the diffidence or passivity the word *derivative* suggests either about his pronouncements, about his poetics, or about his poems."[1] "A Seventeenth Century Suite in Homage to the Metaphysical Genius in English Poetry," which appears in Duncan's penultimate collection, *Ground Work: Before the War*, is an exemplary example of the kind of work Duncan often composed in which homage and antagonistic rewriting of poetic precursors lead to a new type of poem, a "world-poem," which can be defined as a "multiphasic work in which various times and places interpenetrate," or, as Ezra Pound said in his *Spirit of Romance*, a work that makes "all ages contemporaneous."[2]

Acknowledging one's indebtedness to tradition also means accepting the communal nature of life and of language. This is especially true in the structure of the "Suite," a long poem that is structured around the appropriation of entire poems by certain Metaphysical poets; Duncan's "method throughout the *Suite* is to quote in full the seventeenth-century poem in question . . . and to follow it with his own variations upon specific themes, phrases, and images found in the poem."[3] The poem, therefore, comes into being through an intense dialectical exchange between the contemporary poet and his precursors, in this case, the poets George Herbert, Robert Southwell, Walter Raleigh, John Norris, and Ben Jonson. This dialectical process of give-and-take gives rise to a poem that is "derivative" because of its communal approach, a "grand collage," to use Duncan's term. In such poems the poet's voice sublimates itself to the demands of a literary tradition—or community—and to a language, both of which transcend the finite limitations of any one subject. In Duncan's later *Ground Work* collections—*Before the War* and *In the Dark*—this realization of one's finitude leads directly to an inevitable reckoning with mortality and to the eventual dissolution of the subject, and it is this "undoing" of the subject that underlines Duncan's conception of community, tradition, and the world poem.

This essay will primarily focus on Duncan's "Up Rising" and "A Seventeenth Century Suite" in order to illustrate how the poet's method of literary appropriation and derivations constructs a poetics of community during a moment in American—and world—history when the very idea of community has been undone. Furthermore, I will squarely place my own reading of Duncan's notion of a communal poetics within the ongoing discussion already begun by critics such as Peter Michelson, Norman Finkelstein, and Nathaniel Mackey. In particular, Mackey's extensive and illuminating essay "Gassire's Lute: Robert Duncan's Vietnam War Poems" has been instrumental in grounding my own understanding of Duncan's approach to community and has been extremely helpful as a point of departure.[4] I will also, primarily, be focusing in on the "Suite" as an example of one of Duncan's late works, works that, as Finkelstein also claims, can be read as a critique of the lyric subject. In the late works one finds a poet attempting to come to terms with the disintegration of metaphysical systems, and this metaphysical crisis is made tangible through the theme of war and the dissolution of language and, by extension, the self.[5] All these themes, I argue, are tangibly felt through Duncan's representation of community.

It is in the work of Jean-Luc Nancy that I have found a theoretical bridge through which to bring into dialogue my own readings of Duncan's poetry and those of previous critics. Nancy writes, "The gravest and most painful testimony of the modern world, the one that possibly involves all other testimonies to which this epoch must answer . . . is the testimony of the dissolution, the dislocation, or the conflagration of community."[6] Using Nancy's work as a foundation, my essay will examine the concept of community in an attempt to illustrate how Duncan's late poetics represents the crisis of the self in relation to tradition and community—or, to use the poet's own words, "*I* go then / into destruction of the grades of me, / to the undoing of those hierarchies."[7]

But how does Duncan define community? There is no singular use of the term throughout Duncan's work, and it can hold multiple meanings at the same time. A static definition would be antithetical to the spirit of the poet's work, so we should simply focus on how the term functions within certain poems. What the "Suite" further suggests is that community can be theorized through metaphorical spaces (what I will later call performative spaces), spaces that I define as *openings* toward realization, even if this process always fails to completely actualize itself. Community in the "Suite" is also, in a sense, ahistorical, which does not mean a denial of history but a denial of the idea that there is a linear, singular logic to it. History does not necessarily exist on a single, historical plane; rather, it occupies a space where all of history is made contemporaneous. Consider Duncan's use of the Robert Southwell poem "The Burning Babe." Duncan's own variation on the poem hinges on the stark image of the burning babe, which, in the original, was a Christian symbol of Christ's birth. Duncan turns this image into one "beyond hate or loss or / Christian martyrdom" and into a ghostly apparition that reflects on the horrors of the Vietnam War: "the broiled flesh of these heretics, / by napalm monstrously baptized."[8] Duncan is not only engaged with Southwell's poem, which he uses as a touchstone to explore the war, but also in communion with Denise Levertov's "Advent 1966," a poem that also uses the same horrible image. This one *movement*—the "Suite" is composed of ten sections or movements plus coda—in Duncan's much larger composition addresses a number of times and spaces, poems and poets, and allows for a myriad of historical trajectories to come together.[9] It is impossible, therefore, to truly ground this one section of the "Suite" in any single historical period, to name but a single community, in other words. This chiasmus-like structure to the poem has us reading Southwell through Duncan and Levertov, a Borgesian turn by which the writer creates his own precursors.

As such, community can never be defined in any singular manner because its existence precedes and transcends our own finite natures—much like language. For this very reason, as Nancy would claim, a community can also be a site of resistance because it resists definition. A community that cannot be defined is one that is always in the process of becoming, of unfolding; such a community exists only as a possibility, waiting to come into existence. Nancy describes "what we are being called toward, or sent to, as to our ownmost future. But it is not a 'to come,' it is not a future or final reality on the verge of fulfillment, pending only the delay imposed by an approach, a maturation, or a conquest."[10] This future that will never arrive allows community to resist any kind of direct political application: "[The community] is not something that may be produced and instituted or whose essence could be expressed in a work of any kind (including a *polis* or state): it cannot be the object or the telos of a politics."[11] In a similar sense, Duncan's poetics also refuses teleology, allowing the work to remain perpetually open and aware of new possibilities.

I will also examine how this constant *openness* speaks to the much larger issue of Duncan's complex relationship to the Vietnam War and how some of his critics have misread his poetics and his stance on the war. My major point of contention with such criticism is that it rests on a positivist critique of "inaction," and it is a criticism based on teleological readings of the concepts of community and self. As such, the easy move is to suggest that what appears to be Duncan's retreat into aesthetics is a retreat from politics; it is far more complex than that. For Duncan, there was no easy dividing line between politics and aesthetics, and a retreat away from the realm of political action could lead to an ethical turn, which could be highly political. As Robert Bertholf and Albert Gelpi write in their introduction to his correspondence with Denise Levertov, "the only resolution, [Duncan] argued, was imaginative and poetic, not political and social; ethics were aesthetic."[12] But what Bertholf and Gelpi also fail to suggest is that ethics can also be the road to the political.

Duncan, Levertov, and the Vietnam War

Duncan wrote frequently and urgently on the issue of the Vietnam War. His voluminous correspondence with Denise Levertov is particularly compelling for the unexpurgated view into his most personal thoughts on the subject.[13] For example, this from a letter he wrote to Levertov dated March 1968: "I see the Vietnamese War (as I saw the Second World War) as a revelation of the truth of the potential evil of 'America' . . . as a revelation of the truth of American Karma, what Commager called the consequences of the unacknowledged, unrepresented crimes."[14] This very same language of denial and unacknowledged crimes would appear often in Duncan's work, as it does in the "Suite," written in the early 1970s:

> And in our nation's store of crimes   long
>   unacknowledged, unrepented,
> the sum of abject suffering, of dumb incalculable
>   injury increases
> the sore conscience we long avoid.[15]

War, therefore, is not simply a destructive force but also that which allows us a revelatory glimpse at the *truth* of what America is. War is a theme that Duncan addressed in a number of contexts. Here is the opening to his seminal essay "Man's Fulfillment in Order and Strife":

> "War is both King of all and Father of all," Heraclites says. Among poets throughout the world or within any nation, men are at war, even deadly war, with each other concerning the nature and responsibility of poetry. Conventional poets and avant-garde poets are at war; within the avant-garde followers of Pound and William Carlos Williams

> find themselves at war with the new gang of concrete or constructivist poets. And within the tribe of concrete poets, sound poets are at war with visual poets who raise the polemics of the letter of the word against the voice. Every order of poetry finds itself, defines itself, in strife with other orders. A new order is a contention in the heart of existing orders.[16]

Consider how quickly Duncan brings in the discussion of poetry. War becomes an extension of poetics, a means by which, ironically, poetry comes to be. Furthermore, Duncan often invokes theosophical readings of war; the poet is torn between that which needs to be spoken of and that which exists beyond our own means of expression and understanding. Many of Duncan's critics have faulted him for this exact reason. As Michael Davidson has written, "Duncan's tendency to mythologize the war seems . . . inadequate. Too often, his cavalier dismissal of social protest is elitist and, worse, ratiocinative in the face of palpable evil."[17] But it is this space between what can and cannot be expressed that is most compelling in Duncan's work and that needs to be examined. Duncan's poetics makes it clear that we must be sensitive to the ways a language constructs us and, by extension, community, even though the gap that separates the subject from its community and its language is impossible to locate and write. A poem, therefore, must be understood as belonging to a much larger body of knowledge known as *Poetry* in the same way that any protest against a corrupt government is best understood as belonging to the very system it seeks to overturn; from this follows implications for the poetry itself.

The following selection from another letter written by Duncan to Levertov is particularly telling: "The protest is only true when it is . . . an expressive act. When it is directed towards a *means-ends*, it is either futile or, succeeding, belongs to a complex of political meanings that can have no 'truth in itself.' This is of the nature of all acts in so far as they are *means*, i.e. not identical with their own intent. Like lines or images of a poem that are not felt as immediacies of 'form' but as a means toward an end of the poem."[18] This is not only a political statement but an aesthetic one as well. In other words, the poem should speak for itself and on its own grounds. As Mark

Andrew Johnson writes, "those who would disallow politics in poetry are as bad as those who would demand it. Poetry must follow its own orders and so cannot serve as propaganda, but at the same time it must be rooted in the 'living body and passion of Man in the actual universe.'"[19] Duncan often valued poetry for the very reason that it did not serve any obvious utilitarian purpose—such as direct protest—within American society.[20]

The poet's stance, therefore, is not an apathetic one when it comes to the realities of war; there are too many instances of indignation and horror in the war poems that contradict such a reading. Rather, Duncan's approach to the war is mediated through his poetics and his use of language. The openness of his poetry is reflected in his attempt to arrive not at a preconceived notion of protest but at a textual and social space that will allow for something new and different to arise—perhaps not so much an antidote to war but a better understanding of its place, and ours, in the universe. Such an attempt is also an aesthetic one, for it requires a type of imagining that has yet to occur—and perhaps never will; this is what Duncan means when he says that it is a poet's job to imagine evil and not to confront it, for such a direct confrontation would still be operating within the confines of the very discourse the poet is trying to undermine.

We can trace this line of thinking back to the notion of community. For Duncan as for Nancy, a community of resistance, for example, would not be one directed toward a "means-end"; what is needed is an open-ended project that will, in its constant unfolding, its perpetual becoming, resist and baffle any specific political end. "Up Rising," perhaps Duncan's most famous Vietnam War poem, can be read, for example, as a straightforward antiwar polemic, a Dantesque screed against the horrors of American imperialism, and a direct condemnation of Lyndon B. Johnson, who "would go up to join the great simulacra of men, / Hitler and Stalin, to work his fame / with planes roaring out from Guam over Asia."[21]

"Up Rising" is concerned with addressing an American community that has allowed the horrors of the war to turn into "the terror and hatred of all communal things, of communion, / of communism."[22] Duncan invokes community through language: "In the poem 'Up Rising' I came close to the demotic voice. In the context of our particular and national crisis of conscience for those of us who even imagine ourselves as members of any community larger than national interests define, . . . for those of us whose sense of our common humanity has been outraged, the poem seems primarily political in its meaning: to arouse the conscience of the people against the existing order of dominion."[23] Consider, also, the following passage from "War," from the introduction to *Bending the Bow*:

> We enter again and again the last days of our own history, for everywhere living productive forms in the evolution of forms fail, weaken, or grow monstrous, destroying the terms of their existence. We do not mean an empire; a war then, as if to hold all China or the ancient sea at bay, breaks out at a boundary we name *ours*. It is a boundary beyond our understanding. Now, where other nations before us have floundered, we flounder. To defend a form that our very defense corrupts. We cannot rid ourselves of the form to which we now belong. And in this drama of our own desperation we are drawn into a foreign desperation. . . . For our defense has invaded an area of our selves that troubled us. . . . When in moments of vision I see . . . photographt details and the daily body counts actual bodies in agony and hear—what I hear now is the desolate bellowing of some ox in a ditch—madness starts up in me.[24]

The use of pronouns here is startling: "we," "us." There is no individual voice but rather a communal one concerned with the horrors of war and its implications for the country, "our own desperation." The voice condemns itself—"We cannot rid ourselves of the form to which we now belong"—as much as it condemns the violence it observes. Duncan is never one to avoid complicity; thus, in the "Suite"—"a kind of hurt that drives into the root / of understanding, their lives / burnd into us we live by" (76)—victim and perpetrator are one and the same.

The individual voice only arises when it is confronted with an image of suffering and death, "the photographt details" of bodies in "agony," and then only madness arrives, an insanity beyond words, a crisis in which understanding is impossible. The mind and our thoughts can only reach a boundary "beyond our understanding," as this implies an epistemological failure;

knowledge of what lies in this "beyond" is always impossible, and that is why it needs to be imagined. Imagining, therefore, can be an ethical act, for it is a means to understanding the suffering of others.

Nathaniel Mackey states that in "Up Rising" "Duncan digs beneath the narcotizing rhetoric that justifies the war, and he also raises the issue of the nation's refusal to confront its true history, its avoidance of such a confrontation through the adoption of cosmetic, jingoistic versions of the past, versions in which it credits itself with the creation of a 'land of the free.'"[25] It is no coincidence that Duncan makes a passing reference in the poem to William Blake, the English poet of revelation: "As Blake saw America in figures of fire and blood raging / . . . in what image? The ominous roar in the air, / the omnipotent wings, the all-American boy in the cockpit."[26] "Up Rising," much like "A Seventeenth Century Suite," is meant to be a confrontation with America itself, a wake-up call regarding culpability and responsibility. We should read the theosophical overtones of these poems as an attempt to construct a space that will allow us to understand the horrors of war and not, necessarily, as a retreat from saying anything concrete or politically oriented. Duncan is more interested in the possibility of a new imagining than he is in direct action.

In this sense I depart from Peter Michelson's reading of "Up Rising." Michelson argues that "Manichaeism reaches a zenith in this poem, which is filled with indictment but is without the critical substance to make indictment either moving or intelligible. Quite literally, and rightly, *everybody* in America is indicted for the Vietnam War, but . . . on what grounds? So great is the level of generality that about all one can say is . . . *evil.* And in Duncan's scheme that amounts to saying that man is guilty of being man, which is no guilt at all."[27] I feel there are a number of problems with such a reading. First and foremost, it proposes, again, a degree of certainty that Duncan's poetics actively questions and commonly resists. Duncan routinely questions the limits of his own understanding and knowledge, and, as such, we should participate in the very same sense of epistemological uncertainty when faced with a decision, no matter how certain we are of our agency and of our goals.

Second, Michelson's critique of Duncan is based firmly on "materialist," "positivist" grounds. Such grounds, however, are strictly teleological. As Duncan once told Mackey, he had a difficult time with Marxism because he could not accept the fact that any dialectical process must come to some end, that the entire project must be born and end in a structured manner, a historical trajectory toward the end of history.[28] For Duncan, there is no end to the structure of things, no end to the ongoing way of the cosmos: "To be alive itself is a form involving organization in time and space, continuity and body, that exceeds clearly our conscious design."[29] Duncan's series of open-ended poems points to this refusal to accept the ending of the dialectical process. War is an eternal essence, something beyond our finite understandings of the concept; but this does not mean that indignation through poetry is not a means to explore the issue, a kind of protest outside of protest. And for a poem that is accused of being too general in its indictments, "Up Rising" does make some very pointed claims in assigning responsibility for the horrors of Vietnam. The poem clearly castigates Johnson, but it also points fingers, as Michelson correctly points out, at the speaker or the poet's self, a further indication of the fact that Duncan never claimed himself to be above reproach or apart from his own community. The poem is replete with tangible and brutal images, making it that much more difficult to understand claims regarding its "generality" or "nonspecificity." While I understand why Michelson would be wary of Duncan's stance on the war and how it can bleed into a politics and poetics that appear to justify any evil, a teleological critique of his work misses the point. It would be like decrying Blake for being too "revelatory" or Dante for being far too Christian. In other words, we need, if we are going to critique Duncan, to do so on his own terms and in his own language.

Mortality and the Dissolution of the Self

As both Duncan and Nancy were aware, community only comes into being when the individual is faced with strife and conflagration. According to Nancy,

> Community is revealed in the death of others; hence it is always revealed to others. Community is what takes place always through others

> and for others. It is not the space of the *egos*—subjects and substances that are at bottom immortal—but of the *I*'s, who are always *others* (or else are nothing). . . . A community is the presentation to its members of their mortal truth. . . . It is the presentation of the finitude and the irredeemable excess that make up finite being: its death, but also its birth, and only the community can present me my birth . . . as well as the impossibility of my crossing over into my death.[30]

This "mortal truth," for Duncan, often takes the form of war, understandably so for a poet who grew up during an unprecedented era of American expansion/imperialism. "A Seventeenth Century Suite" is particularly illuminating because it affords us a view of Duncan in the twilight of his career. As Norman Finkelstein has argued, the late collections *Ground Work: Before the War*—which includes the "Suite"—and *Ground Work: In the Dark* show a poetry that "turns on itself, becoming increasingly attenuated, self-diminishing, even a self-sacrificing body of writing. . . . The writing feeds on both the poet himself and on other poetries."[31] This self-cannibalistic writing—Mackey draws connections to the image of Uroboros, the snake swallowing its own tail—fails Duncan, and his readers, in terms of reaching any definitive conclusions in regard to what can be done against the horrors of the Vietnam War. But such metaphors can also be read as echoes of the poet's own realization of his own death. Duncan's nonproscriptive stance on the war—what he himself calls a "mystical pacifism"—can therefore also be understood, within the context of his later poetry, as the "failure" of the subject; in other words, there is a singular, rational, centered self.[32] In the "Suite" we find a voice that constantly reaches its imaginative limits: "I cannot imagine, gazing upon photographs / of these young girls, the mind / transcending what's been done to them" (76). And further on:

> Victor and victim know not what they do
>   —the deed exceeding what we would *know*;
> the knowledge in the sight of those eyes
>   goes deep into the heart's fatalities.
>
> [. . .]

What can I feel of it?   All hurt
rushes in to illustrate that glare
and fails.   What can I feel of what was done?
All hatred cringes from the sight of it
and would contract into self-loathing
to ease the knowledge of what no man
can compensate.   I think I could bear it.

I cannot think I could bear it. ("Suite," 76)

The disintegration (and thus the impossibility) of the unified subject is felt through the very form of the poetry, since the fragmentary nature of the modern subject necessitates a radical reimagining of poetic forms as well. Finkelstein writes of "what appears to be a significant transformation in Duncan's verse and perhaps a decline in its lyric qualities. . . . Something strange seems to be happening in the last phases of his work."[33] This "strange" turn is an "unmaking or a passage beyond the bounds even of open-form poetry, combined with a shift in what was previously the poet's centering sense of prophetic vocation, [that] results in an unprecedented kind of writing that no longer seems to be lyric poetry in any conventional sense of the term."[34] Finkelstein goes on to argue that Duncan's late works are an attempt to move toward what the former calls a form of "scripture" that escapes the limits imposed on poetry by the lyric. Duncan's late poetry, along with the aforementioned negation of any metaphysical notion of community, initiates a poetry that enacts the death of the author both in the poststructuralist sense of the term and in the actual, corporeal sense of the poet's own mortality. Finkelstein states that Duncan was familiar with poststructuralist theory and read Roland Barthes with care.[35] But even before Barthes, Duncan saw in Freud's work that the modern subject was constructed on faulty ground. Duncan states that Freud was "my master in his profound sense of the nature and operations of language," and it was Freud, of course, who illustrated how the unconscious undermines concepts such as agency and rationalism, concepts that have traditionally grounded the subject. Duncan: "What I would point out in my work as one of its underlying currents is the weaving of a figure unweaving, an art of unsaying what it says, of saying what it would not say. I want to catch myself out."[36] As such, Duncan's late poetry participates in a postmodern aesthetic that seeks to reexamine and abandon any traditional notions regarding a fully unified and centered subject. Duncan, therefore, in his last two *Ground Work* collections, has moved away from his early romanticist notions regarding the individual to give us a subject fraught with fissures and completely unsure of itself.

There are many moments from the "Suite" that show a mind reaching its limits when faced with suffering, pain, and despair that no amount of rational or positivist thought can make sense of: "wounds break open in the crusts above, / pustulences upon the skin love wears; / generations of despair mount up." Or "Terror erodes its own events, / shadows having no more touch in time / than shadows, yet / there's no relief from that knowledge" ("Suite," 72, 80). Nancy writes: "The individual . . . first knows community when it experiences that impossibility of communion or immanence (the self-presence of individuals to one another in and by their community) before the dead other."[37] Only when faced with the other's suffering and death are we exposed to our own "finitude." Mortality is the irreducible line that cannot be crossed, the moment where community begins and ends. Mortality is a theme Duncan confronts in the very beginning of the "Suite." Rewriting Raleigh's poem "What is our life?" and extending Raleigh's conceit of life as theatrical performance, Duncan states that we are "like actors" in this life "who have not been given their lines" nor "the play they belong to." He continues:

> where most inspired,   the scenes of a lasting passion
>   thrill and then pass on to continuities
> in which their promise is undone and lost.
>   It is the event of a momentary sequence
> that depended upon a place it had in common
>   among commonplaces, in the daily routine
> of suffering, pleasure, despite and make-shift companions;
>
> ("Suite," 71)

And, finally, the conclusion that "In death alone *we* are sincere" ("Suite," 72, emphasis added). Death brings with it sincerity and a certain *truth* through the "performative space" of the theater, an idea I will elaborate on below. But this performative space is also a communal space, one where *we* come to know the sincerity and meaning of our own existence through death and the dissolution of the self and of others. Duncan's theater is where "continuities" pass from one to another and where we relate to each other through "commonplaces" of "suffering" and "pleasure." It is a space where the very idea of community is enacted and produced.

As Duncan observes in *The H.D. Book*, we "participate in a community that exists in a time larger than any individual life-time, [and] in a language."[38] There is no individual who can transcend the limits of his or her own community—or language. It is only fitting, therefore, that the last poem in Duncan's final collection, *Ground Work: In the Dark*, would be the elegiac "After a Long Illness," a work that directly confronts the kidney disease, the "high blood pressure / the accumulation of toxins, the / break-down of ratios" that would claim the poet's life. The dialectical process between individual and community continues to the literal end, the end of life. When Duncan writes, "My Death attended me and I knew / I was not going to die, / nursed me thru. Life took hold," one should not read this as a Whitmanesque affirmation of the constant renewal of life through nature or of the poet's soul transcending its corporeal limits and continuing to exist in an afterworld of some kind.[39] Rather, I see it is an acknowledgment that language itself will go on without the poet, that despite all our own fears about death and mortality, the community will continue its attempts to actualize itself without us.

Performative Spaces

In conclusion, I would like to focus on the relational spaces that Duncan constructs in the "Suite" as a kind of metaphorical opening through which the operations of the community are examined. Spatial metaphors and dimensions are abundant in the "Suite," and they almost always suggest a coming together of radically different zones of contact. I call these openings of the possibility of community "performative spaces" due to their self-reflexive and metaphorical dimensions. The "Suite," for example, begins with Duncan contemporizing one of Walter Raleigh's conceits of life as theater, a "play of passion," turning it into "but shadows upon / a moving picture screen" (71). The self-reflexive nature of such language—and of the metaphor—brings the artifice of it all to our attention. The "Suite" is replete with such moments where the scaffolding of the poem's language is represented through spatial metaphors:

> I know but part of it and that   but distantly,
> a catastrophe in another place, another time,
>   the mind addresses
> and would erect within itself   itself
>   as Viet Nam,   itself as Bangladesh,
> itself exacting revenge and suffering revenge,
>   itself the Court and before the Court
> where new judges disloyal to the Spirit of the Law
>   are brought.   All forces conspire
>   to seat them there. (80)

We have a variety of spaces here: Vietnam, Bangladesh, the mind (the subject's interiority), and the court. Each space, in essence, acts as a synecdoche for any other space appearing in the poem and yet retains its distinct particularities as well. Here, Duncan blurs the distinction between the mind's ability to wield power and to be a victim of that very power, "itself exacting revenge and suffering revenge." I would like to further suggest that such different spatial metaphors bring forth a variety of heterogeneous subjective positions. Here and elsewhere, Duncan's spatial metaphors act as transports to other modalities of thinking and being. We are asked to imagine—even if we are aware that such an enterprise will fail—the positions and sufferings of others, to place ourselves in the space, place, of the Other.

Consider the following lines. Again, the imagery of the court appears as an example of what a performative space enacts. Duncan writes:

> I'd like to clear the air,
> take on a "modern" stance, Poetics 1924,
> a language without ornament,
> a measure   functional thruout,

nothing fancy,   all
without excess,   expressive,
recalling an archaic mask,
the gesture stylized,   to speak
    from energy alone.

The essential, nothing more!
The temper, fire and ice.
Line, hard cut,   without device.
Eyes, hierarchical, straight forward.
Having that rigor
testimony before the Court demands. (87–88)

This passage comes from section 9 of the "Suite," where Duncan quotes and writes variations on a masque written by Ben Jonson for the "honor of the wedding of the Earl of Essex with Lady Frances Howard . . . performed at Court on 5 January 1606" (84). Every court, whether it be juridical or monarchical, is a space where certain well-known roles are enacted and performed, and in an overdetermined manner. In this part of the "Suite" Duncan plays on such performances and uses them to suggest how language allows us different modes of being, for it is nothing but a "mask," if even an "archaic one." The poetic voice is free to "move" about within the performative space in order to foster different subjectivities, to take on different positions: the taking on of a "modern stance," to give another example, or the awareness of the fact that the gaze constructs and defines identities, that "eyes" are "hierarchical."

There is also an urgent movement inward, toward interiority, suggesting in this poem—and much of the late poetry—a sense of constant inward collapse, as one can find with the notion of the mind constructing "within itself itself." This inward turning is the self being turned against its own existence. From the "Suite": "My heart / caves into a space it seems / to have long feared" and "What can I feel of it? All hurt / rushes in to illustrate that glare / and fails" (75–76). What we have is an imaginative faculty seeking an escape route out of corporeality, out of language, out of community. One can consider the "Suite" a flow chart on which the poet's wandering mind is shown in the process of *thinking* and how this process slowly turns: "Now darkness overtakes my thought of dark, / rifts of Our Father blot me out. I'm near / extinguisht. Return . . . Return" (93). The poem's coda ends with a descent "into the infancy of a darkening bliss," a space with intangible dimensions in it. We are with a mind attempting to imagine the impossible: its own end.

I contend that such moments are meant to alert us to the (im)possibilities of a totally revelatory opening in language. Duncan explains: "Today, many use marijuana or LSD in order to come into a reality larger than their own personality or case history or their one family or one city or one nation or one species. But I do it on language. *Words* send me."[40] In this sense, the spatial metaphors in the "Suite" are much easier to understand: they are transports to places where thinking is possible, where a *breakthrough* may actually occur. For this very reason, these spaces form a resistance against conventional modes of thinking and of being (in the same way that community does for Nancy). They challenge what we have come to know—in regard to war, in regard to language—and afford us, at the least, the possibility of thinking more, of thinking differently.

Following Duncan's claims of escape, I see a poet not so much interested in the metaphysical transport that words may be able to provide but, rather, resisting the ways of the world. The metaphorical and performative spaces that are examined in the "Suite" are sites of resistance in that they posit alternatives to the ways of this current world.

DERIVATIVENESS IS the means through which Duncan examines a range of crises—the dissolution of community, the end of the self, the limits of language. Ironically, what is most liberating about Duncan's late poetics is that it does not offer any easy solutions. As G. Matthew Jenkins has suggested, "Duncan's paradoxical form keeps opposites interpenetrating, deconstructing, and reconstituting: narrative/poetry, self/Other, order/disorder, chord/ discord, and so on, but not just on the level of thematic motifs. This poetics, which for Duncan amounts to an oscillating process as much as a typographical shape for his poem, pervades every level of his writing, from singular poems to long series to entire books and, ultimately, to his entire corpus. Duncan never stops contradicting himself or unsaying something he had previously said."[41] It is in this process of undoing and redoing that one of Duncan's most singular virtues rests: that his is also a highly ethical project, and one that never stops interrogating conventional attitudes to our most vexing issues. We would do well to reread Duncan as a poet concerned not with a hermetic retreat from reality but as a writer deeply concerned with weaving together the social, the political, the ethical, and the aesthetic.

Notes

1. Mackey, *Discrepant Engagement*, 70.
2. Mackey, *Paracritical Hinge*, 125; Pound, *The Spirit of Romance*, 8. My equating Duncan's poem with Pound's dictum is simply to suggest that tradition—and, by extension, history—is not simply situated in a "past" that we can easily isolate at a careful proximity from what we may call the "present" or the "future." In this sense, tradition may be a means to critique static notions of time and place as well.
3. Mackey, *Discrepant Engagement*, 95.
4. Mackey, *Paracritical Hinge*, 71–178.
5. The ongoing disintegration of Western metaphysics and the far-ranging implications of this process fall far outside the goals of this essay. My argument, rather, rests on what I see as the much simpler historical trajectory from romanticism to modernism to postmodernism, all of which are historical moments Duncan, in some way, had a stake in. I am, therefore, simply interested in the overall epistemological uncertainty that grounds these historical paradigm shifts and their broader implications for poetry.
6. Nancy, *The Inoperative Community*, 1.
7. Duncan, *Ground Work: Before the War*, 72.
8. Ibid., 75.
9. The poem's intertextuality and self-referential nature are further emphasized by Duncan's use of section 8 as a sequence for his open-ended series of *Passages*, this one being number 36.
10. Nancy, *The Inoperative Community*, 71. This also echoes Duncan's own conception of what can be of virtue in poetry: its very lack of utility, its existence on the margins of society.
11. Ibid., x.
12. Duncan and Levertov, *Letters*, xxii.

13. As is now common knowledge, it was in the way they viewed their own commitments to the antiwar effort that ended the close relationship between Levertov and Duncan. Through the disintegration of their relationship, one gets a better idea of where the two poets stood in terms of their own poetics.
14. Duncan and Levertov, *Letters*, 608–9.
15. Duncan, *Ground Work: Before the War*, 76. Hereafter cited in the text as "Suite."
16. Duncan, "Man's Fulfillment in Order and Strife," 111.
17. Davidson, "Review," 555.
18. Duncan and Levertov, *Letters*, 558.
19. Johnson, *Robert Duncan*, 18.
20. See Mackey, *Discrepant Engagement*, 95–96, for a further examination of Duncan's appreciation of poetry's nonutilitarian role.
21. Duncan, *Bending the Bow*, 81.
22. Ibid.
23. Duncan, "Man's Fulfillment in Order and Strife," 129. The use of the term "demotic" is especially compelling here as further evidence of Duncan's concerns with communal language.
24. Duncan, *Bending the Bow*, i.
25. Mackey, *Paracritical Hinge*, 120.
26. Duncan, *Bending the Bow*, 81.
27. Michelson, "A Materialist Critique," 35.
28. Mackey, *Paracritical Hinge*, 113.
29. Duncan, "Towards an Open Universe," in Duncan, *Fictive Certainties*, 83.
30. Nancy, *The Inoperative Community*, 15.
31. Finkelstein, "Late Duncan," 344.
32. "Mystical pacifism" is from Duncan, "Man's Fulfillment in Order and Strife," 115.
33. Finkelstein, "Late Duncan," 341.
34. Ibid., 341–42.
35. Ibid., 347.
36. Duncan, "The Self in Postmodern Poetry," in Duncan, *Fictive Certainties*, 231–32.
37. Nancy, *The Inoperative Community*, xvi.
38. Duncan, *The H.D. Book*, 157.
39. Duncan, *Ground Work: In the Dark*, 89.
40. Duncan, "Man's Fulfillment in Order and Strife," 121.
41. Jenkins, *Poetic Obligation*, 121.

CHAPTER THREE

Textual Poetics and the Politics of Reading in Duncan's "Night Scenes"

SIOBHÁN SCARRY

Robert Duncan's 1964 collection *Roots and Branches* opens with the figure of the Monarch "tracing out of air unseen roots and branches of sense / I share in thought."[1] It is a fitting way to begin a collection in which the poet will so thoroughly and with such a capacious vision explore the literary and personal influences on his work. True to the movement of the Monarchs, which "sail" and "[flit]" in the opening poem, the derivations and inspirations throughout *Roots and Branches* range widely, from H.D. to Charles Baudelaire and from William Blake to Jesus to Erik Satie.

Michael André Bernstein suggests that critical traction for highly intertextual work such as Duncan's can best be gained through a "willingness to attend to the intricate and enormously diverse modes of its realization."[2] In the case of Duncan, this diversity of modes can occur even within a single poem, as the text and textual history of "Night Scenes" attests. This essay explores this single poem from Duncan's 1964 collection, tracing its derivations and its genetic history and opening a reading of the poem that may help to expand the critical conversation about both the textual practices and political import of Duncan's derivative poetics.

"Night Scenes," a three-part serial poem that explicitly takes up the affective and material practices of gay male cruising, is a derivative poem in myriad ways, engaging in a textual practice that, as Duncan himself later describes, pulls from "multiple kinds of source."[3] Part 1 of the poem, which opens onto the New York streets at night where those "seeking to release Eros" must contend with the pressing threat of the police, exists in fascinating relationship to an epistolary corpus between Duncan and Bay Area poet Mary Fabilli.[4] Letters and an unpublished poem of Duncan's reveal the interpersonal context and the body of accompanying texts around which Duncan composes and frames "Night Scenes."

In the second part of the poem, Duncan provides a rereading of Shakespeare's Ariel from *The Tempest*. Genetic study of this section also uncovers a revisionary praxis that submerges the "textual derivations" of early drafts in service to bringing forth the sexual content of the poem as material fit to stand on its own. References to and quotes from André Breton pepper the third section of the poem. More than simple appropriation or citation, Duncan's use of Breton is also that of literary interpretation and, as it turns out, prototranslation. Duncan pulls both text and context from Breton's poem "Pleine marge" ("Full Margin"), refashioning, dislocating, and reinterpreting the poem in ways that not only produce a rereading of the source text but also serve the larger vision of "Night Scenes." Duncan's translation of "Full Margin," which he produced in the year following the first publication of "Night Scenes," was never published, though others of Duncan's Breton translations found their way into print.

Though "Night Scenes" proceeds through the disjunctions and discontinuities one often encounters in serial poems, and though the derivations range in catholic fashion from Renaissance drama to contemporary surrealism, Duncan's use of derivations within the poem reveals a surprising unity of vision. Michael Davidson, among other critics, has pointed to the ways in which Duncan's use of literary texts within his poems permit him "to write himself into a tradition . . . [and] [refigure] the tradition as sexual."[5] Whether choosing the placement of a phrase from Breton or working to revise the punctuation in part 2 of the poem, at every textual turn Duncan puts derivation to the task of writing homosexuality back into the canon. In "Night Scenes" this is not simply a celebratory or uncomplicated move, nor is it merely an end in itself. With cruising as the through-line among the three parts of the poem—from the New York streets at night to the sexual consummation "stumbling, / into whose arms" ("Night," 7) to the morning streets of Paris, where "half-naked men" (9) draw the speaker's attentions—Duncan figures desire throughout as mobile and circulating, all within the mediated space of urban environments. In linking mobility, sexuality, and urban modernity, "Night Scenes," for all else that it does, may also attend in revealing ways to a particular historical matrix of material and social realities.

THE COMPOSITION HISTORY of "Night Scenes" begins in the spring of 1959, when a draft of part 2 of the poem appears in Duncan's notebooks.[6] The most sexually explicit section of the poem, part 2 follows "green lovers" through the "knotted tides of dark" as they fall into each other's arms at "four o'clock in the morning, stumbling," and then proceed to pleasure each other until "Fatigue spread[s] back" and the "thin spire of longing / perishes."[7] The poem is an unabashed celebration of pleasure and sexual release. Thom Gunn provides this fitting summary: "In the second part [of "Night Scenes"] the innocent boy's orgasm is seen, simply, as lovely in itself."[8]

Genetic study reveals that the poem was not always so at ease with allowing the sexual content, its graphic nature especially, to stand on its own. Duncan's revisions, including those that surround his use of Shakespeare's Ariel, reveal that the sexual matter of the poem was inextricably linked in the early drafts with what one might call Duncan's own "textual derivations," writing that is aware of itself as text and that serves to grant the writer a kind of permission.[9] Duncan excises these portions of the text as the poem moves closer to publication, more confidently putting forth gay desire, and gay sex, on the page as stand-alone material.

One of the signal moments in the poem in which these energies of revision are most evident occurs in the opening lines. When Duncan first composes the draft of part 2 in his notebook, he begins with a double-columned text that appears to be two poems, or a single poem in which multiple reading practices are available. Here is Duncan's original draft from 1959:

How it goes   where the poet can take hold, and
together   in what tempers restore that current
syntactics   which forth-flowing goes

has in each   a wholeness green lovers know
directive   as each in each a fearful happiness
to everywhere   sees the resolute eye in which
        opposites

reason is
still moving   spring twined forth right
song of arrest,
        A light, toward the dark of fucking
scale of souls: I saw the Prince of Morning fall,

and from the Beast a man that was Day came
shaking my heart like a storm in old trees[10]

When "Night Scenes" first appears in print, in a 1962 issue of the journal the *Floating Bear*, the text that hugs the left margin is altogether gone. So too is the one line from the right-hand portion of the poem that explicitly references writing, the first phrase "where the poet can take hold." These changes, which expunge the originary twin impulse of the text as taking up the movements of syntax *and* the movements of desire ("that current which forth-flowing goes"), remain a fixed editorial decision of Duncan's. The same excisions remain in the version of the opening stanzas that appears two years later in *Roots and Branches*:

and in what tempers restore that current
    which forth-flowing goes
a wholeness green lovers know
    as each in each a fearful happiness
sees the resolute eye in which
    opposites
spring twined forthright.

A light toward the knotted tides of dark,
into the tenderness of the crown, night's dominion,

I saw the Prince of Morning fall,
                    opening in fucking a door of Eros.

And from the Beast a man that was Day came
shaking my heart like a storm in old trees. ("Night," 6–7)

What had allowed the poet a way in to his material (the energies of syntax, the very act of writing itself), concerns that in Duncan's oeuvre are often made explicit if not central to the meaning of his poems (and which one could argue are as much the subject of the first draft as anything else), are here removed from the published versions. The effect of this revision is a foregrounding of the erotic and sexual energies that drive the work. The writing process and the permission it grants to "take hold" of the page serve to birth the poem but then recede as ghostly progenitors.

The last lines of the poem similarly give way from a textual to a sexual focus through Duncan's revisionary praxis. Part 2 of "Night Scenes," which moves inexorably toward orgasm, in the last stanza celebrates postcoital bliss—"fatigue spreading back, a grand chorale / of who I am, who he is" (8). In the published versions of the poem, the ending lines read: "this single up-fountain of a / single note around which / the throat shapes!" (8). Given the images of fellatio that have preceded these lines, the poem seems clear about what exactly this "single note" is around which the throat—in exclamatory excitement—is eager to shape itself. But in the original draft, the poem ends quite differently: "this single up fountain of a / single note around which / the throat shapes lines of a poem to come."[11] Though the build-up of previous text, together with the obvious double entendre of the last word "come," do work to sexualize these last lines, the notebook version nonetheless reveals the original importance of writing and text as central to the ideas of the poem. In the draft, part 2 ends with the throat shaped ready for *text*. Duncan's revisions, here again, foreground the sexual content by wresting it free of its textual twin.

Revisions of a similar nature surround the portion of the poem in which Duncan makes use of Shakespeare's Ariel. Attending to this textual history proves integral to understanding how Duncan is using Shakespeare and rewriting the character of Ariel within his poem. Two texts from *The Tempest* make their way into part 2 of "Night Scenes," both from act 5, scene 1. The first is a portion of Prospero's speech to the royal party from Milan who stand charmed before him and who in short order will come to know that it is his white magic that has brought them to the island. Duncan pulls the language exactly from the text of the play and imports it into his poem as citation, which he makes clear through the typographical choice of italicization:

> *The charme dissolves apace*
> *And as the morning steales upon the night*
> *(Melting the darkness) so their rising sences*
> *Begin to chace the ignorant fumes that mantle*
> *Their cleerer reason* ("Night," 7)

In the play, as Prospero speaks, time is suspended for the royal party, who remain "spell-stopped."[12] Duncan places this block of text after the "green lovers" of his poem connect but before they experience sexual release. Prospero's charms seem to provide a function consonant with the "maiden hours" that "dance" and circle to "slow down ecstasy" ("Night," 7). The sensual is figured as taking place while under a charm or spell bestowed by a beneficent magician and thus participating in a radically different temporality —what Duncan calls "an inner temple of durations"—than that of linear time (7). Prospero's white magic, then, is put to use as an intertextual spell in "Night Scenes" that authorizes the sensual pleasures of a gay hook-up.

At the end of Prospero's long speech in act 5, he turns to his servant, Ariel, requesting the retrieval of certain garments from his former life in Milan so that he may reveal himself to his captives; he also reminds the "airy spirit" that he will soon set him free from *his* captivity. Ariel sings the following lines in happy expectation of his freedom, and it is this passage that Duncan takes up in his drafts of part 2 and through which he will ultimately rewrite the character of Ariel:

Where the bee sucks, there suck I.
In a cowslip's bell I lie;
There I couch when owls do cry.
On that bat's back I do fly
After summer merrily.
Merrily, merrily shall I live now
Under the blossom that hangs on the bough.[13]

Duncan writes two radically different versions of the stanza in which Ariel's text will appear in "Night Scenes." In the first draft, the writing is self-reflexive and seeks a kind of permission, not unlike the other portions of part 2 that Duncan ultimately cuts before publication. Note that the same revisionary praxis holds true here. Below is Duncan's original draft from the handwritten notebook, followed by the version that appears in *Roots and Branches*.

can you suck a cock in a poem?
where does the bee sip,
sips I? at the ledge[14]

Where the bee sucks, there, the airy spirit sings, *suck I!*
Where does the bee sip? harvest what honey
    in what beehive?
In a Cowslips bell, I lie —at the ledge ("Night," 7)

In the lines that follow both versions, the poem goes on to do precisely what Duncan worries in his first draft may not be permissible within a poem at all. "Youth spurts, at the lip the flower / lifts lifewards," and, even more explicitly, "we see one lover take his lover in his mouth" ("Night," 7–8). That Duncan submerges the "writing about writing" by the final draft is consonant with his other revisions of part 2, which work toward foregrounding the sexual content as material able to stand on its own. But in this case, the edits are not simply excisions. As Duncan removes the overt and rather vulnerable questions of the first draft, he adds in Ariel's exact lines from the play, and the tone of the stanza markedly shifts into greater confidence and, one could argue, celebration of the sexual content. Even following the changes in punctuation is instructive, as the two question marks that begin the stanza move away from any attachment to the "I" of the poem in the published version; in fact, the first line moves from ending with a question mark to ending with a period (in the intervening draft of the poem's first publication in the *Floating Bear*) to the effusive choice of the exclamation point.

Part of what accounts for the increasing confidence of the text has to do with Duncan's reading of Ariel, a deeper understanding of which is made available by considering Duncan's first draft of the stanza. There, his forthright question—"can you suck a cock in a poem?"—is answered in the affirmative by Ariel's very entrance into the text in the second line. Duncan reads Ariel's plans for freedom, which (in a literal reading) include sucking nectar from flowers, as the longed-for textual antecedent of male-male fellatio that will allow him permission to continue with his own text. When Duncan turns back to the play itself to gather Ariel's exact lines, an interesting lexical transposition occurs that one can only imagine would have delighted Duncan. The verb "suck" from Duncan's own question is, in fact, the same word that Ariel uses to describe his gathering of the nectar; this may give the exclamation point of the finished draft an additional valence, as the quote in the first line could be read as containing both voices.

When Ariel sings of his freedom in the play, he imagines himself as increasingly mobile and free to move about the island as he wishes. This is an unsurprising desire, given his having been trapped for years within a cloven pine, followed by his servitude to Prospero. But Duncan's reading of Ariel, which links this desire for roaming and mobility to decidedly gay sex acts, situates him within "Night Scenes" and reads him back into literature as a kind of proto-gay-cruising figure. In an interview in 1978, Duncan offers insight into perhaps why Shakespeare emerged as a fitting source for a poem such as "Night Scenes": "Shakespeare seems to have indwelt on imagining who any of us readers were going to be that we all discover ourselves in him. . . . Almost anyone who gets into him finds that he was really writing for you, whoever you are."[15]

That Duncan transforms his source texts in such a way that allows him to write himself, and homosexuality, back into the canon is an aspect of his derivative poetics that has been noted by critics, though there is not a unitary textual practice that Duncan employs to this end. Davidson offers a careful reading that delineates the relationship in Duncan's work among scenes of instruction, which open into places of first permission and which then allow suppressed meanings—often dealing with "a sexual mystery . . . that has been suppressed within canonical books"—to emerge.[16] In part 2 of "Night Scenes," Duncan's revisions of his own "textual derivations" and his use and edits surrounding the Shakespeare text work to foreground the "suppressed meaning" of homosexuality but do so by submerging references to the text itself, those places "where the poet can take hold." Where these places of instruction and permission, in Davidson's formulation, not only inaugurate the poem but, as he rightly suggests, often "[become] one of its central subjects," in part 2 of "Night Scenes" Duncan carefully works to dismantle this material in later drafts, allowing the sexual content to arrive on the page as a subject needing no permission.[17] That this content is linked specifically to the context of cruising, and that Ariel is reutilized with this specific practice in mind, become clearer when Duncan joins the text with what will become the opening section of the larger serial poem.

IN JUNE 1959 Duncan composes what will become part 1 of "Night Scenes." Emerging in his notebook in near-final form, this first part of the serial poem follows those touched by the "blunt nose of loneliness" as they "restless move toward the deserted streets" of the city at night, which are lit alternately in the poem by the moon, the speeding light of passing cars, merchants, street lamps, and the threat of "police-cars cruising."[18] The poem revisits, in a very material way, some of Duncan's own lived experiences from his time in New York during the 1940s. An ongoing tension regarding religion and homosexuality between Duncan and his longtime friend from those early years, Bay Area poet Mary Fabilli, reached an apex in the spring of that year, when a flurry of letters and an abandoned poem served as the fiery context in which Duncan forges the first part of "Night Scenes."

Duncan and Fabilli became friends during the 1930s, when both attended

UC Berkeley as undergraduates. When Duncan moved to New York in 1938, he and Fabilli began a correspondence that would last for the rest of Duncan's life. When he returned to the Bay Area in 1945, the two resumed their friendship in person and continued to send letters across the Bay. Fabilli, a visual artist as well as a writer, produced the drawing of Duncan that serves as the frontispiece to his first book, *Heavenly City, Earthly City* (1947); Duncan helped usher Fabilli's book *Aurora Bligh & Early Poems* (1968) into print through his work with Berkeley Miscellany Editions. The mutual support they offered one another was often material—helping each other with publications, enclosing poems for comment—but as the letters reveal, their connection elicited deeply personal responses as well.

In the spring of 1959 Duncan sent Fabilli his then-recent book *Letters, Poems 1953–1956* and, as was the custom between them, asked for her comments. The letter that Fabilli sent in return, dated May 17 of that year, set into motion a veritable firestorm of letters and other writings. The letter begins by excoriating Duncan's poetry, calling it overly derivative of Stein and Pound; she even jokes that she may *burn* his book. Fabilli goes on to strike an even more personal chord when the subject turns to religion. She had, by this time, converted to Catholicism, and she is forthright in expressing her concern for Duncan's soul. Here is an excerpt from that letter:

> The affection between us has survived somehow. I suppose it's partly because I pray for you, and partly because you rely on me to pray for the salvation of your soul. But you have to want to be saved; you have to cooperate with God's grace. If I manage to get to heaven and find you have gone to hell, I will sing Alleluia just the same. So don't be delaying things too long, and don't give way to human respect; and for heaven's sake, *pray, pray, pray* that God help and save you, and change you!
>
> You may come to see me if you wish. But if my very serious faults and irascibility and lack of charity will delay your conversion, then it is better that you do not come to see me.[19]

Duncan fairly reels from the letter. Over the course of the next few weeks, his correspondence with Fabilli becomes an almost daily occurrence, he writes and then discards an angry poem in which he quotes from the letter directly, and the first part of "Night Scenes" appears in his notebook.

Duncan composes his initial poetic response on the very day Fabilli's letter arrives in the mail. "In Perplexity" provides a raw look into Duncan's thinking on religion, orthodoxy, and homosexuality, and, in the last stanza in particular, it includes his own visionary rejoinder to Fabilli's concerns, which serves as a rehearsal for the poem to come.[20]

In Perplexity

in the name of Love this pious female
suffers the thought of me in hot hell.
"The affection between us has survived somehow"
she writes
"*pray, pray, pray* that God help and save you,
and change you."
Not liking
the way I am, she keeps her concern alive.
She gives a damn. In good faith. O Christ,
wondrous is your new dispensation!
that gives the righteous ring
to her condition.
This all-forgiving love that threatens
him who does not obey its ordering,
and casts into a lasting perdition
whatever's obstinate and non-Christian.

Now I shall never come honestly into that fold.
For I love well the goods of this world
and dwell in spirit in its Other
that still is not heaven but a culture
where the imagination has its hold.
All arts furnish the language that is its ground.
All actual things are realized there.

In which such arrangements as this bigot speaks of,
continually appear within the orders of Love.
This is my perplexity:
I maintain this dame is most right.

I shall eternally suffer in her sight
and bear upon my bottom a special lasting flame
and a cold corruption to my heart hold in Christ's name
because I am a Sodomite
and, moreover, have denied obedience to Jehovah
—Lord knows I don't deny His power
He knoweth how to blight the fig and the flower.

But in this imaginary other kingdom
whereof I speak, the name of Love
includes even such hell-blasted souls as mine
for they are notes in a sort of
all-summoning scale where no man
is excluded from its harmony.
Blasting Jaweh along with Pan
and this old friend who threatens me
are parts in a designing heart and mind
of the music that sets the cosmos free
and in the place of all we bless and damn
bringeth whole a joyous Adam.[21]

That "In Perplexity" responds so directly to this interpersonal crisis gives the poem particular force, especially when the full context of Duncan's connection to Fabilli is known.[22] But it is precisely this same quality of direct and un-worked-through reaction that causes Duncan to ultimately shelve the poem. He writes Denise Levertov in mid-July that he has reevaluated the piece as participating in a kind of "gratuitous protest" that ultimately "avoids roots and feeling, substituting attitudes and hysteria."[23] The interchange between Duncan and Levertov regarding the poem is ironic, given their own falling-out-to-come over Levertov's protest poems, and even more poignant if one agrees with Albert Gelpi that the rupture surrounding the political differences between Duncan and Levertov was ultimately rooted, as Duncan's and Fabilli's was, in "different religious sensibilities and theological stances toward reality."[24]

It is nonetheless Levertov to whom Duncan sends the poem a week after its composition, and it is she who both steers him away from the "tone of anger or indignance" that she feels mars the work *and* directs his attention to the last stanza as material capable of lasting value.[25] Here is the kernel of Levertov's assessment of "In Perplexity," sent to Duncan in a letter dated May 25:

> The poem doesn't seem fully alive in its own right, it is still so much attached to your immediate feelings on receiving someone's letter. So that tho the last stanza is so beautiful the rest of the poem puts me in mind of the long, indignant protesting or scornful letters I have often written in response to some criticism but next day have thrown out. Yet there's so much substance there—I would hate to see the poem rejected by you yet I don't feel it is a free thing as it stands.[26]

While Duncan ultimately rejects "In Perplexity" as a stand-alone poem, he does in fact salvage its last stanza. When Levertov writes him again in early June, this time with even greater candor—the poem, she writes, "doesn't seem up to you perhaps"—part 1 of "Night Scenes" follows hard upon this last missive, emerging as a draft in his notebook a few days later.[27] This first section of the poem, *its* last stanza in particular, bears fruit from the seeds of the abandoned poem.

Part 1 of "Night Scenes" broadens its gaze from the interpersonal and discursive quality of "In Perplexity" to take up the broader social context and material conditions of those whom Duncan in the earlier poem calls "such hell-blasted souls as mine."[28] It is set in the very real world ("the place of all we bless and damn") of New York's urban cruising scene in the first half of the twentieth century, and Duncan reveals more than the singular experience of a "Sodomite" whose "old friend . . . threatens [him]."[29] The poem's lens expands outward with an ever-increasing view to reveal that "terror / touches my heart, our hearts, all hearts / that have come in along these sexual avenues / seeking to release Eros from our mistrust" ("Night," 6). The threat posed by one friend in the first poem is figured here in "Night Scenes" as the menacing Panopticon of the larger society: "police-cars cruising," which are "part of the old divine threat"—even the city itself, which "roars / and is a lion. / . . . a treacherous leviathan" (6). In *Cruising Modernism* Michael Trask describes the historical and theoretical shifts in early twentieth-century America that linked anxieties about perverse and illicit sexuality with fears about cross-class contact, immigrant workers, and the unsettling of stability and categories in general. Trask hones in on the ways in which certain modernist texts take up "mobility and dynamism" such that they link "radical erotic energies" with "the central conceits of class."[30] While Duncan's work straddles modernism, and while this representation of New York in the 1940s is a retrospective look from the vantage point of the late 1950s, it is nonetheless important to acknowledge the very real ways in which the text focuses on mobility and desire; the exigencies of cruising, which, by its nature, connotes cross-class contact; modern urbanity; and the policing of sexuality—all within this same historical matrix.

In the closing stanza of "In Perplexity," Duncan offers his rejoinder to Fabilli, a vision of a place in which even "hell-blasted souls . . . / are notes in a sort of / all-summoning scale where no man / is excluded from its harmony."[31] In that poem, he offers up his vision in full, a "music that sets the cosmos free . . . and bringeth whole a joyous Adam."[32] In the final stanza of part 1 of "Night Scenes," this "all-summoning" or "all-including scale" and its music are revisited, but here Duncan's particular prelapsarian vision is tempered by the full context of the societal parameters. The moon, whose light first draws the reader's eye into the traffic and lights of the city in the opening stanza, returns in the final portion of the poem as a natural force among the material and social realities of police cars and terror-filled hearts; its light moves democratically as it "climbs the scale of souls" ("Night," 6) who have walked along the night streets. But given the real forces that press in, the music of this scale is not a certainty but rather something longed for. In the final lines of part 1, Duncan uses the heightened voicing of apostrophe to reassert the vision of an inclusive music and harmony but also to measure the distance between the vision and its realities, which include threats of arrest and violence, "nerves respond[ing]," and the "blunt nose of loneliness" over it all: "O, to release the first music somewhere again, / for a moment / to touch the design of the first melody!" (6). Duncan effectively transforms the "substance" that Levertov recognizes as a promise in the final stanza of "In Perplexity" into a poem that no longer relies on indignation for its "roots and feeling" but rather uses the interpersonal antecedent of a crisis in friendship to inform a poem of broader concerns.

The particular vision put forth in the last stanzas of both "In Perplexity" and the first section of "Night Scenes" is Duncan's own formulation, and while it may draw from a number of traditions, it does not owe its allegiance to any particular orthodoxy. As Davidson points out, Duncan "gained a good deal of his polemical energy from establishing an apostate relation to what he perceived as orthodoxy," and, further, a particular "antipathy to the organized Christian church . . . can be found throughout his writings."[33] Even his friendships, Davidson relates, "were charged with conflicts over violations of (imagined or real) orders."[34] This is certainly true of Duncan's friendship with Fabilli, where struggles over orthodoxy generate the polemical and ultimately textual energies that produce a fit of letters and an abandoned poem and serve as the context in which the first section of "Night Scenes" is composed.

THE THIRD AND FINAL section of "Night Scenes" appears to have been composed fairly close to the poem's first publication in 1962. It does not have as clear a genetic history as the other two sections in the sense that there are no drafts of the poem in Duncan's notebooks, and what typescript pages do exist do not contain dates. It is perhaps for this reason that the full extent of the poem's textual negotiations with André Breton and his poem "Pleine marge" has not yet been brought to light.

Part 3 takes the reader on a morning walk through the streets of Paris, where the early markets make a "temple of produce" and the attentions of the speaker turn to "the savor of men's bodies"—"the torsos of men and trucks in their own light, steaming" ("Night," 9). It is the morning after, as it were, and somehow the speaker has awoken in Paris, a city that "compels" him, "wandering from Breton and towards him by the plan of her streets" (9). This "wandering" speaks to the through-line within the poem as a whole—the cruising that has taken the speaker through the streets of New York, to consummation at four in the morning, and now to a dawn stroll through Paris that reads as an admixture of modern urban cruising and—borrowing from the repertoire available in the new location—a nineteenth-century Parisian notion of *flânerie*; given Duncan's infusion of homosexual desire into the concept, he taps into Priscilla Ferguson's characterization of the *flâneur* as "something of a deviant in emerging bourgeois society" for whom the feeling of "disapprobation never entirely dissipates."[35]

But when the poem's speaker tells us he is compelled to wander "from Breton and towards him," it is also a revelation of the poem's compositional practice. Part 3 of "Night Scenes" is in constant negotiation with Breton's 1940 poem "Pleine marge," leaning on the Breton text for concepts and context, importing direct citations from the poem in French, and dislocating and reenvisioning those lines in ways that serve the larger vision of Duncan's own poem. This derivation is made even more complex by the fact that Duncan would work to translate "Pleine marge" in the months following the publication of "Night Scenes," opening a reading of part 3 as an act of prototranslation as well.

In Duncan's early years in New York, he met scores of European artists, many of whom had come to the United States to flee the Nazis. Ekbert Faas notes in his biography that Duncan had personal contact with a number of surrealists, Yves Tanguy among them. While Duncan apparently did not know Breton well, he did meet him at least once, at a party filled with surrealist émigrés from Paris. Duncan describes his experience at that party in a letter to Sanders Russell: "I felt absolutely brilliant, a genius, in their company. . . . Thank god we're not Surrealists."[36]

Duncan's vexed relationship to surrealism is well documented, perhaps most pointedly by Duncan himself. In his now-famous 1947 attack on the journal *View*, Duncan takes to task editor Charles Henri Ford for what Duncan reads as a politically vacuous editorial vision in which evils are not so much exposed but simply exhibited as ends in themselves—"not a rejection but an acceptance, more than that, a tremulous embrace of what was horrible, a sensation which may be tasted by the reader for the vicarious thrill of it."[37] Duncan essentially accuses Ford of packaging the magazine's political material in ways that made it palatable to the bourgeoisie; it is in this vein that Duncan extends his invective to the surrealists, and Breton is one of two writers singled out in the attack. Duncan calls Breton and Nicolas Calas "romantic revolutionists" who "rediscovered . . . revolution for the sheer sensation of it," playing out "the real political world . . . in charade to give excitement to the boredom of the rentiers"; Duncan saw them as sellouts who "capitalized upon their revolutionary personalities" and allowed themselves to be "taken up and taken in by the culture collectors."[38]

Duncan's engagement with Breton in "Night Scenes" is all the more interesting given this history, and it seems no accident that a poem so steeped in Duncan's New York of the 1940s would revisit a writer and a text from that same time and place in his life.[39] It is also fitting that he chooses "Pleine marge" with which to engage, a poem of Breton's that has been noted specifically for *not* playing at the political world but instead addressing Breton's very real "anxieties about the fate of Europe, the rise of religious conservatism in Vichy France, and his fears for his and his family's safety."[40] Breton wrote the poem in the summer of 1940 while staying in Provence at the home of his friend and doctor, Pierre Mabille (to whom the poem is dedicated); at the time, Breton was awaiting passage to America and worried —given his political affiliations and the possibility of Vichy repression— about his family's safety. Breton and his family did get out of Vichy France in 1941, arriving in New York in June of that year.

The poem "Pleine marge" was published in France in *Cahiers du sud* in the same year as its composition; in 1943 it appeared as a clandestine edition within France as well as through the Nierendorf Gallery in New York, which produced fifty copies or so of the poem in French.[41] Given the overlapping circles in which Duncan and Breton moved in New York, it is conceivable that Duncan saw the poem in this early gallery publication, though it is more likely that he became aware of the text when it appeared as "Full Margin" in its first English translation by Édouard Roditi in the journal *View* in December 1944.[42]

Regardless of when Duncan first encountered the poem, it is clear that by the time he composed part 3 of "Night Scenes," he had an intimate knowledge of the poem. Part 3 is so infused with Breton's text conceptually, imagistically, and linguistically that the relationship between the two warrants a fuller study than can be provided here. But like other of Duncan's derivations within "Night Scenes," his use of Breton, while employing a variety of textual strategies, works toward the larger vision of the serial poem. Duncan uses Breton's context of France, the city merchants, and the poem's persistent imagery of "low-lying lamps" (26), "torches" (11), and "embers" (44) to inform his own poem, which he sets in Paris amid the "early markets" (16) and where a "raised lamp" (18), "flashes" (6), and "the harp of the sun" (10) begin the day.[43] But where Breton's poem ranges all over France and turns its erotic attentions toward "women at odds with their time" (8) and "above all others that Queen of Byzantium" (12), Duncan's text keeps within the bounds of the Parisian streets and looks longingly toward "these grails" (21) that are "not breasts or lions of the Queen of Byzantium, / but men working" (20–21). The poem's descriptions linger over the "torsos of men" (17) as they work, attending not only to the beauty of their bodies, which makes the speaker's "heart [smoke]" (25), but to the material results of their labor as well—"from the muscles of men working in fields [we] see / cathedrals rise" (14–15).

Duncan implicates Breton by reenvisioning his text as one available to a gay-cruising reading and interpretation. Part 3 begins with two lines in French that appear to be a direct citation from the Breton text, but Duncan includes one sly alteration. The first stanza of Breton's poem ends with this line: "La lampe de mon coeur file et bientôt hoquète à l'approche des parvis" (3), which Roditi translates as "My heart's lamp smokes and soon splutters on nearing a parvis" (3). Duncan replaces "mon" or "my" with Breton's name, so that part 3 of "Night Scenes" begins with the heart of André Breton now smoking, and it is his heart that will be forced to smolder over images that "savor . . . men's bodies" (38).

In the other instances of direct citation, Duncan similarly uses Breton's text to write homosexuality back into the source text and forward into his own, a practice that is similar to his use of Shakespeare in part 2, though I would argue Duncan makes a less overt claim on Breton's text as containing material that signals gay cruising; here, Duncan sees the source text as containing material that in various ways makes itself available to or lends itself to this interpretation. Where in the Breton it is women who "arose towards me borne up by the mists of some chasm" (10), Duncan's employment of this line (in French) links the text to the "Flashes" that "seize the eye's grey" (6), a precursor to the cruising glance exchanged with the eyes of the working men, "from which lamps like women fume" (22). In Breton a passionate line of text that refers to place—"The beautiful the ravished the submissive the overwhelming La Cadière" (72)—drops the place-name "La Cadière" in Duncan's text and links its affect to the "Outer Court" (23), where "half-naked . . . men [are] mounting and dismounting" (24). With the original text dislocated and altered in this way, Duncan's speaker experiences the same ravishment but links it to the working bodies of potentially available male lovers. If there is any textual practice that organizes the way in which Duncan uses Breton, it might best be described as his cruising the very text of "Pleine marge," picking up and bringing home certain of its French lines and otherwise borrowing some of its clothes.

Duncan's engagement with "Pleine marge" for the composition of "Night Scenes" was likely a rehearsal, if not what garnered his interest, in the project of translating Breton's poem into English. In the year after "Night Scenes" first appeared in print, Duncan began translating the poem within his notebook.[44] He produced numerous typed drafts, some with extensive notes. While it is clear from the typescripts that Duncan worked from the Gallimard text of 1948, he did not do so from the copy of *Poèmes* in his personal library; in that book, "Pleine marge" is inaccessible due to its being trapped within a sixteen-page signature; the pages remain uncut to this day. Nonetheless, it is clear both from the notebook entry and from markings on the typescript copies that Duncan took up this project in 1963, not 1943, as was previously thought.[45] Part 3 of "Night Scenes," then, is an act of proto-translation as much as it is a text of citation and interpretation, a fact that Duncan himself may point us to in the last lines of the poem: "Out of André Breton /—these things translated from her savor into the savor of men's bodies / we return to her parvis."

In a letter to Mary Fabilli from the 1950s, Duncan defends his poetic practice, and, in fact, his way of life, against the orthodoxy that he sees as a "[crusade] toward oneness." He writes: "I would leave, not a record of something realized . . . but I would leave, as I do, a vast nervous contradictory record of the worldly life I have come to celebrate, almost to worship. Not to seek a synthesis; but a melee."[46] Duncan's poem "Night Scenes" provides us one of these vast records, a single poem that becomes, through Duncan's derivative poetics, a multiply palimpsestic text that is perhaps best understood by attending to the particulars of its many threads without a forced critical crusade toward "oneness."

But even as "Night Scenes" *is* a melee in its many and varied textual trajectories, Duncan's abilities to "trac[e] out of air unseen roots and branches of sense" reveal a surprising consonance even within as varied a text as "Night Scenes."[47] From the very personal context within which Duncan takes up the "threat" that he and others who "c[a]me in along these sexual avenues" ("Night," 6) faced in the New York of the 1940s to the intertextual contexts of his putting writers as different as Shakespeare and Breton to similar use, Duncan's "Night Scenes," like many successful serial poems, gains a kind of unity by gathering its materials using different angles of approach. The poem attends, in serious fashion and in ways that may offer additional ways of thinking about the historical matrix of sexuality, mobility, and urban modernity, to the material and affective history and practice of cruising. If the vision in Duncan's poetics, and his derivative poetics in particular, offers us much to synthesize, it is because Duncan himself is after nothing less than allowing *everything* into the poem. In *The H.D. Book* Duncan writes, "I read *Ulysses* or *The Tempest* . . . as I read cards, water, signs in dreams or the tenor of life around me—not to find what art is but through the art to find what life might be."[48]

Notes

1. Duncan, *Roots and Branches*, 5–6.
2. Bernstein, "Bringing It All Back Home," 178.
3. Duncan, "a little endarkenment," 43.
4. Duncan, "Night Scenes," in *Roots and Branches*, 6, line 17. Hereafter cited in the text as "Night."
5. Davidson, "Marginality," 286.

6. The draft pages are not dated, but adjacent entries indicate a composition date between March 22 and May 9 of that year.
7. Robert Duncan, "Night Scenes Typescripts," Robert Duncan Collection, Poetry Collection, State University of New York at Buffalo (hereafter cited as RDC), pt. 2, lines 3, 8, 36, 48, 50–51.
8. Gunn, "Homosexuality," 155.
9. Michael Davidson provides perhaps the most cogent exegesis on Duncan and permission in his essay "Marginality"; see also his "Cave of Resemblances."
10. Robert Duncan, Notebook 26, RDC, 57.
11. Ibid., 58.
12. Graff and Phelan, *The Tempest*, 77, lines 64–68.
13. Ibid., lines 88–94.
14. Duncan, Notebook 26, 58.
15. Duncan, "a little endarkenment," 44.
16. Davidson, "Marginality," 279.
17. Ibid.
18. The "blunt nose of loneliness" is from Duncan, Notebook 26, 58.
19. Mary Fabilli to Robert Duncan, May 17, 1959, RDC.
20. Duncan revised his handwritten draft from the May 18 notebook entry (Notebook 26, 80–81) into a typescript copy a few days later. It is the typescript copy that is reproduced here.
21. Robert Duncan, "In Perplexity," in Notebook 26, typescript copy, 80–81.
22. For a closer look at the trajectory of Duncan and Fabilli's friendship and a more expanded selection of letters, see my "Capable of Devotion."
23. Robert Duncan to Denise Levertov, July 1959, in Duncan and Levertov, *Letters*, 189.
24. Gelpi, "Poetic Language," 180.
25. Denise Levertov to Robert Duncan, May 25, 1959, in Duncan and Levertov, *Letters*, 174.
26. Ibid.
27. Denise Levertov to Robert Duncan, June 1959, in ibid., 176.
28. Duncan, "In Perplexity," line 35.
29. Ibid., lines 31, 42.
30. Trask, *Cruising Modernism*, 192.
31. Duncan, "In Perplexity," lines 37–40. In Duncan's original draft of the poem, the "all-summoning scale" is instead an "all-including scale" (Notebook 26, 80–81).
32. Duncan, "In Perplexity," lines 44, 46.
33. Davidson, "Marginality," 278; Davidson, "A Book of First Things," 72.

34. Davidson, "Marginality," 278.
35. Ferguson, "The Flâneur," 24.
36. Quoted in Faas, *Young Robert Duncan*, 91.
37. Duncan, "Reviewing *View*," 64.
38. Ibid., 66.
39. Duncan was also, no doubt, aware of the homophobic climate within surrealist circles as well as Breton's role in creating that atmosphere.
40. Mark Polizzotti, introduction to *Andre Breton: Selections*, 28.
41. Sheringham, *André Breton*.
42. The poem in French finds its first wide circulation when *Poèmes* is published by Gallimard in 1948, a book Duncan had in his personal library; it is not until 1969, with Kenneth White's translation in *Selected Poems*, that "Full Margin" becomes widely available in English. The poem also appeared in translation that same year as part of Breton, *Manifestoes of Surrealism*, which included *Soluble Fish*.
43. The line numbers following "low-lying lamps," "torches," and "embers" refer to Breton, "Full Margin," trans. Roditi. All subsequent line numbers cited in the text, unless otherwise noted, refer to Duncan, "Night Scenes," part 3, 8–9.
44. Duncan, H.D. Notebook #6, 11, RDC.
45. An erroneous translation date of 1943 is listed in Bertholf, *Robert Duncan: A Descriptive Bibliography*.
46. Likely an unsent, undated letter from Duncan to Fabilli in the 1950s, RDC.
47. Robert Duncan, "Roots and Branches," in *Roots and Branches*, 3.
48. Duncan, *The H.D. Book*, 492.

CHAPTER FOUR

The Airs of Duncan and Zukofsky

JEFFREY TWITCHELL-WAAS

No one was more responsible than Robert Duncan for initiating the remarkable public reemergence of Louis Zukofsky during the late 1950s and 1960s, yet in many respects the elder poet's poetics were antithetical, indeed antipathetic, to Duncan's own. Zukofsky would appear to represent those tendencies of modernism that Duncan characterized as "Puritan," against which he posed his own poetic values.[1] Whereas Duncan advocates mythopoetics, esoteric knowledge, romanticism, extravagant poetic rhetoric, and an insistent dramatization of the poem within a cosmic framework, Zukofsky is this-worldly, rationalist, rigorous, and restrained and projects a deheroicized role of the poet. That Duncan placed Zukofsky in his pantheon of mentors was, however, more than merely another instance of the infinite elasticity of his self-declared derivative poetics, for in many respects Zukofsky was important to Duncan precisely as a challenge and poetic antagonist.

By Duncan's own account, he came upon the objectivist Zukofsky early, in the late 1930s, digging in libraries for an alternative modernism to counter the conservative version being established under the aegis of T. S. Eliot. In this context, Duncan's advocacy may have been nothing more than that Zukofsky was associated with the right party, so to speak, sponsored by Pound and representing the next generation of an intrepidly experimental American poetry pushed underground by the conservative realism of the war emergency. By the late 1940s Duncan was in correspondence with Zukofsky, and in the spring of 1955 he carried several of Zukofsky's works with him to Mallorca, where he shared them with Robert Creeley, who immediately became a lifelong enthusiast. Zukofsky's appearance in the *Black Mountain Review* a few months later was his first significant appearance among the as-yet-undesignated "New American" poets, and Creeley publicly advocated Zukofsky's works whenever and wherever he could. Duncan also urged Jonathan Williams to publish Zukofsky, resulting in the beautiful Jargon Press edition of *Some Time* (1956). Both of these publications alerted Cid Corman to Zukofsky, eventually resulting in the Origin Press publication of "A" *1–12* (1959) and the collection of short fiction, *It Was* (1961), as well as featuring Zukofsky in the second series of *Origin* magazine (1961–64). For Zukofsky, now well into his fifties, these volumes represented his first books that were not more or less vanity publications and laid the groundwork for his remarkable renaissance among young poets throughout the 1960s. Meanwhile, Duncan himself was responsible for Zukofsky's invitation as poet in residence at the Poetry Center at San Francisco State College in the summer of 1958, for which his major statements on poetics were gathered together as 5 *Statements for Poetry* and published in a mimeograph edition. Duncan's role in such familiar networking is merely a small example of his lifelong endeavor to uncover and promote an alternative, underground modernism as a context for his own work, which always relied heavily on the idea of a conducive, if contentious, sense of poetic community and tradition.[2]

In Duncan's various critical comments on Zukofsky—never extensive and often found in interviews—he frequently places him in antithetical relation with Charles Olson.[3] As Duncan liked to say, these two poets could not read each other, yet for him and many of his contemporaries they defined a range or field of "what poetic consciousness might be" (*Fictive*, 213). While the older modernists defined the tradition within which Duncan identified himself, their achievements were already largely complete, whereas Zukofsky and Olson, slightly older bridging figures in the 1950s and 1960s, were still very active in forwarding the developments of experimental modernism. Yet in Duncan's mind they virtually spawned each other as necessary and dialectically related mappers of the way forward from the heroic generation of modernists. At various times Duncan describes their effect on him as "a call to order," although in very different senses.[4] Olson's explosive, brilliantly speculative explorations of the repressed unconscious repositories of psychic energy contrast sharply with Zukofsky's disciplined, rigorous formalism. While Duncan knew both poets personally, his relationships with them were asymmetrical: obviously, in the case of Olson he was much closer in terms of friendship, exchanges, and a general sense of collaborating in a larger poetic scene, whereas Zukofsky insisted on a formal distance and had no interest in public involvement beyond occasional readings and journal publications. There is no doubt that Duncan's natural inclinations and interests were closer to Olson's than to Zukofsky's, especially within the context of a poetic community in large part defined and motivated by Olson. So it is interesting that later Duncan would suggest that Zukofsky had more to teach him—the way he put it is that he understood and could anticipate Olson's poetic moves, while Zukofsky was capable of decisions and "fine distinctions" that were still beyond Duncan.[5] Zukofsky represents a poetic craft that is in many respects antithetical and therefore a continuous provocation to Duncan's more natural propensities, and there is evidence that Zukofsky exerts a greater presence in the poetry of Duncan's later years.

Zukofsky's questioning presence is evident in the first and best-known poem that explicitly evokes Zukofsky, Duncan's "After Reading *Barely and Widely*," written probably in early 1959 and included in *The Opening of the Field* (1960). This poem was composed not long after Zukofsky's residency at San Francisco State College during the summer of 1958. In a July 9, 1958, letter to Denise Levertov, Duncan says he had hoped that Zukofsky would be a needed "contradiction to my own doctrines and Spicer's" for the students of the poetry program but that he had been disappointed by Zukofsky's lack of openness to their (and his) more extravagant rhetoric.[6] As soon as the Zukofskys returned to New York, Celia Zukofsky brought out the limited edition of *Barely and widely*, and no doubt copies were sent to Duncan, prompting his poetic response. It is worth keeping in mind that at the time Duncan composed his poem, Zukofsky's revival in the larger public consciousness had barely begun: virtually nothing aside from his short poems had been published outside of scattered journals (*"A" 1–12*, effectively the first appearance of "A"-12, only came out in September 1959), and few readers of *The Opening of the Field* would have had access to or even heard of *Barely and widely*.

Although the poem's title advertises this as one of Duncan's more overt derivations, its relationship to Zukofsky is oblique, and here I will draw out a dialectic that passes back and forth between homage and critique. This is apt, since the poem's most persistent concern, formally and thematically, is doubleness.[7] The opening lines ("will you give yourself airs / from that lute of Zukofsky?") pick up the quaint poetic manner that both Zukofsky and Duncan were not averse to using as nods to the tradition.[8] Aside from its more literal, albeit obsolete, poetic sense, "airs" characteristically takes on a range of other meanings: atmosphere, aura, impression, personal manner, or even an affected pose that in some sense Duncan will activate. Yet understandably this initial invocation of Zukofsky has been read as merely the occasion for a poem that then pursues Duncan's own interests and manner. The introduction of a cluster of Greek words and their definitions in the first strophe clues us into the etymological method that the poem will persistently ask the reader to consider. For Duncan, as for Zukofsky, etymology proliferates meanings and associations but is not, as for Olson and many other modernists, a means of revealing some more authentic, original meaning.[9] However, for Duncan, etymology and its close kin, the pun, tend to be seen in terms of a repressive model, so that hidden antithetical meanings are always implied or embedded in words. Duncan found strong support for such symptomatic readings in Freud, and he tended to take the repressed antithesis as the psychological motivation behind any given verbal act. Duncan was heavily invested in the repression model that he projected out across history and knowledge, aligning himself with traditions of the underground and esoteric knowledge. In this respect, Duncan differs sharply from Zukofsky, who certainly was not averse to puns but did not read them in terms of depth models and disliked psychological explanations. Rather, for Zukofsky, puns and etymology are means of evoking recurrences and resonances across the textual surface. Especially after the 1930s, Zukofsky, no doubt assessing what was happening to Pound, rejected paranoid versions of history and as a reader could hardly have been more classically canonical. But for all Duncan's trafficking in esoteric traditions and texts, he is remarkably self-conscious that he is engaged in poetic and textual practices, that the antitheses of words, meanings, histories are structurally implicated in each other and must be kept in dialectical motion to creatively move on. In the latter half of "After Reading," when the poem swerves heavily into occult and alchemical texts and references, Duncan quotes from Olson's cautionary "Against Wisdom as Such"—"'an école des Sages ou Mages / as ominous as Ojai'" (*Opening*, 91)—as if momentarily reminding himself not to take these concerns too dogmatically.

Returning to the opening of "After Reading," Duncan responds to his own question by setting into play a cluster of words and associations:

> Yes, for I would have my share
> in the discretion I read from certain jews,
> not ʻιδιώτης but standing apart
>
> from or before, (*Opening*, 88)

"Discretion" is the term chosen to characterize Zukofsky's work, suggesting discreet/discrete, both careful distinctions and reserved manner, as well as fine judgment.[10] "Discretion" is hardly a tag one would hang on Duncan. It is Zukofsky's rigorous and nuanced formalism that Duncan admires, but there is also a sense of distance that Duncan will tend to read psychologically as implying a certain fear of intimacy. That Duncan associates this "discretion" with Zukofsky's Jewishness will manifest itself in the sense of the Jew as outsider, "standing apart," an historical condition, both imposed and self-imposed, that presumably conditions the terms of this "discretion." Duncan here touches on a stereotype, particularly virulent in his youth, of the Jews as overintellectual, as infected and infecting a cerebralism that has fatally alienated Western culture from itself. Duncan identifies by complicating this stereotype, insisting "not ʻιδιώτης," that is, not private or individual (*idiôtês*) specifically in the sense of divorced from public involvement and responsibility. The word can also be taken in the sense of a layperson or someone who is unskilled, thus ignorant, from which the English "idiot" is derived. Duncan finds juxtaposed in his Greek lexicon ʻιδιώ (*idiô*) or ʻϊδος (*idos*), meaning "sweat," thus introducing a sense of fear and uncertainty that lies behind or motivates this standing apart.[11] From this initial cluster of ideas and suggestions, Duncan generates the poem through verbal associations. So in the first section, he pursues the root of 'ιδιώτης in 'ίδιος (*ídios*), which means "private," "pertaining to oneself," or "separate, distinct, peculiar"—qualities of discretion that, however, in their social context take on other senses:

> but queer,
>
> crossd, athwart, fated, fey
> is a man with a quick odd look,
> cousin to idiocy, that strains to see. (*Opening*, 88)[12]

Duncan obviously is referring to himself as gay, as poet, as cross-eyed (seeing double), and yet all of this could as easily refer to the decidedly difficult and peculiar Zukofsky, who had poor eyesight. This is not, in fact, profitably decidable, since the "airs" of Duncan and Zukofsky are texts in which precisely these ambiguities, queernesses, and cross-eyed senses predominate. The rest of the poem, divided roughly into two halves, pursues the theme of doubleness, first in terms of the writer/reader's relationship with poetic language and then in more explicitly social and Jewish terms.

In the first half, what primarily concerns Duncan is poetic address, poetry's tendency toward emotional appeal and identity, or, contrarily, its distance and otherness. Often enough, especially when posing his argument against the powers of reason and responsibility, Duncan insists that, properly, poetry is such a surrender of the self, a possession by the text, even to the point of sentimentality as a movement beyond the strictures of what is taken for granted and approved. Yet he also recognizes the dangers of such surrender, so, for example, when acknowledging the importance of his adopted parents' theosophy to his own outlook, he invariably points out the naive credulity of their hermetic readings. To maintain the antithetical tension in language, its doubleness, it is necessary to resist such surrender or identity, which always masks a difference, a hostility, an uncertainty. Yet the rejection of this identity and certainty is not in the end an option, given its integral role in the structure of uncertainty and otherness. So a Jewess's casual address, "dearie," is felt to combine "a careless hostility and affection" (*Opening*, 88), until the tension transforms her into a "hag" who grasps "without discretion," violently threatening to erase all difference. But, finally, she reemerges a page later as "this outrageous old woman" who will "not be driven off; / [since she] shall claim in the first nature a lasting part" (*Opening*, 89–90). We recognize here the typical demands reading Duncan makes as figures reappear in strangely differing guises. The metamorphoses from Jew (double) to hag to outrageous old woman are typical Duncan personifications of the poetic line or text. If in some sense emotional identity ("a touching line") is the initial lure of poetry, there also is the need to maintain distance and difference, Zukofskian discretion, to resist that emotional lure that threatens to swallow us up as we respond with mere passivity. So Duncan recognizes in Zukofsky a distance and difference that may appear to repress the emotional, although, in fact, it is "of violence and obedience a delicate balancing" (*Opening*, 89). Duncan quotes a brief passage from "4 Other Countries," the major poem in *Barely and widely*:

> "That song
>   is the kiss
> it keeps
>   is it
> The
>   unsaid worry
> for what
>   should last." (*Opening*, 89)[13]

The kiss of poetry that makes claims on the reader and for a certain transcendence, a kiss that lasts, contains a mute worry that it cannot, that it is no more than ephemeral. The manner in which these lines draw out the discreteness of rather ordinary words and their subtly articulated music in a syntax that doubles the sentence back on itself, enacting the tension of its sense, is exemplary of what Duncan meant by Zukofsky's "discretion." In this characteristically muted articulation that Duncan finds tucked within an extended travelogue poem, there is an expression of the tension out of and about which poetry perpetuates itself. Duncan juxtaposes this delicate passage from Zukofsky with a sharply contrasting quotation from H.D.:

> "Goot, gut and good and surely God,
> and so we play / this game
> of affirmations / and"
>
> of names. (*Opening*, 89)

This is more in Duncan's own manner, a somewhat indiscriminate cluster of associations, affirmatively eager to accumulate affinities: "For there is that to which we would give ourselves / wholly." This is the lure of identity that desires to leap to the cosmos, which, however, can never be bridged and against which Zukofsky asserts cautious rigor and distinctions.

The latter half of "After Reading" more explicitly picks up on Jewishness but associated with all manner of "*bæddel* [hermaphrodite] mixtures" (*Opening*, 90), that is, the social other so often stigmatized in the effort to repress. Duncan quickly accumulates a series of manifestations of this repressed other: dwarves, trolls, Pan, fairies, occult and alchemical traditions, and Shylock as the outsider who pleads his commonness with his accusers. Again Duncan sets in motion etymological connections, since the Old English *bæddel*, meaning "hermaphrodite" (Hermes + Aphrodite) or "effeminate," with implications of homosexuality, is the root of the modern "bad." But the very doubleness of the word reveals its necessary and constituent relation with that which would repress it, so again all these underground figures and traditions are themselves merely manifestations of the doubleness everywhere in language, which endlessly generates transformation. Duncan concludes the poem with a foregrounding of the Jewish tradition as a perpetual song within which the poet participates:

> a tradition, a caution, a string of the lute
> from division and union whereon
>
> this air. (*Opening*, 92)

In circling back around to the "lute" and "air" from the outset of the poem, which specifically addresses Zukofsky, the particular quality that distinguishes the elder poet has been recontextualized as intrinsic to an entire tradition and possibility of poetry as Duncan understands it.

Beyond the obvious surface differences between the two poets, what most significantly distinguishes Duncan's manner from that of Zukofsky is his incessant talking *about* something, usually in one sense or another the poem itself. Zukofsky's poetry tends to aspire toward a condition of music, a poetry that rarely *says* but works with recurrences to create interactions, a textual space shared between people in the act of writing/reading: "'all who eat there / inseparable'" (*Opening*, 90).[14] This follows from Zukofsky's adherence to the Imagist principle, as espoused if not always practiced by Pound, of presenting rather than saying or telling. Not surprisingly, Zukofsky advised Duncan to "stay off'n the poetry about poetry."[15] Yet Duncan's endless talking about his poetry in his poetry constantly circles around on itself, rereading and revising itself so as to undermine any grounds for the stance from which his statements are made—the perspective becomes multiple or, as he liked to put it, "multiphasic." Near the end of "After Reading," Duncan explicitly addresses this circling:

> The beauty is mind,
> a discretion circling round
>
> a containd danger, an impending mystery. (*Opening*, 91–92)

Circling back to the opening suggests that Zukofsky's "discretion," his need for rigorous distinctions and a distancing of the self, hides tensions that necessarily motivate his writing. "Danger" and "mystery" are not the sort of terms one would expect to find Zukofsky using, yet from Duncan's perspective this is what is implied in Zukofsky's manner: his formalist rigor and experimentation indicate a need to contain disorder, excess of emotion, or sensuality, which drives his perpetual exploration of form.

Zukofsky's response to Duncan's "After Reading" came in the poem "Her Face the Book of—Love Delights in—Praises," which opens by echoing Duncan's question and responding with another, "How will his praise sound back to him?"[16] Not surprisingly, the rest of the poem does not offer any straightforward or paraphrasable answer to the question. Zukofsky's poem was instigated by the coincidence that within a six-month period he found himself praised in poems by two poets, the other being Henry Birnbaum, at a time when Zukofsky was just beginning to emerge from two decades of almost complete public obscurity. While undoubtedly expressing a certain delight at such praise, he turns this praise toward yet another poet, Lorine Niedecker, by incorporating a collaborative poem of sorts from their correspondence. Niedecker had not only praised Zukofsky through his obscurity but of course very much shared it, so here he acknowledges the importance of their poetic collaboration and their "praises" in the sense of responding to and reflecting on each other's work over many years. As a specific response to Duncan's poem, it is doubtful too much should be read into this beyond its acknowledgment, although he does deflect the praise back to Duncan by quoting Birnbaum's praise, which it is evident Zukofsky does not think much of as poetry.[17] The point perhaps is that "praises" as poetic homage, influence, or allusion is unpredictable and may not have altogether happy results, however well intentioned. Of more importance is the sense of belonging to a community of poets, as much or more of the "past" as of contemporaries, who, like the legendary tree of Father Huc that Zukofsky mentions, are each distinct-tongued leaves yet fed by the whole in a manner too complex and subtle to separate out.[18] We see here Zukofsky's long-held suspicion of the idea of influence, not because he or other poets are unique, but precisely because the materials of poetry, if properly appreciated, are so historically and personally overdetermined.[19] Finally, we should note Zukofsky's deliberately low-key, even intimate manner, which contrasts sharply with Duncan's compulsive circling around poetic profundities. Curiously, in sharp contrast to Zukofsky's standing apart and restraint, Duncan's career is strongly marked by his sense of poetic community, yet the quiet intimacy of which Zukofsky was capable was largely beyond Duncan, who, although often directly addressing friends and lovers, always tends to boom in the poetic cosmos. However, in his late work Duncan would realize a more intimate voice as he attempted to adequately express the centrality of his domestic life with Jess.

It strikes me as telling that in the decade immediately following "After Reading *Barely and Widely*"—the period of *Roots and Branches*, *Bending the Bow*, and *The H.D. Book*—Zukofsky seems to largely disappear from Duncan's work, which at the time is strongly preoccupied with occult and hermetic materials. Although *The H.D. Book* is Duncan's major survey and assessment of his modernist inheritances, Zukofsky is rarely mentioned. The lone sentence of significance appears when Duncan discusses the chilling establishment of official "modernism" in the 1940s and 1950s upholding the principles of the "rational imagination": "There is one lonely acolyte of poetry where Louis Zukofsky perfects his art, wrapped in the cocoon of an 'objectivism' derived from Pound and Williams, a hidden zaddik in a thicket of theory, to emerge in the myrrh and light of 'A,' to keep the music, and in the working hive of his thought in *Bottom: On Shakespeare*."[20] However, while Zukofsky certainly was erased from the scene, it is somewhat ticklish to present him as champion of an underground repressed by the forces of reason and realism, which Duncan's effort to deck him with mystical Hasidic associations does not altogether hide. In any case, Zukofsky's presence will assert itself in the darkened period of *Ground Work*. With no pretense of being explanatory but merely emblematic, we might note the shift in emphasis from "myth" in "The Truth and Life of Myth" (1968), Duncan's most coherent and major statement of his poetics, to the more linguistic "IT" in the preface to *Bending the Bow* (1968) and thereafter to indicate that totality or significant design that cannot be said or seen.[21] The very gestural character of this "IT," its jarring inadequacy as a signifier of what it would reference, indicates Duncan's progressive self-critique of his own key terms and an attenuating confidence that any word or articulation can avoid the illusion of nomination. In this context of increasing linguistic fragility, we can begin to appreciate the significance of Zukofsky in Duncan's late work where various references to Zukofsky proliferate.[22]

A striking example of Zukofsky's centripetal presence in Duncan's late work is one of the last *Passages*, "With In," which at first glance may not appear to explicitly evoke Zukofsky. However, the pencil-thin lines down the page are signature Zukofsky, and each of the concluding centered lines, "A // music / at rest" (*Ground*, 253), touches on key Zukofskian motifs. The poem once again concerns boundaries or form as defining tensions between inside and outside, but the real effect of the poem can only be appreciated in relation to the set of *Passages*, "The Regulators," among which it appears. This set represents the extreme of the late Duncan's sprawling expansion of his lines, which here are hardly contained even by the oversized page.

The line, if we can still call it that, has become more visual than aural, an effort to score a resounding space that in doing so everywhere manifests its fragility, the sense that broken words and phrases are merely scattered about the white of the page. Immediately preceded by two apocalyptic *Passages* of disintegration, "In Blood's Domaine" and "After Passage," which address the pathologies of disease and nuclear annihilation, respectively, "With In" stands in overt contrast as a pivot around which the diastole and systole of the entire set are anchored. In this context, "With In" sticks out as a point of rest, as the regulating countertendency Duncan always acknowledged, and leads into the more composed and balanced concluding two poems of "The Regulators." Who more appropriate than Zukofsky as the figure of salutatory rigor and restraint that nonetheless generates enormous expansion?

Although Duncan wrote a critical piece of homage shortly after Zukofsky's death in May 1978, in which his intention was to assess Zukofsky's importance in the poetry of Duncan's own generation, the only part that was published and presumably written is a rather limited introduction.[23] A more consequential statement of Zukofsky's specific significance is found in the introduction Duncan wrote for John Taggart's Pythagorean-inspired book of poems, *Dodeka* (1979). Taggart's own indebtedness to Zukofsky gives Duncan the opportunity to more rigorously define Zukofsky's work, which he characterizes, particularly as it culminates in "A"-22 and -23, as pursuing a mathematical approach to poetry, a radical linguistic formalism where the most basic and literal particles of writing, letters and numbers, are foregrounded as the primary materials of the text. Such a poetry eschews sense as ordinarily understood for the evocation of a universe of language that "divines the content of a life-world-mind poem as household" (*Fictive*, 212). What Duncan previously designated as "discretion"—rigor, discipline, discreteness—is now more cosmically characterized as "ecological," a non-aggressive and balanced sense of being in the world: "The poem in its transmutations of the music proposed emerges as a measured consciousness of self and world, tempered throughout by a scale of feeling and inspiration—not cautious, but considerate, ultimately, economical, in the root-meaning of the word—ecological" (213). This is an astute insight into the late Zukofsky as manifest in "A"-22 and -23, where a compacted poetry has been constructed out of hundreds of quotations that have been submitted to the full spectrum of Zukofskian reworking: collaging, severe pruning, grafting, homophonic transmutations, and so on. The result is not a poetry that eruditely alludes to other texts on an epic scale but an attempt to create a density of verbal resonance evoking a sense of embodied language across linguistic time and space as manifest in the specific material elements of language. The aspiration of such poetry as activated by and with its reading is, as Duncan suggests, a heightened recognition of the adequacy of the given, of the world as textually mediated. Whereas Duncan inclines toward an expansiveness and revelation through the perpetual questioning of limits, Zukofsky's sensibility focuses on the immediacy of textual detail as an activity of adjustment and proportion, of discovering local complexities and harmonies, without denying the considerable dissonance that inevitably counters such desire. While the Taggart essay offers no overt criticism, once again Duncan inevitably evokes Olson as Zukofsky's antithesis: "a primordial, titanic, unaccountable spirit in poetry, beyond measure, where one could only take soundings and carry the compass in a boundless space" (213). Duncan himself needs this violent dissolving of measure as well, yet in an important sense his later work, with its acute sense of mortality, will tend to increasingly acknowledge limits and the need for balance. If this represents something of a move toward Zukofsky, it is in the sense of the continuing "reprimand" Zukofsky presented as a poet/mentor to Duncan's natural propensities.

Duncan's major late poetic engagement with Zukofsky is "Jamais (*Passages*)," presented in "Homage to the youthful Zukofsky, his looking forward in the 1920s to prove his Art in *A-23*" (*Ground*, 151). Duncan expressed relief that Pound, despite his long-implied intention, did not impose closure on the *Cantos* in the final installment, and the unusual prefatory note to "Jamais" suggests it was written in response to the publication of the concluding sections of "A" in "A" *22 & 23* (1975).[24] This note proposes that the poem might be read as an imaginative reconstruction of Zukofsky, thinking through the implications of his poetics, or the poetics implied by the young poet's understanding of his "now" considered in light of his final achievement in "A"-23. Duncan imagines something like the underlying dynamic that gives continuity to Zukofsky's long, generative career at a point when Duncan himself was self-consciously considering the groundwork for his old age. Yet we would hardly expect the poem to be concerned with anything other than Duncan's own preoccupations, so that to the degree that it addresses Zukofsky it is in terms of that derivativeness whereby the other poet becomes the occasion for allowing differences into Duncan's textual space. The poem in fact rehearses Duncan's long-standing concern with tensions on a cosmic scale: between now and eternity, chance and determinacy, the particular and the whole.

We notice that "'a'" appears in the first line, and the poem concludes with "'the'" suspended on its own, a gesture spanning Zukofsky's career from his initial public appearance with "Poem beginning 'The'" through his just-completed lifelong work, "A." Zukofsky famously insisted on the importance, the potential "epos and historical destiny," of such seemingly insignificant words as the articles, and he makes this claim in the context of denying poetry's need for myth.[25] Duncan's poem proposes a movement or transformation from "a" to "the" as that from open possibilities, the indefinite, to definiteness, the sense of inevitability "beyond chance." The poem's title evokes Stéphane Mallarmé's *Un coup de dés jamais n'abolira le hasard* (1897), perhaps the emblematic modernist poem of intellectual rigor and textual precariousness. Duncan is not the first to suggest an affinity between these two poets, and Zukofsky himself draws on Mallarmé extensively in "A"-19, although *Un coup de dés* is only alluded to in passing. Duncan's own engagement with nineteenth-century French poetry was intense and is especially felt in the *Ground Work* volumes, where a few poems are largely written in or out of French. So Mallarmé's presence here is not so much something Duncan takes from Zukofsky as a recognition of the similarity in the two poets' grasp of the scene of writing, which manifests in analogous compulsions of rigor, formalism, and impersonality. Or perhaps one could suggest that Mallarmé is a space where Duncan and Zukofsky meet: the former in the lush and exotic imagery and the latter in the formal and intellectual rigor.

However, the opening of Duncan's poem appears to reject the central "statement" of Mallarmé's poem:[26]

JAMAIS
must extend beyond the throw of the dice "a" just now, yet
no throw of the dice may chance IT. (*Ground*, 151)

The poem begins by facing the indefinite; it is merely "'a' just now," but if it is fully realized, it becomes "the," establishing a sense of the definite and of inevitable existence, although in Duncan any "the" necessarily opens up again into the infinite "a." Since Duncan conceives of poetic composition as process, as responsiveness in its enactment, it is like a throw of the dice without an end that can be predicated, always working "in the dark." However, Duncan repeatedly insists he does not believe in chance as a compositional method, such as deployed by John Cage or Jackson Mac Low, since there is an assumption of ultimate order even if our position is necessarily always immanent, inside, and in the process, so that that order can never be known except as participation in its acts of self-creation. So "no throw of the dice may chance IT," can reduce "IT" to mere chance or randomness. The preceding poem, "Empedoklean Reveries (*Passages*)," identified "never" with "infinite" (*Ground*, 147), a definition echoed later in this poem, and of course "jamais" also translates as "ever," so again we encounter that omnipresent play of antitheses. While Duncan rejects chance, it inevitably fascinates him and is a recurring theme in his work because it is implicated in any conception of design and the necessity of transformation—it remains a nagging "Demon of Incident," as he puts it later in the poem.[27]

The poem then proposes the quality of "lucidity" as a quintessential poetic value, surely indicating the Poundian and Imagistic aesthetic that marked Zukofsky's starting point but whose implications he will rigorously follow through, since what we see in poetry is inevitably the words themselves. Lucidity, then, is always complicit with the duplicity of language as exemplified in a sentence from Heraclitus:

"*Reason being such always*
men fail to understand"
All ways men fail to understand. (*Ground*, 151)

Duncan is quoting a passage from Aristotle's *Rhetoric* on the problems of punctuation. Where Aristotle, seeking lucidity, finds it undecidable whether "always" belongs with the opening or terminating clause of Heraclitus's sentence, Duncan is pleased to find the ambiguity of a pun in the English translation.[28] Aristotle was a major interest of Zukofsky's, as Duncan would know from reading "A"-12 and *Bottom*, while Duncan often proclaimed himself a Heraclitean. The type of ambiguity Aristotle is thinking of, where the statement can in a sense be read in both directions, was favored by Zukofsky, particularly in the late movements of "A," while the antithetical pun is more Duncan's style. But in either case, the inevitable play in language is recognized, and in Zukofsky's case the recognition that the poet cannot move beyond the image as words in order to stabilize it is the starting point of his distinctive development from the Poundian poetic principles to which he remained loyal.

The first half of the poem proceeds with its rejection of chance:

> Now   is wedded thruout to   the Intention of a Universe.
> Verse,   linkt to the Idea of that Governance,
> moves "beyond" (*Ground*, 151)

Zukofsky's own recurrent resort to the image of music is here raised as a traditional assertion of universal design, which is echoed by

> —Man's Art,   an other   arbitration of the whole
> "Nature of Sound"   in which
> the "sameness" of the note   is dismisst.

Poetry is "an other," whether in the sense of echoing the whole or an othering of the poet/reader, an act of arbitration that mediates the disjunction between part and whole, now and eternity. The arbitration of the "'Nature of Sound'" here literally echoes its initial articulation a few lines previous, and, as frequently throughout the poem, the phrase's iterability and doubleness are marked in signature Zukofsky style with quotation marks. Similarly "the 'sameness' of the note" can mean the identity of the note to some original ("the octave the first") or an identity among notes; in either case, the composition of music/poetry harmonizes through its differences.

The second half of the poem, marked off by an extended pause, pivots sharply but not unexpectedly to the darker side of this projection of cosmic and poetic harmony:

silence . the eternal . inertia (*Ground*, 152)

As always, without antithetical resistance, without self-reflexive questioning, there is the risk of inertia where that "'sameness' of the note" that was harmoniously "dismisst" asserts itself as mere sameness. This counterforce, unquestionably felt as a threat to complacency, appears initially as "the granite massif," a massive, inanimate disruption of the "overtones of Universe," which in turn introduces the image of modernist musical dissonance that shattered "'the stability of the central triad'" (*Ground*, 152). This somewhat cosmic scale of disruption manifests itself "in the particular now" as the reappearance of chance and randomness, "the Demon of Incident" where the inert "reorganizes" the particular such that we are haunted by the sense of no organization whatsoever.

The concluding sentence of the poem imagines the young Zukofsky—but it could just as readily be Duncan or the reader—confronted with this situation and accepting it, choosing to write in the acceptance of the duplicity of "lucidity": "What! I do not 'know' what I see?" (*Ground*, 152). The signature references to Zukofsky are found in the riming pun on "see," "C," and "sea" as well as, of course, in the final dangling "'the.'" Such verbal play, so central to Duncan's poetics and practice, was a permission Zukofsky offered in contrast to the strictures of elder modernists: Eliot, Pound, and Williams. Duncan found this see/C/sea pun in Zukofsky, particularly "A," where C, aside from referring to the musical note or scale, always indicates Zukofsky's wife, Celia, and therefore is also buried in "see" and "sea."[29] The sea appears particularly in the early movements of "A" as an image of inert being, albeit always in motion, while seeing, which here echoes the earlier "lucidity," is arguably Zukofsky's most persistent concern or image: from Imagism, to the optical definition of "An Objective," to that compulsive and lengthy examination of seeing in Shakespeare, *Bottom*.[30] Although, literally speaking, C was not yet in his life at the time, "Love / flings itself forward // at sea in its work," and the young Zukofsky begins his first poem "Poem beginning

'The'"—not of course literally his first poem but his first Zukofsky poem. This "the" upon which so much will depend for Zukofsky is left dangling in Duncan's poem, both suggestive and fragile.

The juxtaposition of the Zukofskian diminutives "a" and "the" with the Duncanesque "IT" risks being unintentionally comic and certainly highlights the contrasting temperaments of the two poets. It is unlikely Zukofsky would have been entirely comfortable with the grandiose gestures of this homage. The contrast between "A"-22 and -23 and "Jamais" is striking: the former with its flattened textual surface in which semantic sense is vigorously undermined and subsumed into the flow of signifiers across the surface, whether conceived in terms of pure aural sound (non-sense) or overdetermined proliferation of possible semantic (etymological) threads, the latter persistently discursive and self-reflective in manner, however elliptical and multidirectional. Zukofsky's materialist poetics meant that his musical ideal of the poem strove for a subsumption of ideas in a sensory immediacy between poem and reader, a tangible affect of proportion within a very present and specific world. Despite Duncan's disapproval of the Platonic split between mind and body, his residual Platonism is strong and manifests itself in his endless talking, the poems endlessly talking about themselves enacting cosmic creativity as thinking about "IT" thinking. It is not surprising, therefore, that Duncan feels no compunction in the introduction to Taggart's *Dodeka* in quoting from "A"-22 and -23, as if Zukofsky is making discursive statements, yet Duncan also makes the remarkably perceptive claim that in these poems "the 'feel' of actual speech has been enlarged for us to include in its range not only how we hear others talking but how others could talk" (*Fictive*, 214). In their distinct ways, both poets are profoundly immanentist, so that making poetry is a matter of working with and within what is given or found, which implies the acceptance of design in a totality forever beyond our ken. In Duncan this results in a poetics of process, an active participation in the designs of the cosmos endlessly realizing itself without telos, and therefore an acceptance of the necessity of perpetual transformation and conflict. Zukofsky, as Duncan recognized, aspires to a sense of proportional balance in what is given, so that the problem is that we are insufficiently aware of the adequacy of what is before us—we keep looking beyond and therefore fail to see. Duncan's sometimes violent belief in a desire that can never be satisfied inexorably put him at odds with Zukofsky, yet, consistent to his own dialectical principles, he incorporates Zukofsky as an antagonistic presence within his own work.

Notes

1. Duncan, "Preface to a Reading," 54.
2. For the information in this paragraph, see Duncan, "As Testimony"; Creeley, "For L.Z."; Corman, "Meeting in Firenze"; and Scroggins, *The Poem of a Life*, 273–74, 280–81, 289–92.
3. For comparative considerations of Zukofsky and Olson, see Duncan, *Robert Duncan: An Interview*, [25–26], [30]; Duncan, "As Testimony," 421–22; Robert Duncan, "An Introduction: John Taggart's *Dodeka*" (1979), in *Fictive Certainties*, 213 (hereafter cited in the text as *Fictive*); Faas, "An Interview," 6. Duncan later interpolated into his key critical piece on Olson, "Notes on Poetics Regarding Olson's *Maximus*" (1956), a paragraph on the equivalent critical importance of Zukofsky, specifically *Bottom: On Shakespeare*, to the development of his own poetics (*Fictive*, 72). I am not aware that Duncan ever commented in any detail on *Bottom*; it is mentioned twice in *The H.D. Book* and occasionally elsewhere but only to reiterate its importance.
4. Duncan, "As Testimony," 421; Duncan, *The H.D. Book*, 217.
5. Duncan, *Robert Duncan: An Interview*, 25–27.
6. Duncan and Levertov, *Letters*, 125–26.
7. Johnson, *Robert Duncan*, 81.
8. Duncan, *The Opening of the Field*, 88 (hereafter cited in the text as *Opening*).
9. Kamenetz, "Realms of Being," 11.
10. On Zukofsky and discretion, see Duncan, *Robert Duncan: An Interview*, [12], [26].
11. Duncan is evidently consulting H. G. Liddell and Robert Scott's standard *A Greek–English Lexicon*. For remarks on *idiôtês*, see Duncan, *The H.D. Book*, 559.
12. On the various etymological senses of "fey," including its relation to "fated," see Duncan, *The H.D. Book*, 124–29.
13. As printed, two quatrains are run together, which is why "The" in the fifth line is capitalized; see Zukofsky, *Complete Short Poetry*, 180–81.
14. Duncan is quoting from "4 Other Countries" in *Barely and widely* from a passage describing a Fra Angelico fresco depicting the Communion (Zukofsky, *Complete Short Poetry*, 185). The quotation a few lines previous in Duncan's poem is from #2 of *Barely and widely* (ibid., 163).

15. Duncan relates this remark in a letter to Robin Blaser dated June 29, 1958, which would have been when Zukofsky was poet in residence at San Francisco State College (Duncan, "Letters," 123).
16. Zukofsky, *Complete Short Poetry*, 206.
17. Birnbaum's eight-page poem "Orizons" appeared in *Poetry* 94.3 (1959): 156–63, in which also appeared the first three of the Zukofskys' *Catullus* translations.
18. See Zukofsky, *Bottom*, 192. Zukofsky explicitly associates Father Huc's tree with William Carlos Williams's "The Botticellian Trees" and then replicates this passage in his homage to Williams in "A"-17 ("A," 387).
19. For Zukofsky's thoughts on influence, see the brief statement "Influence" in *Prepositions +*, 135, which was extracted from a 1930 review of René Taupin's *L'influence du symbolisme sur la poésie américaine de 1910 à 1920*.
20. Duncan, *The H.D. Book*, 216–17.
21. Both essays were written around the same time in the latter half of 1967, and "IT" appears in the former as well (*Fictive*, 33, 50), but the overall change in emphasis is notable.
22. Aside from the more significant instances that will be discussed below, there are a number of more or less explicit passing references to Zukofsky and/or "A" in *Ground Work: Before the War/In the Dark*, 227, 237, 246 (hereafter cited in the text as *Ground*). "*Passages* 33" (*Ground*, 24) clearly echoes Zukofsky, most obviously the title I's (pronounced "eyes"), which are mentioned in the preface to Duncan, *Bending the Bow*, iv, although the play on "I" and "eyes" is also found throughout Zukofsky, *Bottom*.
23. Duncan, "As Testimony," was written on request for a large memorial issue of *Paideuma* brought out shortly after Zukofsky's death and concludes with a note projecting three further parts, the second of which would specifically address "Marx, Marxism and Stalin in 'A.'" In the published piece Duncan already mentions his disappointment with Zukofsky's "praise of Stalin" in "A"-8 when it first appeared in 1938, which provoked a defense of Zukofsky by Burton Hatlen ("Stalin and/or Zukofsky"). That the eighteen-year-old Duncan read "A"-8 as pro-Stalin is, in the context of the times, both inevitable and correct, especially given that Duncan's own early politics were anarchist-influenced and instinctively suspicious of any socialism associated with Stalin and the Comintern. Zukofsky concludes a litany of fascist atrocities in "A"-10 (1940) with the Stalin-Hitler Pact ("A," 121), although in characteristically oblique manner and in "A"-12 (written in 1951) there is, by Zukofskian standards, a more clearly anti-Stalin passage (ibid., 203–4). Duncan's point is simply that as he read "A"-8 in 1938 he could not but feel Zukofsky was uncritically pro-Stalin, but he concludes that, as with Pound, "whatever a poem meant in its truth of particulars it was not a political directive" ("As Testimony," 427).

24. "Jamais" was first published in *New Poetry* (Australia) in 1976. Since "A"-24, a musical arrangement of selections from across Zukofsky's writings assembled by his wife, Celia, had already been published in 1972, "A"-23 marked the completion of "A."
25. Zukofsky, *Prepositions +*, 10.
26. Finkelstein, "Late Duncan," 357.
27. Other significant poetic considerations of chance include "Risk" (Duncan, *Roots and Branches*, 56–59) and "The Missionaries (*Passages*)," which is a response to Jackson Mac Low's *The Pronouns* (*Ground*, 139–40). For remarks on John Cage and chance, see the Duncan interview in Faas, *Towards a New American Poetics*, 79–81.
28. Judging from the specific translation of Heraclitus's sentence, Duncan's source is Aristotle, *On Poetry and Style*, which is a translation of Aristotle's *Poetics* with selections of relevant passages from the *Rhetoric*. The preceding two lines (beginning with "whether a certain word") are adapted from Aristotle's text.
29. For example, see Zukofsky, "A," 190.
30. For the sea in "A," see especially the opening pages of "A"-6 (21–23). The optical definition of "An Objective" is in *Prepositions +*, 12.

CHAPTER FIVE

Is the Queendom Enough (without the Queen)? Poetic Abdication in Robert Duncan and Laura Riding

GRAHAM LYONS

The best writers . . . have succeeded because they chose to enter the prison house of language. It is, of course, where we all live, but only those who inhabit it deliberately are able to tell the truth about it.—Jerome McGann

The privilege of individual freedom of word that poetry bestowed could not be itself a warranty of truth of word.—Laura (Riding) Jackson

I don't seek a synthesis, but a melee.—Robert Duncan

In his 1953 "Statement on Poetics" appended to Donald Allen's pathbreaking *New American Poetry* anthology, Robert Duncan lists Laura Riding among his poetic sources. She is one of the "heros, gods and models" he wished to "emulate, imitate, reconstrue, approximate, duplicate."[1] In his characteristically multivalent way, Duncan is quite right: on several counts, Duncan followed Riding's example. Most in evidence, I suggest, is the way both poets problematized their authorial identity—Duncan by way of a "derivation" from the poets who came before him (undercutting his own originary voice) and Riding by way of a renunciation of a poetic self that fluently "expresses" (an abdication of poetic authority in the service of "truth"). In the only extended examination of the interface between Duncan's and Riding's work, Jeff Hamilton points to another "emulation" (or perhaps a "reconstrual") when he claims that the productive confusions and conflations in their poetics stem from a shared understanding of the limitations of the symbolic and from the humanistic responsibility attached to this knowledge; according to Hamilton, both Duncan and Riding encouraged a poetic oscillation between "communal and inner lives" and saw this structured indeterminacy as a profoundly social obligation—an obligation to articulate the problematics of representing truth.[2] Indeed, we could say that Riding foregrounded the problematic tripartite relationship between self and collective and language for Duncan, who then picked it up and sought to attenuate its difficulties through a radical (though "derivative") poetics. The responsibility—one is tempted to say the burden—of this task led both poets to take a poetic hiatus of sorts for an extended period of time: Duncan waited sixteen years (1968–84) between major publications, and Riding abandoned poetry altogether in 1938 and never returned to it.[3] Riding was convinced in the end that poetry unnecessarily and amorally valorizes the poet as subject, that it ultimately fails in an idealized "attempt to make language do more than express; to make it work."[4] Unfortunately, as Riding informs us in *The Telling* many years later, "Art, whose honesty must work through artifice, cannot avoid cheating truth."[5] Because of this inherent dishonesty, Riding "ended, in [her] movement in the poetic path, at no-end."[6] That Duncan chose to reenter the realm of mainstream publishing in spite of the compromises and frustrations that came along with that process suggests that his faith in poetry—in his compositional apparatus, in its potential effects, in its participation in a community of readers, in poetry's claim on "truth"—endured Duncan's doubts in a way that Riding's, up to her death in 1991, did not.[7] One might speculate, then, that Duncan found a way to "reconstrue" Riding's "model" into a poetics that could move beyond the singularity of the "poetic path" Riding lays out for him. Indeed, Duncan's poetics move toward a "field" wherein the singular voice of the poet could join in a sort of collective participation of readers and writers that makes up the idealized and complex space of poetic composition.

I would like to sketch out further this as yet infrequently explored relationship between truth, poetic identity, and composition strategies in the work of Laura Riding and Robert Duncan, to begin to work out how Duncan's poetics manage to incorporate and answer Riding's critique of poetic identity and her call for "abdication" in *Anarchism Is Not Enough*. What enables Duncan to return to that broader audience with the publication of *Ground Work* yet still hold himself to Riding's standard? Can we read Laura Riding's abdication—the aporia of her poetic hiatus—in Duncan's derivations from her work? As a schematic starting point, I propose that Duncan's "imitat[ion]," "emulat[ion]," "approximat[ion]" of Riding's poetics take on at least three intersecting strategic trajectories, directed toward a dialectical "abdication": (1) a slippery or confounded gender identity, buttressed by a complex symbology; (2) a power-fraught oscillation between self, text, and reader through notions of permission, obedience, mastery, and law; and (3) the incorporation of a spatialized or "field"-based composition strategy that eschews closure in favor of an indefinite openness. While this essay focuses on the latter two, these three poetic techniques, among others in Duncan's repertoire, build toward an abdication of the poetic voice—in the sense of both sapped individual power (the poetic self subsumed to an abstracted notion of Poetry) and self-reflexivity and formalism (poetic lines that call into question the poetic line as such, what for Riding can be called "designed waste"). I argue that Duncan's poetry—especially in his series of linked poems, *Passages*, constructs a poetic voice that is simultaneously enabled and undercut by a premeditated design that keeps the contradictions of poetic power in play. In *Anarchism* Riding gestures toward the first two of the strategies above (slippery gender and oscillating power relations), but she abdicates, literally and figuratively, before she can integrate them as Duncan does. Riding fulfills the fatalism inherent in her poetics, while Duncan embraces the destructive potential of his "reconstrue[d]" texts and leaves them open. Here, we reach the crux of their relationship—the competing possibilities of abdication: where Duncan, thanks to innovative field-based poetics, maintains a tenuous and provisional hold on his poetic power, Riding releases the rei(g)ns and bequeaths them to her successors. Indeed, Duncan's idiosyncratic "reading" of Riding—less as a source from which to derive than as a poetic identity with whom to grapple—reframes Riding's abdication as an open question, as a justifiable choice, as a reminder of the danger (and the relevance) of the poetic word.

Anarchism Is Not Enough:
Poetry, Truth, and the "Impossible" Self

Ever polemical, Laura Riding lays out her central problematic—how to tell the truth in language—in nearly all her texts, and *Anarchism Is Not Enough* frames politically her programmatic skepticism toward the "potentiality" of poetry to do the job, a skepticism that ends in an abdication. Indeed, even that ostensible political commitment to the social act of poetry as truth teller and as anarchic force is disavowed. The reader encounters in the text a confrontational, staunchly individualist, and antirepresentationalist poetic, a tissue of frustrating yet productive half-explanations and self-contradictions presented in short pieces of criticism with such titles as "What is a poem?" and "An Important Distinction" and in playful prose poems like "In a Café" and "An Anonymous Book." The modular and disjunctive text is dominated in the middle by "Jocasta"—a long essay that articulates Riding's strong skepticism toward "systematic thinking" and "professionalized literary traditions" and, in many ways, points forward to the extended philological engagements of Riding's writing after her renunciation of poetry (introduction to *Anarchism*, xi–xii). Riding's alternative to received tradition—in a form of response to T. S. Eliot's impersonalized "Individual Talent"—is a series of contradictions and paradoxes with no clear resolution. And this irresolvability is by design; as Riding tells us in her "Letter of Abdication," which closes the text: "We are all in an impossible position; which you handle by making less, myself more, impossible" (*Anarchism*, 211). Riding's language here sets up an ambiguity where both the "position" and "myself" are made more impossible—a feedback loop of modernist difficulty making that turns on a doubled sense of the poetic: as a participatory form based in the "we" and as an abstracted and individual form based on formal innovation. Working her way through a number of dialectics—birth and death, expression and communication, the individual and the collective, the real and the unreal (9, 13, 42, 45)—Riding unravels the idealized aesthetics and criticism that dominate her poetic community. She establishes poetry as the only route to the impossibility she seeks to embody, an unarticulated ideal of its own. For Riding, a poem "is the result of an ability to create a vacuum in experience—it is a vacuum and therefore nothing" (17). Again, Riding stages a slip between creator and thing created: the poem is a passive "result of an ability," not something willed or created but still dependent on a certain aptitude for the task. This paradoxical and yet ideal "vacuum," in Riding's account, counteracts the corrupt "flattery" she saw in romantic poetics (which wallowed in "overfeeling") and contemporary criticism (which flouted experience in favor of the intellectual "expert") (16). Riding puts forward what one might call a reverse neo-Platonism, asserting that "as nothing—well as nothing [a poem] is everything in an existence where everything, being effect of effect without cause, is nothing" (18). Because "cause" is sidestepped, "there is nothing for which the poet can flatter himself or receive flattery" (17).[8] Thus poetry fulfills its purpose when it mimes the nothingness of existence, flattening out effects and causes into a self-referential "vacuum" where the poet is mere vessel, on the one hand, and refined and impossible figuration, on the other. In this contradictory position, says Riding, "the only productive design is designed waste" (18).[9] *Anarchism* presents poetry as the most effective means of using language honestly, forgoing "flattery" of the self in service of an impossibility that the poet imagines or creates a priori, before the poem is composed. But this preordained wastefulness, set in motion as an "effect" of the depersonalized poet, unsettles received modes of expression and gnaws at the foundations of traditional senses of the truth. Good poetry, she implies, is anarchic, and even good poetry is not enough.

Indeed, several decades later, in an interview in 1955, Riding responds to this conundrum, suggesting that the "difficulty—apart from that of the inherent unlendability of poetry to the articulate resolution of anything—was involved in a difficulty centered in the question of the nature of human identity."[10] And while poetry cannot resolve this identity, it certainly can point us toward the source of the "difficulty": representation or, in Riding's terms, "appearance." Near the end of *Anarchism*, again in her "Letter of Abdication," Riding invokes the image of a circle and asserts that "appearance is where the circle meets itself, where you live and do not live, where you are and are not dead. Appearance is everything and nothing" (*Anarchism*, 219).

Foregrounding the paradoxical difficulty of "appearance" allows one to avoid Riding's accusations: "You stop half-way round the circle in order to spare yourself the humiliation of missing the true end, which is not perceptible in the ordinary way. Indeed if it is not perceived, it makes no difference, the circle goes round and round upon you" (212). Built into the circularity of Riding's language here and elsewhere (the poem as a "vacuum and therefore nothing," appearance as "everything" and "nothing") is the call for a new order of perception that moves beyond the selfishness of criticism—the fear of "humiliation"—without shirking individualistic discovery.

For Riding, the problem of representation, of "appearance," never resolves itself; the circle must continue to slowly revolve around the paradox of impossibility, the "not enough" of any codified system. Duncan, to his credit, recognized that this critique begins with the system of the singular self. In the introduction to *The Years as Catches* Duncan recounts the way he personalized his early encounters with Riding's "polemical and logistical rhetoric, the argumentative fantasies of her war with false poetry and her doubt of the truth of poetry, [which] were to depress and haunt my mind for the coming years, until I would make that resolve to make up a poetry in order to sing. . . . Laura Riding scolding poets seems, even today, most to be scolding the poet I knew myself to be, scolding my very thinking to know and presuming to be."[11] Duncan interiorizes Riding's general attack on aesthetics, on "false poetry," and takes her "scolding" to be directed squarely at his own presumptions and at his very identity as a poet. But he also displays an understanding of Riding's ultimate goal in the process of composition: the expression or embodiment of "truth"—refracted through the abdicating poet—and the inherent impossibility of that goal. If for Duncan truth telling came from "mak[ing] up a poetry in order to sing," for Riding truth telling came from withdrawal; truth came from a self-righteous "scolding [of] poets . . . presuming to be" seeking and finding a resolution of identity and representation, a scolding of poets presuming to be breaking out of or making concentric the circle of "appearance." For Riding, the point of poetry is to seek this end, this identity (the truth teller), but not to achieve it. Those who presume to achieve it are fair game for her criticisms.

And so, Riding's individualistic and confrontational quest for the "true end" of an endless circle works against the "warm middle" of centralized subjectivity and a presumption of fulfilled truth, and a carefully formalized series of paradoxes becomes her most productive rhetorical mechanism—a mechanism that asserts, ultimately, the impossibility of represented truth in poetry (*Anarchism*, 213). Riding summarizes this technique (while simultaneously undercutting it) and its productive possibilities for the poet in a characteristic and "scolding" passage:

> I will argue further against what I am arguing for. The you which is you is only you, and not only dead but invisible. And you can never be this you unless you see the you which is it and every one hard round the circle to the end, where you can no longer see, and you are alone. And the result, if you do this? You will be so alive that you will be deader than ever; you will have achieved the identity of opposites; you will have brought two counter-processes to rub noses, and the you which you are not, which is you alone, and the you which you are, which is it, every one, not you—and much good may it do you, except to make you deader than ever. (213–14)

Through accusative rhetoric that continually turns in on itself, building binaries upon binaries, Riding celebrates an "identity of opposites" as an impossible and paradoxical ideal fraught with the blindness of death, but an ideal nonetheless. What Riding makes explicit here is the productive non-sense of her argument—a "scolding" to prospective poets that points out the pitfalls of what she calls "flattery." But her dialectical method here is not merely a negative (nor even a negation of a paradox) because she offers a properly doubled poetic method: though it means poetic death—or at the least a necessary abdication—Riding impels "you" to bring together "two counter-processes to rub noses" as a route to that ideal impossibility she both celebrates and abhors throughout the text. It is an impossibly singular subject position to occupy, consisting of "you alone"; and the dialectical flip side—the "you which you are, which is it, every one, not you"—is an equally impossible and idealized community from which Riding's queen is unalterably apart. Further on, Riding scolds "ignoble and indecent" individuals who "begin with contradictions instead of ending with them; efface them instead of developing them" (217). So, through a call for a poetic "identity of opposites" that builds negation upon negation—and through a demonstration of that paradoxical form of argumentation and way of being—Riding offers simultaneously in *Anarchism* a support and rejection of poetry: it is a "vacuum and therefore nothing," but it can emulate the nothingness of reality and make the circles of appearance "concentric" in the right circumstances (19). However, if that truth telling is achieved, the poet—"you," the truth teller—is "deader than ever." Truth telling, in Riding's schema, is coextensive with the death of the poet. For Riding, the only alternative to this unavoidable contradiction is abdication, a self-removal that acknowledges the inevitability of death and—as Duncan demonstrates in his rereading of her work—initiates further production in the anarchy of the singular poet's absence.

Duncan's Areas:
Instituting an Order of Orders in Order to Sing

Duncan recognized the vitality of contradiction in Riding's work and in "Pages of a Notebook" connects it to sexual fulfillment, to the Lion (an important figure in his poetic cosmology), and to his "Atlantis" dream of the field and the cave: "For me, the Lion is sexual appetite that knows no contradiction within itself. The dream of myself as Emperor of the World. Laura Riding suggests that in Story one is Emperor of the World, creator of all things; that wisdom comes in abdicating. The freedom of the individual lies in his institution of anarchy where before he was ruler."[12] Here, although the spirit of opposition remains, Duncan conflates Riding's poetics with his own in at least three ways—a dialectical sort of derivation that keeps the contradictions in play. First, as with Riding, individualistic poetics takes precedence, at least as a point of departure: according to Duncan, one becomes "creator of all things," then chooses to abdicate. Problematically, perhaps, Duncan also acknowledges that one acquires "freedom" through the "institution of anarchy"—a syntactically ambiguous phrase that implies both agency (one institutes anarchy) and structure (the process is institutionalized; a firm structure replaces one's rule). Importantly, the possessive, "his," attaches both the active and passive forms of "institution" to the storyteller.

Like Riding, Duncan plays with pronouns and verb tenses as a way to reveal the inherent multiplicity of linguistic meaning and to connect the struggle for meaning to the desiring subject. The wisdom of abdication, then, is a wisdom of withdrawal from the assumptions of queenly control, an acknowledgment of the slipperiness of linguistic plenitude and of the need for continual movement, reframing, rereading. We can also sketch a rhetorical line here between this doubled sense of "institution" and Duncan's assertion in *The H.D. Book* that the poet "make[s] up a poetry in order to sing"—but here the structure precedes the expression, the song. Duncan thus sets up a tension between the "creator of all things" and the creation that affords one a "Queendom," to use Riding's term, or venue in which to "sing." The poet is free, Duncan implies, only when he has (wisely) abdicated, only when he has extricated himself from the work, from the institution he creates.

Duncan develops further the relationship between poet, poem, and the "field" of language in the introduction to *Bending the Bow*: "The artist . . . works with all parts of the poem as polysemous, taking each thing of the composition as generative of meaning, a response to and a contribution to the building form"; further on, he celebrates the resulting potentialities: "So the artist of abundancies delites in puns, interlocking and separating figures, plays of things missing or things appearing 'out of order' that remind us that all orders have their justification finally in an order of order only our faith as we work addresses."[13] Again, poetic creation for Duncan turns on tensions, this time between "each thing of the composition," the "building form," and the "artist of abundancies." Puns reappear, a source of "delite," their origin unspecified. Duncan implies that the poet's work requires a collective "faith" that mediates thought and language and reveals an already-present "order of order"—a metapoetic structure that the poet can "address" but cannot create. But Duncan still posits an artist who conceives of words as "generative of meaning," a prime mover that must see the possibilities and recognize that "the totality of creation" proffers a complex space of order and disorder. Duncan's "Structure of Rime I," something of a poetic manifesto from *The Opening of the Field*, draws out this very tension under the rubric of "obedience":

> I ask the unyielding Sentence that shows Itself forth in the language as I make it,
>
> Speak! For I name myself your master, who come to serve.
> Writing is first a search in obedience.[14]

Although it cannot be willed to fruition but rather "serve[d]" with "obedience," Duncan forcefully seeks the elusive "Sentence" and implores it to "Speak!" Thus, if language broaches meaning and allows for poetic complexity, the artist "search[es]" out its powers and "delites" in what transpires: "the building form." The result is poems such as "Often I Am Permitted to Return to a Meadow," where meaning continuously oscillates between the striving poet who is "permitted to return" ("By whom?" one might ask) and the multiplied meaning of the words and forms his poems reveal as they enter the "eternal pasture folded in all thought."[15]

Duncan's spatial tropes—the "field," the "meadow," and the "pasture"—provide a space for these tensions to multiply productively. In what is once again an abdication of his own poetic voice in the introduction to *Bending the Bow*, Duncan asserts: "The poem is not a stream of consciousness, but an *area of composition* in which I work with whatever comes into it."[16] In what might by now be a familiar process, the poet initiates the poem but relinquishes his diction to language, which enters the "area" seemingly without coercion; once that nebulous "whatever" enters, Duncan can "work with" it. Critic Andrew Mossin succinctly frames the inherent openness of this spatialization: "For Duncan, who consciously referred to himself as a 'derivative' poet, the point is never to attain some true account of a 'personal' voice, but to activate in language the process whereby elements of personhood, voice, and authorship merge in a composite space of writing."[17] Mossin highlights, as Duncan does, the "process" involved, which (to make process the subject here) never assumes that a poem can capture or mime personality or "truth" but rather that it can reveal the nature of the problem itself—or, at the least, to move away from the source of the problem, away from the autonomous self. As such, the merger of "personhood, voice, and authorship" emerges as self-referentiality, as self-reflexivity. But Duncan saw more in the writing of poetry than the either/or of solipsism and poetic death, of individuated autonomy or undifferentiated chaos; as Mossin intimates, the poet has an opportunity to "activate" the words, to keep their play in play—indeed, very like Riding's "identity of opposites" above, a subject position that makes counterprocesses "rub noses." Duncan relates his struggle to find the compositional approach that resulted in his *Passages* series: "Having grown up in a period when you had to listen to quite a lot of flack about how did the poem end, and so forth, it took me quite a struggle to realize it didn't have to end at all—we participate in it and these are participatory forms. The actual form they belong to just extends infinitely in time and space and content and the poems are areas—areas I'm in when I write."[18] Time and space collapse ("fold") into the "pasture" of poetry for Duncan. Regardless of the fact that he writes the words in 1963 and publishes them in 1967, for example ("The Currents" in *Bending the Bow* even marks the specific composition date for single lines and stanzas), we can always "participate" in the "forms." Duncan creates a profoundly democratic space for composition and for interpretation, and that space activates the poetic oscillation of poet and text beyond what is inherent to form and composition. In another productive tension, however, the marking of composition dates creates an historical specificity that rubs up against the open timelessness that "extends" in these spaces. We can juxtapose pendulum swing toward contextualization with Riding's poetic "vacuum," which seems to exist outside language and to be unchanged by time or space. So, as a response to the linguistic fatalism of Riding's poetic abdication, Duncan's poetics manages to trace an "area" of agency—for the poet and for the reader—that does not betray Riding's "scolding" critique of systematized aesthetics. Paradox returns full force here, as for Duncan poetic composition functions as a doubled "institution" of control and of abdication, a "process" and an "order of orders," an initiation of composition and an "obedience" to whatever might transpire in the making. In spite of (or perhaps due to) these oscillations, Duncan embraces "abundancies," as he calls them above—the potential for activity inherent in a passive action like abdication, the possibility for growth and movement in the death or withdrawal of the pure poetic voice.

Tracing the Passages of Poet, Text, and the Sentence

While Duncan's analyses of his poetics—and its relationship to Riding's work—describe and "approximate" the problematic Riding adumbrates in *Anarchism* (and in more ways than what I've sketched above), the lines of his poetry at once enact the developmental contradiction(s) that Riding demands *and* the participation and abundance of his own poetics. In particular, as we have seen in the paradox of the "master, who come to / serve," the dispersal of authorial voice returns again and again as the work (or language itself) is given rhetorical prominence—though the poet continues to dwell in his "queendom" of "delite." Indeed, Duncan's open-form *Passages* provide one of his more innovative attempts to move beyond pure authorial abdication. *Passages* are implicitly related free-form poems that, like the *Structure of Rime* series, span several volumes of Duncan's poetry. The *Passages* commence in *Bending the Bow*. Duncan explains their genesis in the introduction: "I number the first to come one, but they belong to a series that extends in an area larger than my work in them. I enter the poem as I entered my own life, moving between an initiation and a terminus I cannot name."[19] We might notice, once again, the way that poetry is spatialized here; *Passages*, as a "series that extends," even seems to encompass those potentialities heretofore unseen—the "field" continuously expands. Duncan "cannot name" the "initiation" or the "terminus" for *Passages* because he refuses to close the series (or the series refuses to close itself). Perhaps another poet will pick up *Passages* and continue their development; perhaps a reader will track down an intertext (a source of the "derivation") that will enrich the "area" in which the series dwells. Time and poetic intention (e)merge into a timeless space of writing. Duncan's strategy here, which is another abdication, wraps another layer of textuality around his poetic identity; not only does Duncan allow language to "come into" his writing area—to control word choice, puns, and so on—but he muddies the connections between the poems in an ostensibly interlocking series. His "Notes" to open the first volume of *Ground Work* elaborate further: "Passages themselves are but passages of a poem beyond that calls itself Passages and that is manifest only in the course of the book in which it appears, even so phrases have both their own meaning and yet belong to the unfolding revelation of a Sentence beyond the work."[20] Here, Duncan once again invokes the mythical (and capitalized) "Sentence," the word, a "revelation" that empowers the series to "[call] itself Passages." His rhetoric—particularly the use of passive voice and the personification of abstractions—removes self completely from the process. But Duncan still holds the rei(g)ns of defining their appearance (definitively: they "are but" what he says they are). As he says in "Pages of a Notebook," "I have 'selected' my works, weeded out the poetry, which is not all of a tone, and composed a work that has a remote consistency."[21] In "The Self in Postmodern Poetry," Duncan suggests that *Passages* is "a work in which I seek to lose myself in the hearing of the voice of the work itself, a work not of personality or oneself but of structures and passages."[22] Who is making these choices? Who decides ("selects") when the poems begin and end, what gives them "consistency"? The structure of *Passages*, beyond the basic tenets of Duncan's poetics outlined above, simultaneously saps and reinscribes authorial power: it gives him a say in the interaction of his corpus, if only to express what might seem to be vague equivocations (or productive contradictions?). As he attempts to explain *Passages*, at least, Duncan confounds and implies interlocking meaning in the same gesture.

In "Passages 4 (Where It Appears)," Duncan affirms these simultaneous concerns, with power oscillating between his own poetic vision and the enactive power of the word alone. He avers, "I have in this my own / intense / area of self creation," yet he affirms that he would

let image perish in image,
            leave writer and reader
 up in the air
  to draw
                  momentous
                        inconclusions,[23]

Duncan invests the compositional process with an "intens[ity]" that extends beyond his own work in the "area." Allowing the "image" to "perish" leaves space for the possibility of "momentous / inconclusions." Duncan recognizes that the destructiveness and infidelity of language—which enter into his work, whether he wills it or not—enable a permanent openness, an abdication of final meaning and, by implication, authorial autonomy. The spatialized "field" of time in the series of *Passages*, however, permits Duncan to return to the "area of self creation" whenever needed. Regardless of who initiates such things, the "image perish[es] in image," and the writer and reader merge in the "air" of interpretation. Further, in a poem whose title—"In Place of a Passage 22"—begins as an abdication, Duncan casts himself as a poetic "agent," particularizes his perceptions during composition, and allows the "image" to disperse the experience:

> turning my poet's mind in tides of
> solitude, seductive reveries, fears, resolves, outrage
> yet
> having this certain specific agent I am,
> the shadow of a tree wavering and yet staying
> deep in it,
> the certain number of his days renderd uncertain,
> gathering,
> animal and mammal, drawing such milk
> from the mother of stars. (*Bow*, 75)

Here, Duncan shrouds his poetic voice ("this certain specific agent") in the "shadow" of a "wavering" tree; even so, he remains "deep in it." Vitally, Duncan enjambs "yet" to foreground the tension between multiplied "tides" of individual emotion and the singularity of the "I" as an "agent." In spite of the difficulty of representing the "turning [of] my poet's mind in tides of / solitude," the poem helps him to "[draw] such milk / from the mother of stars." The poet dwells, works, and participates in the liminal space afforded by the "yet," by the possibilities (and attendant difficulties or "shadow[s]") language affords him. The result: an ambiguity that encourages us to "draw / momentous / inconclusions," to "delite" in the "wavering" and "seductive" productivity of the "field" of language—what Duncan calls in "Passages 28 (The Light)" "that great horse Poetry, Rider / we ride, who make up / the truth of What Is" (*Bow*, 122).

As the "Rider" merges with the ridden (the poet with language, and vice versa) in the quest for "the truth," Duncan returns to derivativeness to confound them again in "Passages 31 (The Concert)" as he invokes "that lonely spirit / having in its derivation likewise / the quality of the stars and yet / a severd distinct thing."[24] Truth cannot be fully attained, but one can approximate the "quality of the stars" by remaining derivative; however, because each spirit is a "severd distinct thing," the demands of individuality (in this case, the Wordsworthian quest for solitude) reinvest authorial identity. Later in "The Concert," our "lonely spirit"

> bends his head
> to hear the sound he makes
> that leads his heart upward,
>
> ascending to where the beat breaks
> into an all-but-unbearable whirling crown
> of feet dancing, and now he sings or it is
> the light singing, the voice
> shaking, in the throes of the coming melody,
> resonances of meaning exceeding what we
> understand, words freed from their origins,[25]

Here, the oscillations (or are they "resonances"?)—this time between the "spirit" singing the "coming melody" and the "whirling crown" (symbol of the "queendom") that comprises that "upward" movement of the heart—build toward a Ridingesque abdication. The poet is effectively multiplied, forced to "hear the sound he makes"—the "melody" is extricated from the poetic "voice / shaking." Expression of words is placed at a remove from its "origins," "exceeding what we understand"; Duncan acknowledges, as Riding does above, that language problematizes meaning's pure plenitude—but it also affords the poet his or her "all-but-unbearable whirling crown." As Duncan intimates in "Passages 33 (Transmissions)," productive structure—a meta-"design"—exceeds thematics:

> —no one
> nor poet
> nor writer of words

can contrive to do justice to the beauty of that
design he designs from.
We pretend to speak. The language is not ours
and we move upward beyond our powers into
words again beyond us unsure measures

the poetry of the cosmos[26]

As a final poetic citation, we are "moving between an initiation and a terminus"—but perhaps now we can name it. If the "design" the poet "designs from" (his poetics/aesthetics) comprises the "beauty" of his work, Duncan may be setting himself up for the "scold[ing]" of Riding's antisystematic, anti-idealist critiques. But his dispersal of poetic identity, his abdication—which takes the form of multiplicity ("no one") and dispossession ("The language is not ours") above but serves as a repeated trope throughout *Passages*—ensures that he remains in Riding's "field" of contradictions because in an open form the poetic self can be at once singular and multiple, in control and derivative, Queen and not-Queen.

Towards an Institution of and an Abdication from "Abundancies"

Perhaps it is not so simple as this, but we might initiate a conclusion by noticing the stark difference between Laura Riding's *Anarchism Is Not Enough*, which tends to insist upon a closed reading, and Robert Duncan's *Passages*, which encourages an open reading that extends beyond the poet's own work. Speaking in the language of economies, one could say that Duncan responds to Riding's "scarcity mentality" toward language (particularly the trappings of "appearance") with a doctrine of "abundance"—"Abundancies," in his words. But these are, for better or for worse, conclusions that "efface" the contradictions we might find (and I certainly do not want to receive a "scold[ing]" from Riding for it). What this essay has pursued is the possible avenues (or "areas") of development in Duncan's poetics; how has he engaged with Riding's problematic? In general, Duncan evinces a greater faith in the "Sentence" and its inherent ability to create and enact, to represent materiality, experience, indeed, to represent truth (again, "abundancies"). As such, his abdication leads to contrary results: once Duncan has his or her "queendom"—acquired primarily through an innovative poetics, a beautiful "design he designs from"—he effaces his own poetic identity and bequeaths meaning and potentiality to a community of readers and, more centrally, to language itself. Of course, this general model does not remain closed; Duncan's abdication, unlike Riding's, is not permanent. Riding, in spite of a moderately successful and productive poetic corpus, chooses to abandon poetry—seemingly the last hope in *Anarchism Is Not Enough*—and never returns to it. The impossibility, what I would call the "scarcity," of "truth" she saw in aestheticized poetry drove her from her "queendom," and the nothingness she sought came to fruition; even Riding's "designed waste" could not make appearance into truth. Duncan, as we have seen, took up the impossibility of represented truth and made it a careerlong quest for the elusive "Sentence." His most compelling innovation—a spatialized poetics—allowed him to scatter his poetic identity in a "meadow" of oscillating tensions. If Duncan is right, language will continue to enact a rich field of multiplied meaning; the poet's work, in this situation, is a complex and fluctuating abdication from the desire to control. Faith in the "Sentence"—and its "participatory" possibilities—encapsulates Duncan's ultimate distinction from Riding. And the truth of poetry might constellate around this unending quest for the truth of the poetic self—expressed via (fraught and contradictory) language and delivered to a no less tension-riddled community of readers.

Notes

1. Duncan, "Pages from a Notebook," 406–7.
2. Hamilton, *Drawing the Line*, 238.
3. These are not exact analogues, of course—Duncan's hiatus was far less drastic and permanent—but the correspondences between them pose a productive ambiguity: in the seeking after textualized truth, both Duncan and Riding withdrew for an extended period from communicating through the public forum of poetry. As I will suggest below, the permanence of Riding's "abdication"—a permanence apparent to Duncan even as early as 1953—precisely fulfills the fatalism of her complex poetics. This in mind, I want to suggest that Duncan's return from his publishing hiatus, a return in which he reenters the "field" of his *Passages* series, demonstrates both his fidelity to Riding's vision and his departure from it.

4. Riding, *Anarchism*, 14. Hereafter cited in the text as *Anarchism*.
5. Laura Riding, "Preface for a Second Reading," in *The Telling*, 67.
6. Laura (Riding) Jackson, introduction to *The Poems*, 3.
7. It should be noted, however, that Riding never relinquished her quest for "truth"—though in her later years it took the form of *Rational Meaning*, a decadeslong collaboration with Schuyler Jackson that seeks, so the subtitle claims, "A New Foundation for the Definition of Words."
8. Notice, again, the ways in which Riding (and I, in paraphrasing) remove or defer the subject of the sentence, invoking passive voice verb constructions, pronouns without clear referents, and abstractions as the agents for verbs. Beyond an espoused poetics, the critique of the "subject" occurs at the level of syntax—in Riding and in Duncan, as we shall see.
9. The question of what poetry can be written through a principle of "designed waste" is one that Duncan attempts to answer, though not explicitly, with his *Passages* series.
10. Riding, quoted in Hamilton, *Drawing the Line*, 151.
11. Duncan, *The Years as Catches*, ix–x.
12. Duncan, "Pages from a Notebook," 405.
13. Duncan, *Bending the Bow*, ix.
14. Duncan, *The Opening of the Field*, 12.
15. Ibid., 4.
16. Duncan, *Bending the Bow*, vi, emphasis added.
17. Mossin, "Unveiling Expectancy," 546–47.
18. Duncan, quoted in Hamilton, *Drawing the Line*, 170.
19. Duncan, *Bending the Bow*, v.
20. Duncan, "Some Notes on Notation," in *Ground Work: Before the War*, xi.
21. Duncan, "Pages from a Notebook," 406.
22. Robert Duncan, "The Self in Postmodern Poetry," in *Fictive Certainties*, 227.
23. Duncan, *Bending the Bow*, 15. Hereafter cited in the text as *Bow*.
24. Duncan, *Ground Work: Before the War/In the Dark*, 15.
25. Ibid., 16.
26. Ibid., 25.

CHAPTER SIX

Reading A/Drift: Robert Duncan's Use of Foreign Words

CLÉMENT OUDART

The Silver Rib of the Foreign Word

In his essay "On the Use of Foreign Words," Theodor Adorno vouches for "a determined defense of the use of foreign words," as he is waging a merciless war against purism, on the one hand, and "an immanent, closed organic language," on the other.[1] In his view, a proper defense should not so much try "to demonstrate the harmlessness of foreign words as to release their explosive force: not to deny what is foreign in them but to use it."[2] Displacing the polarity of purity/corruption to more subversive grounds, he wryly asserts that "one must defend them where they are at their worst from the point of view of purism: where they are foreign bodies assailing the body of language."[3] We are indeed reminded that "foreign" words are only alien to homespun words in the eyes of purism, whose proponents, suggests Adorno, should relinquish "the idea of a pure ur-idiom" altogether.[4] Discussing Verlaine's differential principle of nuance in his *Art poétique*, Rilke's use of foreign words and their untranslatability in the *Neue Gedichte*, Adorno celebrates the fact that the modern writer surpasses this primordial pure versus corrupt dichotomy:

> The writer may well proceed in the way Walter Benjamin described in *One-Way Street* when he compared the man of letters to a surgeon who performs a difficult operation on his idea and in doing so inserts

> the "silver rib of a foreign word" into the idea. But the silver rib helps the patient, the idea, to survive, while it sickened from the organic rib. . . . In the foreign word the nuance is both rescued and destroyed at the same time. . . . But while the writer still always thinks that he is quoting from his education and from special knowledge, he is actually quoting from a hidden language that is unknown in the positive sense, a language that overtakes, overshadows, and transfigures the existing one as though it were itself getting ready to be transformed into the language of the future. . . . The power of an unknown, genuine language . . . that arises only in pieces and out of the disintegration of the existing one; this negative, dangerous, and yet assuredly promised power is the true justification of the foreign word.[5]

Adorno's critical prose sheds light on the polyglotic material of modernist palimpsests like the *Cantos*, which served as a model for Robert Duncan's poetics in most of *Ground Work: In the Dark*—a poetics grounded in a "boundless creational field" that produced an increasingly polyphonic serial poem.[6]

Written in October 1979, "In Waking" gathers fragments in Latin and French and foregrounds the act of writing as re-membering. It is also an ephemeral address to the poet's lover:

> the lines coming thru as I find myself
>   speaking,   mouthing them,   "*We* . . ."
> —toes *(mes orteils)*,   naming,   flexing,
>   the calves of my legs *(mes mollets)*   heavy—
> I am remembering.[7]

This tongue-in-cheek allusion to the resurrection of Osiris leads to self-reflexivity (the recording of the poem's gradual making) and on to the blurred borders of the native/foreign binary opposition in language. This entails Duncan's sense of self-estrangement in the experience of writing:

> In the customs of speech I have long known
>   —native to what speech?—
> a few words from an other language
>   I am seeking

come thru you again where
foreign to myself I am
reminded yours in every light.[8]

Interestingly, this poem from October 1979 about the poet's sense of foreignness inhabiting the self and language was written immediately after a journal entry written in French on Tuesday, December 13, 1977. Indeed, Duncan's notebooks from the late seventies testify to a daily practice of *writing* in French, enabling the poet to make his *demeure* (abode) in the foreign language. The poet mixes within the same genetic space vocabulary taken from French classic authors (such as Jules Verne, Colette, Simenon, Baudelaire, Nerval, among others) grammar exercises often bordering on the Steinian mode of repetition (as if to impregnate his own language with traces of the foreign syntax) and phonetic drills (yet another experiment in ciphering and deciphering). In December 1977, then, Duncan was at the peak of his "foreign" reading-and-writing practice after spending the spring in Europe, mostly in England, France, and Belgium. In this note bordering on journal entry and prose poem, Duncan wrote: "Dans ce livre dont les pages blanches, propres, dont la solitude, viennent de m'embarrasser, je doit maintenant faire des taches, prendre à tâche de faire cette écriture, chaque jour, en français. Je dois commencer à parler cette langue mère dont ma langue propre n'est pas né [*sic*]."[9] Translated literally, Duncan's entry reads: "In this book, whose white [blank], clean pages, and whose solitude, have just embarrassed me, I now have to make blots, to set myself the task of doing this writing, every day, in French. I have to start speaking this mother-tongue from which my own tongue wasn't born." The stress is laid on the two homonyms (*tache* for "blot" or "stain" and *tâche* for "task"). The poet thus underlines the etymological root of lite-rature as *rature* (smear or erasure), which inspired in different ways both Derrida and Lacan, since "*literatura* in the singular means writing, grammar, learning or literature. However the latter noun comes from the verb *lino*, whose meaning is contradictory since it calls up 'I smear,' 'I cover' or 'I erase.'"[10] Duncan is also drawing on the literal and figurative meanings of *propre* (my "own," unsoiled and proper)—a word whose polysemy is essential to the poet's inquiry into the (m)other tongue.

Duncan's (m)Other Tongue

This inquiry takes the form of a philosophical investigation into the origin and the other, which materializes as a series of metonymic displacements along the chain of signifiers. Duncan evolves an *écriture* predicated upon the practice of ciphering and deciphering as the meaning of words is anchored in bilingual wordplay. His writing *t(â)che* or "task" may be seen as pertaining to what Derrida calls the *shibboleth* in his glossing of *tout autre est tout autre*, a phrase embedding for him "the essential and abyssal equivocality":

> [T]his play of words seems to contain the very possibility of a secret that hides and reveals itself at the same time within a single sentence and, more than that, within a single language. . . . The essential and abyssal equivocality, that is, the play of the several senses of *tout autre est tout autre* . . . is not, in its literality . . . universally translatable. . . . We have here a kind of *shibboleth*, a secret formula such as can be uttered only in a certain way in a certain language. . . . The untranslatability of this formal economy functions like a secret within one's so-called natural or mother tongue.[11]

Duncan's writing practice as veiling/revealing underlines the indwelling of a *secret* in *écriture*. My sense is that it is epitomized by his relation to the French language and specifically to the work of Egyptian-born poet Edmond Jabès. "Not being French," writes Duncan about reading *Le livre des questions*, "having no permission, no initiation—the mystery but increases everywhere": "Here, in Jabès, I take this French to be my 'Hebrew,' as my *temenos* and dwelling in language."[12] Yet if Duncan holds the other tongue to embody an enhanced sense of mystery within language, the secret (*Geheimnis*) already inhabits what Derrida calls the "so-called mother tongue": "It is there before us in its possibility, the *Geheimnis* of language that ties it to the home, to the motherland, to the birth-place, to economy, to the law of the *oikos*, in short to the family and to the family of words derived from *heim*—home, *heimlich*, *unheimlich*, *Geheimnis*, etc."[13] Duncan does not primarily associate the uncanny (*das Unheimliche*) with the written text but with *voices*—voices always coming from beyond, in his imagination, and epitomized by Jabès's address to the Other in the myriad fictitious prophetic voices of *The Book of Questions*:

> We may be reminded that where paranomasia begins, there may be mirage. This voice and these voices where there are only printed words on the page as I read must be of such a nature, the more so because it is only in the most tenuous reaches of desire, wish, imagination, risk, that I trust I hear, for French is not native to me, it is my "foreign" language, "foreign" to me and then haunting, charged with the over-thereness my native language had only before I could understand and then speak.[14]

While Duncan's *écriture* is rooted in his daily *t(â)che* in the mother's tongue or Mother tongue ("langue mère," as distinct from *langue maternelle*), the play of voices and the materiality of phonemes conjure up a sense of foreignness bound up with a return to the primordial time of infancy.

The consubstantiality of other and mother tongue was famously formulated by Jacques Lacan, for whom "language brings with it a fundamental form of alienation that is part and parcel of learning *one's mother tongue*. The very expression we use to talk about it—'mother tongue'—is indicative of the fact that it is some Other's tongue first, the mOther's tongue, that is, the mOther's language."[15] In speaking of childhood experience, Lacan virtually equates the Other with the mother.[16] Indeed, he insists that the child is born in the Symbolic order of the Other's discourse. "The Other," emphasizes Lacanian theorist and translator Bruce Fink, "is that foreign language we must learn to speak which is euphemistically referred to as our 'native tongue,' but which would be much better termed our 'mOther tongue.'"[17] These comments shed light on Duncan's essay on Jabès, which proceeds as follows:

> Oh yes, I can read; the words on the page and their phonetic transcriptions, and the theories of voice, I can read. But this voice and these voices I must hear in an infatuation. This is the language of the "Other," whose ultimate lure is the lure of an other "me." Close then to the very voice or mode of Poetry, for I know in the courses of my

> work the voice is in one sense more me than I am, in another sense is an "I" beyond me.[18]

Duncan first lays the emphasis on the foreignness of the mothertongue, which the subject tries in vain to make "his own" (*appropriate*), before depicting the polyphony at work in Jabès's poetry as the epitome of "the language of the 'Other'": this last phrase inevitably conjures up Lacan's notorious definition of the unconscious as *le discours de l'Autre*, often translated as "the language of the Other." The Other, explains Lacan, is located in what Freud called before him the "other scene" in *The Interpretation of Dreams*.[19] Spelling out his eerie experience as the *subject of the poem*, Duncan wrote in "Songs of an Other": "I come into / the being of an other me."[20] Beyond the foreign tongue, otherness has become the voice or mode of poetry itself. "It is, after all, in French, in the oracular voice of Rimbaud, that this '*Je [est] un autre*' so strikingly came into our European World Mind, though Baudelaire had noticed that an author is aware that his 'I' is an other. In Jabès's dedication isn't this otherness, now between the I and the Thou, between the writer and the reading, in the last verse fused impossibly in the We?"[21] Duncan's reading of the self through his reading of Jabès is informed by Rimbaud's oracular statement in the first *lettre du voyant* (I is an other: "Je est un autre") as well as Baudelaire's more elusive or fugitive subject.[22] Rimbaud writes Georges Izambard, in a letter dated May 13, 1871, that he is applying himself to become a *voyant* (seer) so as to reach the unknown by way of a systematic unsettling of all the senses. And this sensory disturbance incurs tremendous suffering:

> But one must be strong, must be born a poet, and I recognized a poet in me. It is not at all my fault. It is wrong to say: I think: one should say: I am thought.—pardon my wordplay.—
>
> I is an other.[23]

Rimbaud's critique of rationalism through his shift from a Cartesian *cogito* (*je pense*) to "I am thought" (*on me pense*)—an aphorism that underwrites Duncan's conception of poetic practice as revelation, such as dramatized in the *Structure of Rime*—immediately precedes the syntactic rupture enacted in "I is an other," his visionary formula for the alienation of the ego by or *in* language.[24] Duncan's reference to Baudelaire's alienated "I" in "The Delirium of Meaning" echoes a 1961 chapter of *The H.D. Book* (II, 9), where he quotes the first fragment of Baudelaire's subversive autobiographical writings:

> Here sorting and mixing are functions of a higher organization in which, troubled by my thought of Baudelaire's *Mon coeur mis à nu*, I begin to take thought in Baudelaire's thought. "*De la vaporisation et de la centralisation du Moi*," appears reflected almost as if contrived to fit the composition of my own reflections. And as I read Baudelaire the specter of my trouble with his trouble begins to come forward, as if in a mirror behind me as I work.[25]

In his *Journaux intimes* (comprising "Mon coeur mis à nu" and "Fusées"), Baudelaire's lapidary style befits his bitter diatribe against bourgeois morality and his foray into the stronghold of rational individualism. The poetic fragments actually exhibit his fierce undermining of the traditional autobiographical gesture of self-constitution. Although deeply ambiguous, the opening aphorism taken up by Duncan calls for an impersonal, programmatic disintegration of the subject, just as the (Satanic) other takes his place.[26]

Emblematic of Baudelaire's Satanic verse, the address "Au lecteur" serves as a threshold before the descent into the heart of darkness along a path strewn with the sickly flowers Duncan will savor with "the endlessness of a relentless distaste."[27] Indeed, anticipating Freud's "*it* speaks," Rimbaud's groundbreaking "I am thought" is echoed in Duncan's quotation from Baudelaire: "C'est le Diable qui tient les fils qui nous remuent!" (The Devil himself pulls on all our strings!). This is a shift from the Other's language to the Other's desire. Subjected to the Other's desire (in the guise of Satan or the supreme of vices, *Ennui*), the poet lets foreign matter enter a prose poem following his tribute "À Maître Baudelaire" and fittingly entitled "At Cambridge an Address to Young Poets Native to the Land of My Mothertongue":

> "*Les fils qui nous remuent*" *invisibles*—a line of Baudelaire leaks through —lead me to believe. Soundings and listenings enthrall my belief and steal it away. Bereft, I am still listening. As I had only to believe then, murmuring, *babbling*, whining, howling, shattering the divine columns

> of language surrounding me long ago—yesterday—but a second ago while-where I lay in the house of men and women sounding. I was a serpent. The *seed* of a mind to come coild before language and recoild in the waves of talk-ing around me.[28]

Once again Duncan's experience of the French language as intrinsically "foreign" recalls the infancy of the mind, the primal time where language, through the mother tongue, consists of an alien "babbling," a language "charged with the over-thereness my native language had only before I could understand and then speak."[29] For Lacan, alienation occurs through the utterance of the first babbles. Its vehicle is the mOthertongue, then called *lalangue*, from "lallation, archaic babytalk."[30] As Jean-Michel Rabaté points out: "The Unconscious is fundamentally writing, and the battery of these archaic inscriptions antedates the child's first immersion in a 'babble' of half-meaningful signifiers that Lacan calls *lalangue*."[31] From "babbling" to babel: the *t(â)che* of the translator . . .

A Babel of Words

Duncan's poetics of *transfiguration* is predicated upon a double displacement: quoting a fragment incurs a textual displacement, the wrenching of words from their original co-text, and this, of course, creates a first level of opacification; translating it performs another displacement, which, if no guarantor of transparency, renders the original accessible to the reader.[32] Both displacements could be described as acts of appropriation. In appropriation resonates the word *propre*, used by Duncan in his diary entry. It consists in making what is foreign one's own. When the writer performs such a multifaceted transfiguration, its impact on the reader and the writer alike is that of familiarization, or making the other's text one's home. Yet the trend can be reversed, as Duncan did by choosing to translate into French the first two lines of Pound's Canto I—"And then went down to the ship, / Set keel to breakers, forth on the godly sea, and"—in the opening lines of his bilingual poem entitled "Et."[33] In the process Duncan operates a willful *defamiliarization* of the modernist masterpiece he had read and taught all his life: "Et / puis sommes descendus au vaisseau / avons posé la quille aux brisants / là-bas."[34]

As is well known, Pound's "tale of the tribe" is itself derived from a Renaissance translation of the *Odyssey* in Latin. Like Canto I, Duncan's Passage "Et" proceeds from a defamiliarizing translation, which is a concrete representation of the way in which language contains the past. Both texts take shape through a voyage through language, between texts and languages. Duncan drops a hint: "[I]n these passages / back of Pound's cantos / my keys."[35] In translating Pound's first "song," the poet performs both appropriation and defamiliarization. In the process he creates the possibility to "make it new," for in translating this fragment, both writer and reader rediscover the inaugural magic of a new reading. In steering away from the mother tongue, the poet vivifies the infant mind. The "foreign" tongue resulting from this procedure, I would argue, is the paradigm of the Other language: for the native speaker of English and French alike, the experience is that of defamiliarization. In fashioning a language to which no one is native, Duncan invents a topos for the unfamiliar. With Passage "Et," Duncan is going adrift, slyly projecting his own musings as he sets forth on a godly sea of intertextuality in a timeless sonic flow between waking and dreaming. Predicated upon double entendre—and a welter of (conscious and unconscious) errors—Duncan weaves a bilingual text fraught with paronomasia and mirage. In this poem he nimbly *passes* from one tongue to another through the strategically placed "transparent" words passage/*passage* and derivation/*dérivation*:

la démarrons!   la faisons
        le passage
                        au-delà
  dérivés
                    did not want to
                        drift
    I said yet   this is my drift
dérêvés   O   outside my own dream
        having no tongue of my own,
            no mouth
dreamd here   there
                        le rêve[36]

The poem drifts (*dérive*) from "dérivés" to "dérêvés," from the shores of language (*rive*) to the world of dreams (*rêve*), a Joycean language of the night placed under the *spell* of the Poundian "tone-leading of vowels." In this constellated page the poem hinges on the guarantee of intelligibility, Syntax.[37] Therefore, the poet is free to atomize his materials and to tap into the endless reserve of polylingual polysemy. Lacan reminds us that drift is etymologically close to drive: "Here I will take up the challenge made to me when people translate as 'instinct' what Freud calls *Trieb*—which 'drive' would seem to translate quite well into English, but which is avoided in the *Standard Edition*. In French, my last resort would be *dérive* [drift], if I were unable to give the bastardized term *pulsion* [drive or surge] its point of impact."[38] The poet is driven by the pure *jouissance* of the phonemic treasure-trove of signifiers. In his own words, Duncan seeks to achieve "a disturbance of words within words."[39] Hinged upon the semiotic bar splitting signifier and signified (or the semiotic/semantic), Duncan's poem releases an unsuspected wealth of meaningful puns. We are reminded that linguistic jouissance, or the enjoyment of the words' *signifiance*, is above all a matter of *j'ouis sens*. Here is a particularly apposite passage in Lacan's "The Subversion of the Subject and the Dialectic of Desire" translated by Bruce Fink:

> We must keep in mind that jouissance is prohibited [*interdite*] to whomever speaks, as such—or, put differently, it can only be said [*dite*] between the lines by whomever is a subject of the Law, since the Law is founded on that very prohibition.
>
> Indeed, were the Law to give the order, "*Jouis!*" [enjoy or come!], the subject could only reply "*J'ouis*" [I hear], in which the jouissance would no longer be anything but understood [*sous-entendue*].[40]

Phonemic jouissance dwells in the inter-said of Duncan's polyglotic poem:

"to see and perceive things *here*" to hear in this hearing what sounds
depth appears unfathomable obscure foundations
ses courants du fond[41]

Driven by the homophony of here/hear, the poem drifts from purely phonemic and metonymic shift to paradigmatic substitution: "hearing" leads to "what sounds," which in turn produces a grammatically ambivalent reading ("what phonemes" or "what probes"), the latter solution offering a passage to "depth" and allowing ultimately the reader to hit bottom, so to speak. Shifted from the surface level to the vertical axis of semantic soundings, Duncan's textual derivation leads its readers to "unfathomable obscure foundations," all but deadly undercurrents ("ses courants du fond"). Here again Duncan may be leading us into the Nekuia episode at the onset of the *Cantos*: "Sun to his slumber, shadows o'er all the ocean, / Came we then to the bounds of deepest water."[42] Plunged in the dark, the poet enjoys a *d(é)rive sans fond*, touches upon the bottomless ground of the real (the Lacanian register of phonemic jouissance).

The poet works the ground of the between, or *entre-deux*, as obliquely suggested in the title of an unpublished poem from August 12, 1977, precisely entitled "Entre les Deux":

Langages éloges
Signes sons
les mots arrivent les pas
sages et resonants dans l'échange
entre l'espace et le temps
commencent en français (Notebook, 57)

Duncan liked Saint-John Perse's *Éloges* (1911), which is probably alluded to in this poem. Besides the numerous alliterative or consonantic effects (signes/sons, langages/éloges/échanges), Duncan encrypts a "schibboleth" in the French idiom with "les pas/sages": in addition to the effect of disjointed "passages" (in the pas/sage, or *versus*, from one line to the next), Duncan conjures up the literal meaning of the separate words ("the wise footsteps"), which is reinforced by the use of *résonant* (echoing, resounding). What's more, another reading is possible with homophony (*les passagers résonants*), which may be a slant allusion to the words themselves, echoing passengers in language. In "Le Sonnet où sonne la sonnette" the poet performs another foray into the excessive and awe-filled *enjoyment* of the poetic, where

monstrous sense and sound
transformd
transfounded in this fond

nonsense and unsound
confidence—[43]

By means of its playful paronomasia, Duncan's "Sonnet" conjures up a string of phonemic associations stemming from the verbal form *sonne* ("rings," as in the Celan poem), where *sonne* is in turn contained in "sonnet" and "sonnette" (a sonnet and a ring or bell). It is also *die Sonne* (the sun), and the French bell is in turn a German poem (*Sonnette*). In keeping with this poem, where the death knell is tolled in the background ("dès dernières jours"), another poem composed immediately after "La Sonnette" in June 1977 features the polylingual pun on sun/*sonne*/*Sonne*.[44] In an expanding and increasingly self-referential network of phonemic and semantic rimes, "Pour Souffrir l'Envie jusqu'à l'Amour en Vie" (with its pun on *envie*, "longing" or "desire," and *en vie*, "alive") features the return of the Nervalian "black sun of *Melancolia*": "Au seuil du soleil noir . . ."[45] Paronomasia entails a displacement from the threshold of the dark star (*seuil*) to mourning (*deuil*) in a poem reminiscent of surrealist imagery ("dans l'accident psycho-chimique de la chair").[46] As reveals the sixth complete typescript for "Ground Work: Volume Two" headed with "CONTENTS as of May 1981," the original title of this poem comprised yet another interlingual pun: "Pour souffrir l'envie jusqu'à l'*Amor* en vie." This timeless metaphysical conceit consists in blending love and death, a theme developed by Freud under the auspices of Eros and Thanatos. It is emphasized by Duncan through his use of the Italian (or Spanish) word *amor*, whose homophone *la mort* creates a mirror to the pun on life and desire (*vie* and *envie*).[47] This commingling of opposites (creating a paradox: *la mort en vie*, a "live" or "quick" death) culminates in the expression commonly used in French for a sexual orgasm, *la petite mort*, of which Lacan made the most.

Duncan's interlingual wordplay with *die Sonne* exemplifies a babelization of language in the late writings, where polyglotic puns and a plethora of distortions converge into a "Babelized" language reminiscent of Pound's *Cantos* and Joyce's *Finnegans Wake*—both Duncan's bedside books and touchstones of his reading of modernism. In "The Delirium of Meaning," Duncan elaborates on the pitfall created by a word like *blessure* (wound) and the subsequent bliss of misreadings: "In the accident between languages after Babel, the *blessure* from French appears as a *faux ami* familiar to unwary English readers who read 'blessing.' . . . In the *blessure*/blessing of my uncertainty, my stranger-reading out of French, in no way a native. . . . Once the reading has so wandered, the 'correct' translation remains haunted by the multiplication of meanings only misreading frees in us, who do not misread or mistake carelessly."[48] As always, Duncan's statement finds an echo in a poem, here in "The Dignities," which he wrote in January 1980: "setting up a *demeure* 'in uncertainties, mysteries, doubts.'"[49] In a way, Duncan's critical prose flows back into the poem via the typically Jabèsian notion of *demeure*.[50] In another unpublished essay from 1977, Duncan elaborates in French on the mother tongue as "*Ur-Sprache*" (Notebook, 55) before moving on to oppose the mythic ur-idiom to the plurality of languages in the aftermath of what George Steiner calls the "second Fall."[51]

A/Drift in the Other's Tongue

Arguably the most unbridled inquiry into the multilingual "commune of poetry," Duncan's "In Wonder" is also one of the most tongue-in-cheek of all his language games. Willfully fragmentary, often at the limit of syntax and (non)sense, this poem assembles Duncan's "babblings" as he is seeking "to stir these / latencies":

FOR MICHAEL PALMER who *alzo* may work alone
spracht *our Dee* no language
this writing as such its intercourses
parmi des faux amis ses *erreciónes*
means
Ists gut?
Chaque à son goût exquis arrive à la *SAVEUR*
que la langue désire[52]

Steering away from the seriousness of the earlier intertextual derivations, the poet plunges into a parodic vortex of languages: "Hinter den German ein Traumen-Figures liegt avec des Engeln kasts / speech-shadows / upon the waters."[53] The specters of the Rilkean angels and of Freudian "Dream-Work" seem to hover over this medley of what Duncan wryly names "Ur tterances" (and, further on, "Terrorances"). The resulting "poem-work" is an oblique reflection on (and enactment of) the post-Babel dissemination of tongues by way of a playful tribute to Michael Palmer's language skills and taste for European literature. It is also a defense of the use of foreign words much like Adorno's above. In his attack against purism, Adorno also forcefully argues against the organically developed *Ur-Sprache* with its mythical "ur-words" as opposed to "found" or "made" words. "The true words, fragments of truth, are not the buried ur-words that are mythically evoked. They are found words, the performed words, the artificial words, in short, the made words; just as, according to the account in *Genesis*, god did not reveal the names of things to man; instead, those names were made known to him only when man named them in his human fashion: in the act of naming itself."[54] "In Wonder" offers such a collage of found words, whose distinct sound images and meanings are joyously savored: "Chaque à son goût exquis arrive à la *SAVEUR* / que la langue désire."[55] At his most Barthesian, Duncan's enhanced textual pleasure is adumbrated in the synesthesia of the senses (typical of Baudelaire's "Correspondances"). With the primal metonymy of *la langue*, meaning both "tongue" and "language," the aural pleasures of a cunning linguist, so to speak, are brought to the fore. Duncan scribbled down in a notebook entry from December 1977 that he relished the sounds of the French language, namely, long vowel sounds foreign to English, like the *-eur* in *saveur* (Notebook, 59).[56]

His most vivid depiction of poetic experience was written for the Saint-Hubert symposium in May 1977. As he writes Chris Edwards, his paper was originally written in English and hurriedly translated "from my loaded English by Serge [Fauchereau] at the last minute and sight read in my very embarrassing french."[57] It was, interestingly, never translated back into English. In this speech Duncan evokes the "thrice-great 'petite langue,'" which is reminiscent of the rustle of language, the minor mode of his poetry, as well as of the babblings of *lalangue* mentioned above. His faith in some sense of "measure" à la Williams comes across: "a beat so close to my heartbeat that it seems to be my own heart which is disturbed by the primal shock of this rhythm in which sound thus moves forward, belonging neither to me or to you, you and me, but to this *it*, this *(s)he*, impersonal and neutral, this *ça*, the poetry to come."[58] "In Wonder" configures the story of what cannot be told and yet is slyly *inter-dite*: forbidden therefore leaking through between the lines. Conveyed in the poem's phonic and writerly texture, the insistence on the letter of discourse is placed under the sign of metonymic displacement, that is, the ceaseless drifting from one signifier to another along the signifying chain. This story is the quest of a signifier that lends desire the figure of metonymy, for the signifier one seizes and enjoys is always revealed to be a lure—the trace of what is always already missing, a constitutive (ontological) lack that sets writing in motion. In Duncan's poetics, desire is adrift, it is "A Drift."[59] Endlessly adrift along the signifying chain, desire in language is pictured as a flow pouring meaning ("une poésie dont les vers versent / ce flot des sens") on the slant slope of the versus ("devers/des vers"), all the while bearing in mind that "ni en anglais ni en français / n'existe / cette 'çà'" (Notebook, 46). This "notebook poem" is entitled "Deversations after our conversations / for Michael Palmer, Royet-Journoud and Jean Daive" (written on March 24, 1978). Besides the reference to the translation of the Freudian id (which gave Lacan's *ça* and possibly Duncan's IT), the poet makes up a willfully overloaded signifier. He disturbs the sign by combining the feminine (for the word that embodies the neuter) with a diacritical surplus added to an already ornate word: *ça* becomes "*çà*." Duncan saturates the signifier of the Unconscious by means of graphical overdetermination (underlining, quotation marks, the usual cedilla, and the added grave accent). He playfully suggests the process of depletion in the quest for the object of desire along the signifying chain ("—partout ce vide / évidemment" [vacuum], "déversoir," "déverser" [to pour]) while charging the signifier with plastic and semantic energy to the utmost degree. Duncan's "*çà*" comes to embody the arch-signifier: overflowing with meaning and always on the side of excess. In Lyotard's words, the aural realm of *signification* and the graphic realm of *signifiance* are knotted together in this monosyllable.[60] The plasticity of the "scriptural signifier" demands that the reader's cursive eye pause and pay attention to the energy-construct contained in the sign so as to absorb the figural dimension of its meaning.[61] The Other's desire (both as desire of the Other and desire for the Other) is pulling the strings. "In the heightened awareness of the spelling present in letters along with the evocation present in phonemes and with the casting of what we call meaning, image, content, concept in the semiotic fabric[,] we lose ourselves in the work. The intellect is drawn into the net, lured by the flame, so that the poem is written over an abyss" (Notebook, 66).

Duncan's process of writing is not driven by a teleological aim or an urge to "make it cohere" but, rather, one "to copy this palimpsest."[62] This movement is taken in the double bind of witnessing its continual, processual birth, a movement forward (*archè* as originary principle), and the undercurrents of a drive toward *archè* as origin. The works' genetic bedrock not only lays the groundwork for the poems but also encapsulates Duncan's metamorphic poetics. Further, I would like to suggest that some of the notebooks could be regarded as a work with a plasticity of its own. And conversely, the published poems (the conventional literary product) ought still to be read *as notebooks*, as the groundwork for an illusory Book to come.

Notes

1. Theodor W. Adorno, "On the Use of Foreign Words," in Adorno, *Notes to Literature I & II*, 288.
2. Ibid., 286.
3. Ibid., 288.
4. Ibid.
5. Ibid.
6. Duncan, *A Selected Prose*, 221.
7. Robert Duncan, *Ground Work: Before the War/In the Dark*, 231.
8. Ibid., 232.
9. Robert Duncan, Notebook 59, Robert Duncan Collection, Poetry Collection, State University of New York at Buffalo. Hereafter cited in the text as Notebook.
10. Rabaté, *Jacques Lacan*, 33.
11. Derrida, *The Gift of Death*, 87–88.
12. Duncan, *A Selected Prose*, 217.
13. Derrida, *The Gift of Death*, 88.
14. Duncan, *A Selected Prose*, 210.
15. Fink, *The Lacanian Subject*, 7.
16. Jean-Michel Rabaté ties the origin of "a pervasive Otherness" in Lacan's theory to his shifting interpretation of Hegelian phenomenology from a Kojève-

inspired perspective to one influenced by his interaction with Jean Hyppolite in his Seminar of the 1950s. Cf. Rabaté, *The Future of Theory*, 29, and Rabaté, *Jacques Lacan*, 15.

17. Fink, *The Lacanian Subject*, 10.
18. Duncan, *A Selected Prose*, 210.
19. Cf. Lacan, *Écrits*: "We must establish the notion of the Other with a capital O as being the locus of speech's deployment (the other scene, *ein anderer Schauplatz*, of which Freud speaks in the *Traumdeutung*)" (252).
20. Duncan, *Ground Work: Before the War/In the Dark*, 144.
21. Duncan, *A Selected Prose*, 210.
22. In the original draft of the essay (Notebook, 71) Duncan quotes Rimbaud's famous axiom correctly. It was mistakenly turned into "*Je suis un autre*" in *A Selected Prose* (210), where Rimbaud's disjointed—hence meaningful and indeed revolutionary—syntax was corrected.
23. Rimbaud, *Oeuvres complètes*, 237, translation mine.
24. Rimbaud's self-proclamation strongly influenced Lacan, who repeatedly quotes *je est un autre* in his critique and ultimate reversal of the Cartesian *cogito ergo sum* into "I *am* where I am not thinking" and "I think where I am not." Cf. Lacan, *Écrits*, 23, and Fink, *The Lacanian Subject*, 140.
25. *The H.D. Book*, 469. "On the vaporization and the centralization of the *Self*. All is there" (Baudelaire, *Oeuvres complètes*, 676, my translation).
26. In his study of "Mon cœur mis à nu," Marchand points out that there is "no theory whatsoever in this assertion. Baudelaire sides neither with the self nor with personality. He does not even affirm the unity of spirit" (*Sur "Mon Cœur mis à nu" de Baudelaire*, 11, my translation).
27. Duncan, "Towards His Malaise," in Duncan, *Ground Work: Before the War/In the Dark*, 200.
28. Ibid., 202, first emphasis mine.
29. Duncan, *A Selected Prose*, 210.
30. Rabaté, *Jacques Lacan*, 174.
31. Ibid., 31.
32. For "a babel of words," cited in the subhead, see Baudelaire, "Correspondances": "La Nature est un temple où de vivants piliers / Laissent parfois sortir de confuses paroles" (Nature is a temple whose living pillars / Sometimes give forth a babel of words), in Benjamin, "On Some Motifs," 181.
33. Pound, *Cantos*, 3.
34. Duncan, *Ground Work: Before the War/In the Dark*, 225.
35. Ibid., 226.
36. Ibid., 225.

37. Cf. Mallarmé, "Le Mystère dans les lettres": "Quel pivot, j'entends, dans ces contrastes, à l'intelligibilité? Il faut une garantie— / La Syntaxe" (*Oeuvres complètes*, 2:232–33).
38. Lacan, *Écrits*, 290.
39. Duncan, *The Opening of the Field*, 7.
40. Lacan, *Écrits*, 306.
41. Duncan, *Ground Work: Before the War/In the Dark*, 225.
42. Pound, *Cantos*, 3.
43. Duncan, *Ground Work: Before the War/In the Dark*, 204.
44. Whereas with "dérêvé" and "dérivé" Duncan was unusually accurate, in most instances the accents, which sometimes change a word's meaning, are misplaced. In writing "dès dernières jours" the poet turns "of the last days" (*des derniers jours*) into "as soon as last days" (with an erroneous feminine on *jours*). He may have meant *dès les derniers jours* (as early as [in] the last days), which would convey a sense of urgency related to the romantic topos of shrinking time.
45. Duncan, *Ground Work: Before the War/In the Dark*, 207.
46. Ibid.
47. Duncan's pun on "en-vie" also appears in "Son écrit d'un texte parlé," in Duncan, *Le récit et sa représentation*, 68.
48. Duncan, *A Selected Prose*, 216.
49. Duncan, *Ground Work: Before the War/In the Dark*, 240.
50. "Je bâtis ma demeure" is the key early poem that gave Jabès's first collected volume of poems its title. The blessing of "uncertainties" also leads us back to Duncan's volume of critical prose entitled *Fictive Certainties*.
51. Steiner, *After Babel*, 61.
52. Duncan, *Ground Work: Before the War/In the Dark*, 227.
53. Ibid., 228.
54. Adorno, *Notes to Literature I & II*, 228–29.
55. Duncan, *Ground Work: Before the War/In the Dark*, 228. The syntax is disrupted and undecidable: "each at its exquisite taste arrives at the *FLAVOR* / language desires."
56. "S'il y a des mots de la langue française que je préfère pour leur sonorité, ceux sont les mots dont la sonorité me frappe l'oreille avec quelque chose d'exotique, une voyelle, un phone qu'on ne trouve pas en anglais, comme le /oe/ du mot *saveur*, une voyelle plus longue que les nôtres et, colorée par le /r/, à mon oreille plus foncée, cette voyelle a pour moi une saveur extraordinaire." In English: "If there are words in the French language that I prefer for their sonority [sound], those are words whose sonority [sound] strikes my ear as somewhat exotic, a vowel, a phone[me]

which is not found in English, like the /oe/ of the word *saveur*, a longer vowel than ours and, colored by the /r/, sounding darker to my ear, this vowel has for me an extraordinary flavor" (Notebook, 59).

57. Robert Duncan to Chris Edwards, September 27, 1978, Robert Duncan Collection, Poetry Collection, State University of New York at Buffalo.
58. Duncan, "Son écrit d'un texte parlé," in Duncan, *Le récit et sa représentation*, 66, my translation.
59. "A Drift," uncollected poem from June 23, 1980 (Notebook, 62).
60. Lyotard, *Discours, figure*, 71.
61. Ibid., 216.
62. Pound, *Cantos*, 816, 817.

Part Two

READING DUNCAN

CHAPTER SEVEN

Derivation or Stealth? Quotation in the Poetry of Robert Duncan and Ronald Johnson

ROSS HAIR

> The goods of the intellect are communal; there is a *virtu* or power that flows from the language itself, a fountain of man's meanings, and the poet seeking the help of this source awakens first to the guidance of those who have gone before in the art.—Robert Duncan, *The H.D. Book*

> Plunder, O poet.—H.D., *Tribute to the Angels*

Why do we read? What are our motives for opening a book? Are we looking for pleasure, knowledge, instruction? When Barry Alpert, editor of *VORT* magazine, asked Kansas-born poet Ronald Johnson (1935–98) the same question in 1974, Johnson answered: "I read to steal."[1] For a poet whose resourcefully eclectic "magpie gleanings of song" take in everything from poetry, music, art, and science as well as snippets from everyday life, this admission of stealth is an apt summary of how Johnson's collage poetic operates.[2] As Martha Woodmansee and Peter Jaszi stress, "Authorship does not exist to innocent eyes: they see only writing and texts."[3] Therefore, a level of cunning and artfulness is necessary if one is to see the multiple factors that produce a text. Johnson's own stealthy strategies foreground a number of pertinent questions about authorship, originality, and the creative possibilities and permissions that intertextuality affords the poet.

Johnson's stealth significantly recalls the derivative poetics of his friend and mentor Robert Duncan, who, in *The Artist's View*, famously claims to be "ambitious only to emulate, imitate, reconstrue, approximate, [and] duplicate" an eclectic range of influences and models.[4] But is Johnson's stealth the same as Duncan's poetics of derivation? I want to address this question by examining how Johnson read Duncan in the mid-1960s. "Duncan was more a poet to learn ideas from than technique," Johnson writes in a letter to Peter O'Leary. "Ah how I miss Robert," he continues, recalling his friendship with "the Dunc who was always available to bounce ideas off and talk Cosmos" (*RJ*, 590). But Duncan has given Johnson more than just "ideas" and has played a practical role in his poetry, providing Johnson with poetic techniques and strategies that he applies in *The Different Musics*. This, Johnson's third major collection comprises the poems he wrote between 1966 and 1967 and forms the second half of his 1969 collection, *The Valley of the Many-Colored Grasses*.[5] Duncan plays an important role in the new direction Johnson's poetry takes during this period, with Duncan's poem "The Fire, *Passages* 13"—first published in the April 1965 edition of *Poetry*—providing Johnson a platform for sounding the different musics of his own poetry.[6] As Johnson acknowledges in the introduction he gave for Duncan's reading at the San Francisco Poetry Center on September 22, 1984, Duncan's poetry gave him not only the creative permission he was seeking at the time but also "tools" that would help him find his own voice.

> Like no one else, he ever, too, left room on the page for my own inspiration to grow and flourish. The title poem of my third book, *The Different Musics*, was not only dedicated to him, it used his tools to break new ground for my own poetic.
>
> He is also one of the two friends I have on this earth who knows everything I want to know, and always gives me more than I imagined.[7]

But what are these "tools," and how do they help Johnson "break new ground" in his own poetics? My intention is to consider the range of tropes, images, and techniques that Johnson "steals" from Duncan's work. "The Different Musics" is not, I argue, simply a derivation of "The Fire" but a poem that skillfully assimilates a number of salient sources into its own unique music. By following Johnson's reading of Duncan it is possible to see the wider implications—both in terms of practice and ethics—of Johnson's stealth and the ways in which it differs from Duncan's derivative poetics.

ALPERT SAW ENOUGH of a similarity between the poetics of Johnson and Duncan to prompt the question: "Do you ever think of yourself as a 'derivative poet' in Robert Duncan's sense of the word?" Johnson answers by explaining his own autodidactic sensibility.

> I think everybody learns from their predecessors, and some a lot from their contemporaries. Duncan himself has done this—he once wrote for a period in the style of Gertrude Stein. If I have learned anything it's that living itself is a process, a process of learning. And everyone has something to teach. During the summer vacations from Columbia I was staying at Jonathan Williams' home in North Carolina, and his father had collected oriental porcelain and had many books in the subject. I read them, and then began to study Japanese flower arrangement from books his mother had. Then every day I would go out to the woods and bring back flowers, leaves, or berries—whatever—to make an arrangement for a different bowl. I wrote *The Book of the Green Man* staying with a friend, Mrs. Dorothy Neal, in north Georgia. She knew about birds and taught me. These things have all entered the poems—is that derivative? (*RJ*, 548)

Johnson is derivative only in the sense that his work draws on a range of experiences and examples that have proven instructive in his own education. And while Johnson may very well have derived his skills and knowledge by following the examples of other people, he does not see such resourceful appropriations as imitative. Johnson may take or "steal" other people's intellectual property in his poetry, but he always makes it his own and makes something new out of it. "I have always acknowledged other's ideas when I use them" is Johnson's answer to Alpert's question: "What do you think of the notion of poetry as plagiarism?" "Edward Dahlberg once said something about better writers only being better thieves. Shakespeare seldom used an original plot. Henry James used his friends and friends' stories of friends. Max Ernst and Jess Collins make pictures from pictures. Plagiarism is, I believe, to take other's ideas and offer them as one's own" (*RJ*, 547–48).

These remarks about plagiarism coupled with his initial claim—"I read to steal"—poignantly recall T. S. Eliot's essay "Philip Massinger": "Immature poets imitate; mature poets steal; bad poets deface what they take and good poets make it into something better, or at least something different. The good poet welds his theft into a whole feeling which is unique, utterly different from that from which it was torn; the bad poet throws it into something which has no cohesion."[8] Unlike "imitation or plagiarism," which, Eliot believes, is "the basest, because least conscious form of borrowing," stealing, by comparison, is an activity that takes the stolen goods and makes them into "something better." Seen from the perspective of Eliot's thesis, Johnson's own claims to stealth can be read as a tacit assertion of his own stature as a "mature" poet. This is rather curious considering that Johnson, like so many of the New American poets, establishes his poetry in opposition to Eliot's. Duncan, for instance, in *The Artist's View*, rejects Eliot's values by asserting his willingness to "emulate, imitate, reconstrue, approximate, duplicate," a point Duncan later reaffirms when he declares himself an "adolescent . . . wet behind the ears" who imitates: "Why who cares now, not I, that I imitate or pretend, or sit a great frog in the mighty puddle of my own front room. Here I need not be mature."[9]

The conservative values Eliot promotes in terms of poetry and culture are at odds with Johnson's American sensibilities, his transcendentalist affinities, and his fascination with various forms of folk and outsider art.[10] In saying "I read to steal," Johnson is claiming, like Eliot, that he uses the work of others to develop and enhance his own. Reading becomes the germ of something new and unique, something "utterly different from that from which [the stolen material] was torn." For Eliot the new work contributes to a Eurocentric literary tradition—"an organized view of the whole course of European poetry from Homer"—that underwrites a historical sense, disclosing "our position relative to the past."[11] By contrast, Johnson's stealth displays a pragmatism that values stolen material as resources for new creations. Thus, unlike Eliot's highbrow cultural agenda, Johnson's poetry, as Eric Murphy

Selinger writes, shows a "refusal to distinguish between Highbrow Artist and Common Man" (*RJ*, 332). Everything is potentially worth stealing, be it something from William Blake, Edith Sitwell, a popular science book, or a television advertisement. All that matters is that the material catches Johnson's magpie eye and fires his creative imagination, just as "The Fire" evidently did.

AS A COLLECTION, *The Different Musics* marks a significant advance in Johnson's poetics. Moving on from the apprentice work of his earlier collections—*A Line of Poetry, a Row of Trees* (1964) and *The Book of the Green Man* (1967)—both of which display strong fidelities to the modernist collage modes of Pound, Williams, and Olson, in *The Different Musics* Johnson turns to alternative models to develop his poetics. As the title indicates, *The Different Musics* is Johnson's first extensive engagement with the work and ideas of the American composer Charles Ives (1874–1954), who exerts considerable influence on Johnson's major work, *ARK*. "I think the structure of Ives' symphonies had been more of an influence on me than just about anything else," Johnson tells Peter O'Leary in his 1995 interview (*RJ*, 580). Yet the rudiments of Ives's influence can be traced back to a number of the poems that appear in *The Different Musics*, particularly the collection's title poem and "The Unfoldings," which concludes with the sound of two galaxies colliding (*Valley*, 111).

Ives's use of dissonance and polyphony gave Johnson an instructive model for developing his "many-focused poetry, one which sees the minutiae with as much clarity as the hill it subsists on."[12] Following Ives, Johnson uses collage to hold different kinds of reality—voices, perspectives, time frames, and dimensions—together simultaneously. "Collage is a means of making all art hold more different kinds of reality," Johnson writes in his essay on Guy Davenport. "Charles Ives asked 'are my ears wrong?' when he heard two things at once make music, and stubbornly wrote down what few could hear till now."[13]

Here—and when he tells Alpert that *The Different Musics* refers to "Charles Ives' use of two tunes at once" (*RJ*, 548)—Johnson is referring to Ives's use of polyphony, which allows for the coexistence and superimposition of radically different musics in one composition, "blend[ing] the music of highly diverse traditions in a volatile and provocative blend," as David Michael Hertz notes.[14] This blend consists of popular American music (Stephen Foster ballads, college songs, hymns, and ragtime tunes) and the European classical music of Beethoven, Brahms, Debussy, and Wagner. J. Peter Burkholder suggests that musical quotation is a way of Ives "speaking for himself, in a language that is his own, one that assimilates all the musical tongues he had learned. What he has to say could not be said in any other way."[15] Like Eliot's "mature" poet, Ives is at once both derivative and original in his use of musical references to articulate his own ideas about American music, his New England experiences, his Yankeeism, his religious beliefs, and, as I discuss below, his transcendentalist-inspired cosmology.

But how do Duncan and "The Fire" relate to this Ivesian polyphony? Johnson, no doubt, recognizes in Duncan and Ives a mutual preoccupation with music and its cosmological significance. Music and its corollary, dance, figure prominently in Duncan's work from *The Opening of the Field* onward. "As for Music," Duncan writes in "Moving the Moving Image, *Passages* 17," "to know this is to know the order of all things / set together in a key of diversities // is a sweet harmony."[16] Although this is a paraphrase of Hermes Trismegistus in *The Perfect Sermon or the Asclepius*, it is a sentiment that Ives's music shares.[17] Considering the poem's own preoccupation with music and cosmos, to have Ives and Duncan as the major references in "The Different Musics" is a resourceful move on Johnson's part.

Although Ives and Duncan are integral sources for "The Different Musics," Johnson, in his interview with Alpert, plays down Duncan's presence in his poem: "'The Different Musics' was dedicated to Robert Duncan because I had just read his poem 'The Fire' which begins and ends with a grid of words like *fire leaf fish* which are done at exact heartbeat rhythm—that's the way Robert reads them—in time to the heart. Though the only obvious relation of his poem to mine is the field of stars at the end. But I did want to pay homage to a poem I found so exciting and beautiful" (*RJ*, 549). Johnson refers to the grid of thirty-six words—among them "jump," "stone," "hand," "leaf," "shadow," and "sun"—that begin and end "The Fire" (*Bow*, 40, 45). According to Christopher Beach, these are Duncan's "adaptation of the Chinese ideogram": "Here the words can be read in any direction within their arrangement (either horizontally, as in English, vertically as in Chinese, or even backward or diagonally). Thus, the words themselves, removed from any fixed syntactic or sequential relation to each other, can serve as visual images as well as units of language. . . . The words take shape in the reader's mind both as individual mental images, as parts of a more complex picture made up by the whole square, and as a complex ideogrammic configuration."[18] Interpreting these words as "a field of stars," Johnson sees Duncan's "ideogram" as a visual image. Perhaps, like Peter O'Leary, Johnson saw Duncan's grid of words as "a concrete-poetry-style arrangement," prompting him to conclude his poem with a block of seventy asterisks forming a "field of stars."[19] Despite Johnson's "homage" to "The Fire," the similarities between his asterisks and Duncan's ideogram are tenuous to say the least and not as obvious as Johnson suggests. However, a reader familiar with Duncan's poem is likely to recognize this as an allusion to "The Fire." Why? Because Johnson does in fact "steal" more from "The Fire" than just this field of words.

THE THEME OF conflagration that dominates "The Fire" recalls the fiery cosmology discernible in the fragments of Heraclitus: "The ordering (kosmos), the same for all, no god nor man has made, but it ever was and will be, fire everlasting kindled in measures and in measures going out."[20] This everliving fire, according to Charles H. Kahn, stands for the "principle of cosmic guidance" and for the "cosmic structure of opposition," representing "the system of all elemental forms that emerge as it is kindled and quenched."[21]

These ideas of an everlasting cosmic fire are evident throughout "The Fire" and its implicit reminder that fire is a fundamental element of cosmos as well as chaos. "It is the first named incarnation of Love," Duncan stresses in "Wind and Sea, Fire and Night": "We burn with it. The fire of Hell. Pain. But it is warmth. Demonic. But it is also light. . . . A light to read by. Within us. A time within which all known things exist."[22] Following such polarities, Duncan presents two scenes of conflagration between the opening and concluding ideograms of "The Fire"—the first following the principle of cosmic guidance and the second following the structure of opposition—based upon examples from music and painting.

In the first, reflecting on the Florentine Renaissance painter Piero di

Cosimo's painting *A Forest Fire* (ca. 1490–1500), Duncan constructs an image of the Anima Mundi, or world soul, the intermediary sphere in Neoplatonic thought that exists between the divine world (the intellectual or intelligible universe of eternal ideas) and the material, sensible world. "There is nothing," the Florentine Neoplatonist Marsilio Ficino (1433–99) writes, "so deformed in the whole living world that it has no soul, no gift of soul contained in it."[23] Thus, every living thing partakes in the World Soul and is interconnected through it, establishing concord, proportion, and harmony.

Contrasting with what appears to be an image of a well-ordered and harmonious world—what the Greeks called κόσμος (*kosmos*)—Duncan presents in the second part of "The Fire" a hellish scene of chaos and "Great Evils" (*Bow*, 44) read out of Hieronymus Bosch's painting *Christ Bearing the Cross*. Where Piero's painting represents a music of harmony and concord, Bosch's represents "the *lascivia mundi* of this vain sound" of "plagues—typhus, syphilis, the black buboes / epidemics, manias" and the political corruptions of "Princes, Popes, Prime Usurers, Presidents / Gang Leaders of whatever Clubs, Nations, Legions" (44). The "pagan countryside" of *A Forest Fire* is laid waste as the "the power of this world" burns the woods and grasses of "Pan's land" (44, 45).

In these two scenes Duncan presents familiar antitheses: order/disorder, cosmos/chaos, harmony/discord. However, the elemental grid of thirty-six words that begins and ends "The Fire" suggests that the poem proposes the mutability of a cosmic cycle that perpetually oscillates between chaos and cosmos, with one always emerging out of the other. Thus, "The Fire" demonstrates Duncan's assertion (via Proclus) that

The cosmos will not

dissolve its orders at man's evil.

"That which is corrupted is corrupted with reference to
itself but not destroyd with reference to the universe;

for it is either air or water" (*Bow*, 79)

Consequently, the Anima Mundi and Hell in "The Fire" can be seen as representing two-thirds of what Ian W. Reid calls "a single cosmic triangle" that informs all of Duncan's *Passages*: "Warfare and Harmony are not opposite poles. They delineate, with Love, the sides of a single cosmic triangle, like the deltoid Pythagorean symbol alluded to in 'Passages' 6 or like a triune deity from whom all man's makings proceed."[24]

My own reading of "The Fire" will focus on one side of this "cosmic triangle"—harmony—concentrating on the first scene concerning *A Forest Fire* and the vision of the Anima Mundi it elicits. This is the part of Duncan's poem that caught Johnson's imagination in "The Different Musics," where he uses the poem's tropes of smoke, music, and harmony to articulate the different musics of his own poem.

IN *A FOREST FIRE* Duncan sees a harmonious prelapsarian world: "as if in Eden, in this panic" where "lion and lamb lie down quail / heed not the eagle," and the animals have "gentle mate[s]" (*Bow*, 41). Mark Johnson believes that in this scene "the predator/prey relationships break down as do the division of species."[25] It is not, however, so much the scene portrayed by Piero that Duncan sees as harmonious. After all, Duncan is quick to note the "terror" and "sorrow" of the fleeing animals in the painting (41). Rather, it is in Piero's mastery of *sfumato*—a technique for softening outlines and allowing tones and colors to gradually shade into one another—that Duncan recognizes the suggestion of harmony, both in terms of music and in the Neoplatonic sense of the word, as κόσμος. If predator/prey relationships do break down, as Mark Johnson suggests, and animal species become indeterminable, it is due to the painting's smoky effects. Quick as ever to exploit a pun, Duncan recognizes how the word *sfumato* (from the Italian meaning "smoked") and the subject of *A Forest Fire* "rime." This is something that he takes full advantage of in the course of "The Fire," implying that even in Eden's bucolic "kosmos" Hell can break out an opposing music.

Duncan also finds in the smoke of Piero's painting the intimations of an Orphic theurgy, perhaps associating the painting's smoke with the incense of an Orphic rite. "A glow at the old borders," Duncan writes, "makes / magic":

magic Pletho, Ficino, Pico della Mirandola prepared,
reviving in David's song,
Saul in his flaming rage heard, music
Orpheus first playd,
chords and melodies of the spell that binds
the many in conflict in contrasts of one mind. (*Bow*, 42)

Duncan identifies a tradition of magic and music with the Neoplatonists roughly contemporaneous with Piero. Thus, along with Marsilio Ficino, who would "sing at length from the hymns of Orpheus," Duncan also includes Georgios Gemistos Pletho (ca. 1355–1452) and Giovanni Pico della Mirandola (1463–94).[26] The inclusion of these names reasserts Duncan's notion of the *poeta theologus* or *vates* (a role that he assumes throughout many of the *Passages*) who can, through the power of music, song, and ritual, make the soul ascend to its divine origins. If we note that "concord" derives from the Latin *concors*, meaning "of one mind," Duncan's invocation of "chords and melodies of the spell that binds / the many in conflict in contrast of one mind" evokes Ficino's belief that an individual "who takes no pleasure in concordant sounds in some way lacks concord within."[27] For Ficino, music is one of the most effective ways of initiating the soul's ascent back to the Intelligible universe and beyond, to the One, as Angela Voss explains: "For Orpheus and for Ficino, the function of the priest in leading people to recognize their own divinity was precisely the function of the musician, for music, in imitating or reproducing the laws of the cosmos in sound, may reveal the soul to itself; namely, that it partakes of the soul of the world."[28]

The idea of cosmos and Anima Mundi play throughout "The Fire." Duncan even puns on Piero's last name so that "Di Cosimo's featherd, furrd, leafy / boundaries" become the boundaries of the cosmos itself.

Di Cosimo's featherd, furrd, leafy

boundaries where even the Furies are birds
and blur in higher harmonies Eumenides;
whose animals, entering a charmd field
in the light of his vision, a stillness,
have their dreamy glades and pastures. (*Bow*, 42)

Piero's sfumato also provides Duncan a visual analogue for the consonance of the Anima Mundi. According to the Platonist Thomas Taylor (1758–1835), "the perfect and perpetual harmony of the universe subsists by the mutability of its parts."[29] Such mutability is convincingly conveyed by the sfumato in Piero's painting, which softens the outlines of individual forms through shading and subtle gradations in color and tone. Duncan achieves an equivalent of sfumato through his use of alliteration, assonance, and rhyme, which enable him to bind "the many in conflict in contrasts of one mind." The alliteration in "featherd, furrd, leafy," for example, and again in "boundaries," "birds," and "blur," along with the rhymes in "furrd" and "bird," dissolves borders and blurs boundaries. A hazy charm ensues as words chime and merge with one another. And in the case of "furrd" (referring to both the fur of the animals in Piero's painting and the furry effect of the sfumato), the word gently morphs into other words—"Furies," "birds," "blur"—to evoke their own harmony; "a charmd field" not dissimilar to Duncan's meadow in *The Opening of the Field*. Like that "eternal pasture folded in all thought," "created by light / wherefrom the shadows that are forms fall," the glowing limpidity of Duncan's "charmd field" implies a similar realm of eternal Ideas and forms, of which earthly forms are but shadows.[30]

Duncan's allusion to the Furies (also known as Eumenides) also asserts the notion of a concordant and well-proportioned cosmos, for these vengeful winged "gorgoneion" (*Bow*, 41) deities of Greek mythology are the regulators of order and justice. In the "charmd" music and smoky light of "The Fire," these Furies also suggest Ficino's doctrine of the *furor poeticus*, which derives from Plato's poetic frenzies. Plato in the *Phaedrus*, Ficino writes, "says that no one, however diligent and learned in all the arts, has ever excelled in poetry unless to these other qualities has been added a fiery quickening of the soul," which is experienced "when we are inflamed by God's presence working in us. Such force carries the seed of the divine mind."[31] The soul is vivified and animated by a "fiery" quality, a divine spark that recalls the fire in Piero's painting that, similarly, provokes the forest animals into fleeing their shelter for a "charmd field."

THIS SECTION OF "The Fire" equipped Johnson with a stock of references, tropes, and techniques that he uses to convey the different musics of his poem. In particular, Johnson exploits Duncan's trope of smoke. Although "The Fire" gives Johnson the basic elements, the building blocks, for his poem, it does not give him a structure, topic, or theme for his own poem. Johnson found those things in Charles Ives, whose music he ambitiously incorporates into Duncan's.

In "The Different Musics" Johnson draws on Ives's unfinished work, the *Universe Symphony*, which aspires to "paint the creation, the mysterious beginnings of all things, known through God to man, to trace with tonal imprints the vastness, the evolution of all life, in nature of humanity from the great roots of life to the spiritual eternities, from the great inknown to the great unknown."[32] Ives conceived the symphony as "a musical piece in two parts, but played at the same time—the lower parts (the basses, cellos, tubas, trombones, bassoons, etc.) working out something representing the earth, and listening to that primarily—and then the upper (strings, upper woodwind, piano, bells, etc.) reflecting the skies and the Heavens."[33] Conflating Duncan's smoky imagery from "The Fire" with Ives's notes for his *Universe Symphony*, Johnson establishes the rudiments of his own poem, which, following Ives, presents the music of the earth and the music of the air and their evolutionary course from "the great roots of life to the spiritual eternities."

In the poem's opening stanza, Johnson describes how "The Different Musics," "come simultaneously / across water, / accumulating fume, spray, the flex of ripple" (*Valley*, 84). In these three lines there is a clear echo of the spirit (breath) of God moving upon the face of the waters in Genesis. There is also the suggestion of the first movement of Ives's symphony: "Formation of the waters and mountains." The word "fume" is especially significant in this context of watery chaos, suggesting vapor, steam, or mist. However, when Johnson consults *Webster's* to unfold this word further, "fume" evolves into and assumes the qualities of the poem's different musics: earth (dust) and air (spirit).

> As fume from the Latin *fumus*, Greek
> *thymos*, spirit, mind. "See

> DUST, THEISM: c.f.
> FEBRUARY, FURY, PERFUME, THYME."
>
> (C.f. means 'compare' &
> 'leads to useful, interesting, or related material that is not,
> however, essential to an understanding of the meaning'.)
> (*Valley*, 84)

Johnson's referral to the dictionary is an example of what Michael Davidson calls "the lexical insert": "The poet turns to the dictionary in order to provide a gloss on a word or a phrase, the etymology being included as part of the poem."[34] Although the provenance of the lexical insert is in Pound's philological appropriations in *The Cantos*, Johnson's lexical inserts are more suggestive of Duncan's "earnest mimesis of a classroom exposition" in "Spelling, *Passages 15*" (*Bow*, 48) and the etymological explications of "The Loom, *Passages 2*." When Johnson writes: "I find among DUST / vapor, storm, breath, smoke" (*Valley*, 84), he also evokes Olson the archaeologist hunting among stones in "The Kingfishers." Treating words as material objects, Johnson excavates the lexical field to find and uncover the histories of words, using the dictionary to both "authenticate meaning" and defer it, "deflecting the original intention onto a new process of speculation and conjecture."[35]

"After writing the first lines I looked up the word 'fume' and found the whole poem there," Johnson tells Alpert (*RJ*, 549). Thus, the words "Dust" and "Theism" along with the words they are compared with—"February," "Fury," "Perfume," "Thyme"—become prominent motifs throughout "The Different Musics." These lexical inserts, as Davidson suggests, instigate "a new process of speculation and conjecture" for the poem, but they also give the poem thematic coherence by becoming the elements or building blocks for the poem itself—components from which everything else evolves and ultimately refers back.

By referring back to the notion of smoke, these lexical inserts also recall the rudiments of "The Fire." In addition to smoke, we find allusions to magic (in the form of incense and festivals), beasts, divinity, and even the *furores*.

By unfolding the etymologies and poetic associations of the word "FURY," Johnson uncovers a host of meanings—"(wrath, ire, turbulence, / & madness)" as well as "the hectic *Furies*" (*Valley*, 85). Johnson later refers to a "choric turbulence, to which the worlds [of air and earth] keep time" (88), invoking both the lexical insert "Fury" ("turbulence") and the regulating Furies of Duncan's poem. And by conflating the word "turbulence" with the avian chorus, described in the poem as "wreathing in sibilant expansions // outward" (87), Johnson recalls the birdlike Furies in "The Fire" that regulate the hierarchical worlds—"the higher harmonies"—of a Neoplatonic cosmos.

Those "higher harmonies" were seen in the glow of the *furies* and smoke of *A Forest Fire*. It is, therefore, not surprising that smoke should assume an equally important role as a mediator of air and earth in "The Different Musics." Ficino posits "*the aerial spirit*" as "*the junction of the body and soul*" (*Bow*, 42). That Johnson finds his own smoke in "The Fire" is evident in the acknowledgment he gives Duncan's poem in the lexical insert "THEISM."

> And THEISM out of *theos*, including breath & spirit
> with demon, incubus—*bestia*:
>
> beasts—and smokes. (*Valley*, 84)

In the last line, "beasts—and smokes" is a pithy echo of the beasts fleeing the forest fire in Piero's painting as well as the sfumato Duncan foregrounds throughout "The Fire." For Duncan, sfumato provides a way of dissolving boundaries and blurring forms. Johnson gestures toward a similar kind of shading and merging in "The Different Musics" with his emphasis on Ivesian "confusion," which implies that the musics of the earth and air are not mutually exclusive but continually interacting as a rich "cacophony" (*Valley*, 85, 87).[36]

We can see this in the confusion of the compost—"the earthy remains of bodies once alive"—that Johnson describes. Although the compost represents the music of the earth (which in Ives's schema marks the "evolution in nature and humanity"), it also generates the music of the air, with the "rich, dark / mold" of its humus producing aerial vapors, fumes, and the "Odors of rotted leaves" (*Valley*, 85). From the compost proceeds the different musics of earth *and* air, which Johnson presents simultaneously in two parallel columns of text.

<table>
<tr><td>Sounds come
to the ear,</td><td>I put my ear to
the ground and heard</td></tr>
<tr><td>transformed: pulling themselves up</td><td>the blood
rush to my head</td></tr>
<tr><td>by the boot-straps:</td><td></td></tr>
<tr><td></td><td>thundering where the roots</td></tr>
<tr><td>as if a new critter</td><td>drummed</td></tr>
<tr><td>altogether,
created</td><td>& whispered as they grew: new
delicacies, new</td></tr>
<tr><td>out of the marvellous canaries</td><td>tangle.</td></tr>
<tr><td>of the air.</td><td>And the blood whispered new delicacies, new

tangle.</td></tr>
<tr><td>This exquisite & unending cacophony, sweet</td><td></td></tr>
<tr><td>roar upon roar</td><td>New extremities, new labyrinth
& branching, new inextricable windings.</td></tr>
<tr><td>swelling, out of the silent
shell.</td><td>A new foliage of sensings:
sings & sings. (Valley, 86–87)</td></tr>
</table>

Two columns, two musics. The left column represents the music of air, where intangible acoustics—"lows" and "overtones" (*Valley*, 86)—come to the ear "out of the marvellous canaries / of the air," and cacophonous roars swell "out of the silent / shell." The right presents the music of the earth, where small voices "*slightly out of tune*" rejoice "in earth" (86) and other material phenomena: "roots," "tangles," and "foliage."

There is a vicissitude in these musics that recalls the way Duncan's sfumato in "The Fire" blurs and dissolves boundaries and the profiles of individual forms. For example, when reading the two columns there is a tendency to read across the page, in a conventional left-to-right manner, rather than down the columns of text: "A cow lows, . . . rejoicing," and we see "swirls! . . . in earth" (*Valley*, 86). Instead of being separate from one another, Johnson demonstrates how the air and earth are continually converging on one another. Indeed, the convergence of these voices "*slightly out of tune*" (86) is emphasized toward the end of the passage by the gradual overlapping of the two columns, suggesting the emergence of something new evolving from the confusion and dissonance of the two musics.

As the tangible "sensings" of the earth morph into song ("sings"), an avian collage of birdsong emerges, "wreathing in sibilant expansions // outward" (*Valley*, 87).

> the reiteration of a red-eyed vireo,
> wren & thrasher & thrush—
> the wood-thrush pushing its err-o-lay through the dusk—
> *err-o-lay-ro-lay-ro*
> *—pee-wee, pee-ur-wee, pee-wee—*
> thin scissorings of black & white warblers & whistling robins
> (*Valley*, 87)

Although "messages of the air," these birds also signify the medial space between earth and air, deftly traversing both elements. However, this chorus also signifies a point of transition—a twilight—as the wood thrush, pushing its song "through the dusk," suggests.

Thus these birds merge into the darkness of night, "opening its arms like smokes to enfold us" while metamorphosing into the mysterious "DANCERS" that conclude Johnson's poem. Again, Johnson draws on Duncan's imagery by conflating the smoky imagery of "The Fire" with Duncan's earlier poem, "The Dance" from *The Opening of the Field*. This is evident in the exclamation "THE DANCE!" which reiterates the title of Duncan's poem, and also in Johnson's repetitious use of the phrase "THE DANCERS," which follows Duncan's own similar reiterations (*Valley*, 87). And when Johnson writes how the dancer's "feet touch" and "struck the earth" (87, 88), Duncan's line is recalled: "Lovely their feet pound the green solid meadow."[37] Further suggestions of Duncan are apparent in the phrases "THE DANCE! THE DANCING OUTWARD!" and "A spreading effulgence! / A 'hood' of light!" where Johnson recalls the exclamatory tone of Duncan's writing (88). Johnson even picks up on Duncan's allusions to Olson's *Maximus* in "The Dance" by, in turn, evoking Olson's "Figure of Outward" in his repetition of the word "OUTWARD!" (88).[38] Like the dancers in Duncan's poem whose "circulations sweeten the meadow" until the early hours of the morning, Johnson's dance through the night to greet the "spreading effulgence!" of dawn (88).[39]

And always the full-winged nights advance:
a field of robins erect
their red breasts facing east, into the rising sun,
OUTWARD!

FIRE IN FIRE, A DANCING FLAME, REDOUBLED LIGHT.

* * * * * * *
* * * * * * *
* * * * * * *
* * * * * * *
* * * * * * *
* * * * * * *
* * * * * * *
* * * * * * *
* * * * * * *
* * * * * * *

(*Valley*, 88)

Johnson refers to his grid of asterisks as "a field of stars," but they are also a concrete representation of the "field of robins" that, with their "red breasts facing east," greet the dawn.[40] If the "sun is but a morning star," as Thoreau writes, then Johnson has seventy microcosms of it in this concluding image.[41] Seventy robins singing, a "choric turbulence, to which the worlds keep time" (*Valley*, 88), their red breasts reflecting back the "spreading effulgence" of the rising sun. A "REDOUBLED LIGHT" and a transfiguring one that in Ives's schema signifies "the rise of all to the spiritual."

"THE DIFFERENT MUSICS" is not simply a derivation or imitation of "The Fire." Norman Finkelstein maintains that Johnson's poem "opens itself to Duncan's, perhaps entering its own 'place of first permission' by joining its music to that of the older poet" (*RJ*, 65). This is a useful way to see how Johnson's poem relates to Duncan's, with "The Different Musics" evolving out of Johnson's perceptive reading of "The Fire." However, Johnson reads Duncan through Ives via a readerly stealth more akin to Ives's musical borrowings than to Duncan's derivation. Johnson never directly quotes from "The Fire" or any other Duncan poem in "The Different Musics," which is remarkable, considering Duncan's ubiquitous presence in the poem. Johnson's invocation of Duncan, as we have seen, is through subtle allusions, paraphrases, hints, echoes, and puns. Such indirect quotation is a characteristic trait of Ives. As Hertz explains:

> Ives' use of earlier musical quotations is almost never direct and literal. The quotations are distorted and fragmented. . . . The original musical material is severely altered and forced into a new musical point of view. Paraphrase and allusion, two types of tropes, are actually far more accurate descriptions of what Ives does with his musical sources. *Quotation* is a term usually associated with Ives' use of musical source materials, but it is acceptable only in the larger philosophical sense used by Emerson. There is no quotation in Ives that does not reclaim the earlier musical composition.[42]

Thus, Ives "forces us to hear the old material in a new way."[43] Burkholder reiterates Hertz's point when he suggests that "what is loosely called 'quotation'" in Ives's music "is not a technique at all but the result of several different ways of basing a new composition on one or more existing ones."[44] In this respect, it is possible to see "The Fire" providing Johnson what Beethoven's Fifth Symphony provided Ives for his *Concord Sonata*. "Ives had no compunction about using the motif of the Fifth Symphony as the motif on which he built the *Concord Sonata* (although actually it never once appears in exactly the form used by Beethoven). Ives did this out of no spirit of imitation or competition, but because he feels so great a theme is universal in nature, and that its implications should continue to grow and to be incorporated into new music."[45]

Evidently, Duncan never saw "The Different Musics" as merely "imitation or competition" but saw a poem with its own unique qualities and strengths. In a New Year's card sent to Johnson in 1970, Duncan thanks him for the dedication in "The Different Musics," picking up on the allusions to "The Dance": "Thank you for the Different Musics in the Valley of the Many-Colored Grasses. You are one of the few poets where a dedication is in tune. And tho today each has his own 'bag,' it is nice if the other one dancing *is* really dancing."[46] For a poet who in 1985 told Burton Hatlen and Michael André Bernstein that "I don't like the things that have been influenced by me," this is high praise.[47] And with that assertion in mind, Duncan's positive response to "The Different Musics" is testimony of Duncan acknowledging Johnson as a "mature poet" who, despite stealing the musics of others, has fashioned from them a tune very much his own.[48]

Notes

1. Alpert, "Ronald Johnson," 447. Hereafter cited in the text as *RJ*.
2. Johnson, postscript to "ARK: The Ramparts," 189.
3. Peter Jaszi and Martha Woodmansee, introduction to Woodmansee and Jaszi, *The Construction of Authorship*, 1.
4. Robert Duncan, "Pages from a Notebook," in Duncan, *A Selected Prose*, 18.
5. Johnson, *The Valley*. Hereafter cited in the text as *Valley*.
6. Duncan, "The Fire," 32.
7. Typescript of Ronald Johnson's introduction to Robert Duncan's reading at the Poetry Center, September 22, 1984. Quoted with kind permission of the Ronald Johnson Literary Estate.
8. Eliot, *The Sacred Wood*, 125.
9. Duncan, *Selected Prose*, 20.
10. For a discussion of Johnson's interests in folk and outsider art, see Selinger, "*ARK* as a Garden," 323–42.
11. Eliot, "A Note on Ezra Pound."

12. Ronald Johnson to August Derleth, July 24, 1969. Quoted with kind permission of the Ronald Johnson Literary Estate.
13. Johnson, "Persistent Light," 13.
14. Hertz, *Angels of Reality*, 95.
15. Burkholder, *All Made of Tunes*, 425.
16. Duncan, *Bending the Bow*, 60. Hereafter cited in the text as *Bow*.
17. See Mead, *Thrice Greatest Hermes*, 210.
18. Beach, *ABC of Influence*, 186–87.
19. O'Leary, *Gnostic Contagion*, 80.
20. Heraclitus, Fragment XXXVII, in Kahn, *The Art and Thought of Heraclitus*, 132.
21. Ibid., 273.
22. Duncan, "Wind and Sea," 70.
23. Ficino, *The Book of Life*, 87.
24. Reid, "The Plural Text," 166.
25. Johnson "*Passages*," 184.
26. Ficino, *Meditations on the Soul*, 60.
27. Ibid., 59.
28. Voss, "*Orpheus Redivivus*," 231.
29. Taylor, *Selected Writings*, 163.
30. Duncan, *The Opening of the Field*, 7.
31. Ficino, *Meditations on the Soul*, 70.
32. Charles Ives cited in Lambert, *The Music of Charles Ives*, 187.
33. Ives, *Memos*, 106. Ives also saw the piece as having four sections.
34. Davidson, *Ghostlier Demarcations*, 94.
35. Ibid., 108.
36. Johnson quotes Ives: "An apparent confusion if lived with long enough may become orderly" (*Essays before a Sonata*, 22).
37. Duncan, *The Opening of the Field*, 8.
38. "Maximus calld us to dance the Man," Duncan writes (ibid., 9). Olson famously dedicates *The Maximus Poems* to Robert Creeley, "the Figure of Outward" (Olson, *The Maximus Poems*, 4).
39. Duncan, *The Opening of the Field*, 8.
40. Duncan has also referred to his ideogram in "The Fire" as "a dawn-of-man-scene" (*Fictive Certainties*, 33).
41. Thoreau, *Walden*, 297.
42. Hertz, *Angels of Reality*, 127.
43. Ibid., 137.
44. Burkholder, *All Made of Tunes*, 3.
45. Cowell and Cowell, *Charles Ives*, 148.

46. Robert Duncan, handmade Christmas and New Year's card sent to Ronald Johnson, 1969/1970. Courtesy of Special Collections, Kenneth Spencer Research Library, University of Kansas Libraries. Copyright © by the Jess Collins Trust and reproduced by permission.
47. Duncan, interview with Michael André Bernstein and Burton Hatlen, 121.
48. Duncan's respect for Johnson continued. Later he would write an endorsement for Johnson's *ARK: The Foundations*, included on the book's inner sleeve.

CHAPTER EIGHT

Symposium of the Whole: Jerome Rothenberg and the Dream of "A Poetry of All Poetries"

STEPHEN FREDMAN

World Poetry

For all his justly celebrated internationalism, Jerome Rothenberg owes a major portion of his poetic horizon to the Black Mountain poets, especially Charles Olson, Robert Creeley, Robert Duncan, and Paul Blackburn. In this essay I want to investigate the impact primarily of Duncan upon Rothenberg's anthology *Technicians of the Sacred: A Range of Poetries from Africa, America, Asia, Europe & Oceania* and upon his intellectual project of ethnopoetics.[1] Rothenberg memorializes this impact in a shorthand manner by invoking throughout his work the phrase "symposium of the whole," which he plucked from Duncan's essay "Rites of Participation," first published in *Caterpillar* 1 and 2 (October 1967, January 1968). Duncan imagines the "symposium" to be a new collocation that joins human beings in consanguinity not only with animals but also with all earthly cells—a coming together in "one fate" brought about by the ecological imperatives of our time. He prophesies a global community that has "gone beyond the reality of the incomparable nation or race, the incomparable Jehovah in the shape of a man, the incomparable Book or Vision, the incomparable species, in which identity might hold & defend its boundaries against an alien territory."[2] Such a community would not be hierarchical, as in Plato's *Symposium* (in which

Socrates urges an ever more rarefied sublimation toward ideal Forms), but would be rather a model of equality and wholeness: "To compose such a symposium of the whole, such a totality, all the old excluded orders must be included. The female, the proletariat, the foreign; the animal and vegetative; the unconscious and the unknown; the criminal and the failure—all that has been outcast and vagabond must return to be admitted in the creation of what we consider we are."[3] Accepting Duncan's invitation to speak for a radically expanded totality, Rothenberg characterizes the symposium of the whole as "a complex redefinition of cultural and intellectual values: a new reading of the poetic past and present" in which "culture" is thought of ethnographically and poetry is defined broadly as creative verbal address to any present circumstances.[4] He coins a new term for this encompassing, inclusivist aesthetics—"ethnopoetics"—and titles the anthology of essays he edits with Diane Rothenberg *Symposium of the Whole: A Range of Discourse toward an Ethnopoetics* (1993). Ethnopoetics would be a site of dynamic interchange between contemporary poetry and that of the most far-flung times and places, reincorporating endeavors consigned to the "nonliterary"—such as ritual, shamanism, and bodily display—back into an extended definition of poetry.

The essay that follows discusses Rothenberg's breakthrough anthology of ethnopoetics, *Technicians of the Sacred*, looking especially to Duncan's role as one model and instigator for Rothenberg's redefinition of the categories of "poetry" and "American literature." The first section considers how Rothenberg derives the notion of world poetry from the explorations of Duncan and Ezra Pound, combining their discoveries with ethnographic texts and anthropological thinking to create the unique synthesis of *Technicians*. The second section looks at the anthology as a work of art in its own right, as an assemblage that belongs among contemporary art movements such as Fluxus, happenings, conceptual art, and minimal art. Much of the impact of *Technicians* arises from its complex structure, which juxtaposes "primitive" and archaic works of art with each other and with avant-garde poetry and art. The third section discusses the erotic poetics of the anthology, a topic of intense interest for Duncan as well. Like Duncan, Rothenberg evokes the concept of shamanism to encompass the entire range of an erotic poetics, delineating thereby an interlinked series of practices addressed to the body, to social ritual, and to mystical transport. The final section explores the relationship of the avant-garde to the vernacular. The anthology argues implicitly that a radical cultivation of the vernacular allows poets to speak to one another across cultures on the basis of their personal investments in particular locales, whether ancient China, contemporary Africa, or downtown New York in the sixties. By placing the American poetry and performance art of the sixties and seventies in the expanding contexts first of modern European art and poetry and then of tribal and archaic poetries that represent the widest possible spectrum of human expression, Rothenberg operates within the frame of "deep time" called for by the critic Wai Chee Dimock, who contends that American literature must be seen not as confined to the geographical and temporal boundaries of the United States but as a vital participant in "global circuits" that cut across time and space.[5]

Rothenberg and Duncan first met in San Francisco in 1959, when Rothenberg came out from New York to consult with Lawrence Ferlinghetti on the City Lights publication of his second book, *New Young German Poets* (1959), a volume of translations.[6] This volume signaled immediately Rothenberg's dedication to a model of poetry as a world phenomenon, beyond the confines of American or English-language poetry. In fact, when Donald Allen began assembling materials for his foundational anthology, *The New American Poetry* (1960), he told Rothenberg that he wouldn't be included because he was "an international poet."[7] Duncan suggested to Rothenberg that his internationalism ought to include his own Jewish identity: "The first indication I had that I should possibly be going in that direction was a conversation with Duncan back around 1959 or 60. . . . He was dropping all sorts of hints to me about the possibility of . . . [ellipsis in original] That I was giving up too much in ignoring the Jewish identity, which was something that must have been with me in a very deep sense since my first language was Yiddish."[8] The other poet who insisted that Rothenberg confront Jewish identity was Paul Celan, whom he had translated already in *New Young German Poets*. Rothenberg reports that "Celan was crazy on the question of being Jewish and when I met him in Paris . . . he kept questioning me on that, challenging my credentials to work on his poetry . . . : was I 'Jewish' enough to do them?"[9] The circle turned again when Rothenberg introduced Duncan to Celan's poetry via his translation of "Shibboleth" in the magazine he edited, *Poems from the Floating World*. In a letter from May 25, 1959, Duncan mistakenly assumes that "Shibboleth" is a sentimental Stalinist poem. Rothenberg corrects Duncan's misreading of that "dark / and twin redness, / Madrid and Vienna," pointing out that for Celan the conquest of these cities represented not defeat for international communism but the beginning of the fascist terror. Over time, Duncan developed a profound admiration for Celan, whom he invokes in a late poem, "A Song from the Structures of Rime Ringing as the Poet Paul Celan Sings."[10] It was Duncan, finally, who introduced Rothenberg to Gershom Scholem's epoch-making *Major Trends in Jewish Mysticism* (translated in 1954), which opened up for Rothenberg, as it did for so many other Jewish poets, a window onto the texts and practices of Kabbalah.[11]

In an article discussing how the practice of translation relates to his own poetics, Duncan claims for himself a "poetics in which the poem is thought of as a process of participation in a reality larger than my own—the reality of man's experience in the terms of language and literature—a community of meanings and forms in which my work would be at once derivative and creative."[12] Duncan finds this community of meanings to be so real and absorbing that he has "at times a feeling that there is no real me, only the process of derivations in which I have my existence."[13] Throughout his career, Duncan referred to himself as a "derivative" rather than an "original" poet, espousing a poetics based on finding correspondences between words, images, and artifacts from the repertoire of human cultures rather than on "expressing" his own thoughts, emotions, or insights. For both Duncan and Rothenberg, the ancestor figures for using translation and collage to create a vital world culture are Ezra Pound and Louis Zukofsky. Both later poets look to Pound's *Cantos* and Zukofsky's *"A"* as vast works of assemblage that bring together translated material from around the world to invoke universal aesthetic, ethical, political, economic, and spiritual values. Although wary of proclaiming simple, "universal" values, Duncan and Rothenberg stage conversations and seek correspondences among the most far-flung cultural materials, with the implicit belief that communication between cultures is possible and that experiences of people remote from one another in time and place are not incommensurate.

In the editing of *Technicians*, Rothenberg follows Pound's lead in two ways: he endeavors to make visible in English "primitive" and archaic poetry from around the world by finding or undertaking himself translations that have a currency or audacity like those of Pound, and he sets these translations in juxtaposition to avant-garde works of poetry and performance art. Thus, he accomplishes the brilliant interchange he praises in Pound's *Canto* 1, in which ancient and foreign poetry are made to appear modern and the poetry of contemporaries is set within the oldest known structures of human feeling and interaction. In the body of the anthology, Rothenberg asserts analogies between the tribal and the modern by selecting translations or re-translations that display formal characteristics of the New American poetry: recourse to vernacular and erotic rather than "poetic" diction, avoidance of articles and punctuation, extensive use of abbreviation, and lineation based upon breath rhythms, including multiple indentations. These qualities bespeak a "hip," up-to-date style that brings the translations into the purview of contemporary poetic habits. The "Commentaries" section of *Technicians* follows Donald Allen's practice in *The New American Poetry* of appending back matter to create new contexts for the primary work. In its enlarged second edition, *Technicians* contains 186 pages of commentary, consisting of ethnographic accounts and modern and contemporary works of poetry and art. The dual aims of the commentaries include documenting the original performative circumstances of the translated poetry and demonstrating specific affinities between works of "primitive" and archaic poetry and those of avant-garde poetry and performance art.

In a suggestive table in the "Pre-Face" to *Technicians* that maps out his expanded vision of poetry in 1968, Rothenberg makes explicit a set of analogies between "primitive" poetry and a whole range of avant-garde practices. The correspondences Rothenberg highlights suggest a number of models for poetry beyond the current standard of the self-contained lyric that dramatizes the dilemmas of a self-reflexive subject: poetry as public performance addressed to a specific occasion; poetry as a vehicle for probing states beyond the conscious mind; poetry as convening a creative social context; poetry as participating in intermedia or multimedia events; poetry as instigator of erotic engagement; and poetry as a shamanic or visionary activity. Likewise, Rothenberg identifies six qualities that "primitive" and avant-garde works share: they emphasize oral poetry and performance; they think through images rather than through rational discourse; they tend toward minimalism; they participate in intermedia art; they insist on the primacy of the body and the erotic; and they demonstrate how shamanism underlies poetry. Rothenberg contends that this greatly enhanced poetics reincorporates into the modern world long-buried human capacities. Like Duncan, Rothenberg takes a position similar to that of the Freudian Left (a term that refers to radical psychoanalytical thinkers such as Wilhelm Reich, Herbert Marcuse, and Norman O. Brown), inviting the return of the repressed in both political and psychological terms; he links *Technicians* to "the recovery in our time, of the 'long forbidden voices' invoked by Whitman over a century ago, the 'symposium of the whole' set forth in Robert Duncan's 'rites.'"[14] Like Duncan and Whitman, Rothenberg summons a "sense-of-unity" (*Technicians*, xxviii) that highlights shared forces within tribal and avant-garde poetries—forces of darkness, of the body, of the unconscious, and of the visionary. By setting the poetry and art of the most far-flung cultures into juxtaposition with the modern arts, Rothenberg creates a "grand collage" whose sense of wholeness allows it to claim the status of "a poetry of all poetries."[15]

Assemblage

For Duncan, the grand collage makes its strongest appearance within the composition of his poems. The poems of the *Passages* sequence, for instance, which begins in *Bending the Bow* and continues in *Ground Work*, act as assemblages of cited materials and contribute to the larger assemblage of the sequence. By increasing the scale of citation from passages to entire poems, Rothenberg assembles not poems or sequences but anthologies; for his innovations in the anthology form he has garnered a reputation as one of the great anthologists of our time. He composes anthologies as an act of *poesis*—not to establish or reinforce a canon but rather to introduce new possibilities into literary creation and new ways of thinking about literary study. The dazzling array of his provocative anthologies includes *Technicians* (1968, 1985), *Shaking the Pumpkin: Traditional Poetry of the Indian North Americas* (1972), *America a Prophecy: A New Reading of American Poetry from Pre-Columbian Times to the Present* (1973), *Revolution of the Word: A New Gather-*

ing of American Avant Garde Poetry, 1914–1945 (1974), *A Big Jewish Book: Poems & Other Visions of the Jews from Tribal Times to the Present* (1978), *Poems for the Millennium: The University of California Book of Modern and Postmodern Poetry*, volume 1, *From Fin-de-Siècle to Negritude* (1995), and volume 2, *From Postwar to Millennium* (1998), *A Book of the Book: Some Works and Projections about the Book and Writing* (2000), and *Poems for the Millennium*, volume 3, *The University of California Book of Romantic & Postromantic Poetry* (2009). Rothenberg's anthologies do a variety of things: "Because I don't like to write discursive prose or essays, I find the anthology is a vehicle for saying certain things about poetry that I really can't manage to say otherwise . . . through selection, through juxtaposition, through presentation of types of poems, through defining by pointing at something. The presentation of examples is a kind of definition. And it's a fantastic big form sometimes—like collage but on a super scale."[16] Within *Technicians*, for example, Rothenberg makes two kinds of juxtapositions. In the body of the anthology he collects poems from every sort of tribal and archaic culture under the headings of "Origins & Namings," "Visions & Spells," "Death & Defeat," "The Book of Events (I)," and "The Book of Events (II)" in order to point out common poetic strategies in disparate cultural situations. In the "Commentaries" section he makes analogies between works from the body of the anthology and those of modern and contemporary poetry and art. Through selection, juxtaposition, and recontextualization in his anthologies, Rothenberg asks us to think anew about poetry and literary history. The anthologies intervene actively, calling into being fields of inquiry (such as ethnopoetics), operating as manifestos (arguing for a "tradition" of avant-garde poetry), and standing up as works of art.

As in any work of collage or assemblage, what is most striking about Rothenberg's anthologies is the surprising selection of materials for inclusion and the unexpected juxtapositions among them. In conceiving of his anthologies as assemblages, Rothenberg engages in one of the primary aesthetic practices of the postwar period, one that Duncan pursued avidly as well. During this time, many poets and artists turned away from the unified or monumental work of art and toward an art of contexts, retrieving vernacular materials from everyday life and combining them into new, provisional wholes. As Duncan says of the contextual practice of poets, artists, and filmmakers in San Francisco, "we began to see ourselves as fashioning unnamed contexts, contexts of a new life way in the making, a secret mission."[17] This contextual practice was given its most visible showcase in a landmark exhibition at the Museum of Modern Art, *The Art of Assemblage* (1961), in which groundbreaking works of cubist, Dadaist, and surrealist collage supplied a lineage for postwar works of assemblage by artists like Joseph Cornell, Bruce Conner, Robert Rauschenberg, John Chamberlain, George Herms, Robert Indiana, Jess, Jasper Johns, Edward Kienholz, Marisol, Robert Motherwell, Louise Nevelson, and David Smith. The curator, William Seitz, also argues that the newly designated performance art of "Happenings" partakes of this same contextual aesthetic. Seeking to dissolve the defensive rigidity and self-enclosure of postwar American society, the contextual practice of assemblage at this time entailed an opening out to otherness. Like Duncan's art of "derivations," it demanded not mastery but a careful situatedness and a noncontrolling, id-affirming vulnerability that seemed all the more risky in a sociopolitical climate that valued restraint, containment, rationality, and self-protection.

In New York in the early sixties, Rothenberg joined with a number of performance artists exploring a new contextual practice, including most particularly the Fluxus group, whose publisher, Dick Higgins, issued two of Rothenberg's books. What ultimately became the *Technicians* anthology received an impetus from a conversation with Higgins about Rothenberg's sense of "the closeness of primitive rituals (when stripped-down to the bare line of the activities) to the 'happenings' & 'events' [Higgins] was presenting" (*Technicians*, xxxi). More generally, it drew sustenance from the Artaud-inspired explorations of "primitive" rites and images by groups such as the Living Theater. In this context, Rothenberg reports that the anthology "grew directly out of a pair of 1964 readings of 'primitive & archaic poetry' at The Poet's Hardware Theater & the Café Metro in New York," in which the readers included Rothenberg, David Antin, Jackson Mac Low, and Rochelle Owens. From the perspective of assemblage, *Technicians* also bears comparison to a pioneering anthology from the previous decade, Harry Smith's *Anthology of American Folk Music* (1952), which launched the folk music revival and has been a primary source for the music and imagery of rock 'n' roll. An enigmatic artist, filmmaker, musicologist, and anthropologist living mostly in New York, Smith (1923–91) practiced assemblage as a form of archaeology, excavating for occult patterns in the present moment and in the arts of many different times and places, seeking solutions to what he called "the problem of rhythm in relation to thought."[18] Smith's unprecedented anthology gathered forgotten music from the catalogs of "hillbilly" and "race" records of the late twenties and early thirties, ordering it not according to folkloric categories but as an assemblage in which songs call out to one another along multiple axes of meaning. Visually, the booklet that accompanies the anthology contains a remarkable mélange of musicological annotation, mock-summaries of the songs, and visual motifs; one critic describes it as "a bricolage of printed ephemera that like junk sculpture incorporates many alien forms, each set off in its own character against all the others and against the whole."[19] As Smith acknowledges, "the whole *Anthology* was a collage. I thought of it as an art object."[20]

Like Smith, whom he thanks for assistance in the "Pre-Face" to *Technicians*, Rothenberg chooses the works in his anthology because of their aesthetic toughness and challenging imagery, not their "representativeness": "My intention from the start was to find translations that would 'translate,' i.e., bring-the-work-across or be a living work in English, & that's a very different thing from (in the first place) looking for representative 'masterpieces' & including them whatever the nature of the translations. I also have (no question about it) my own sense of what's worth it in poetry, & I've tried to work from that rather than against it. I haven't gone for 'pretty' or 'innocent' or 'noble' poems so much as strong ones" (xxxi). The anthologies of Smith and Rothenberg have had such staying power because they were composed as works of art whose component parts are enigmatic, often disturbing, and sometimes even uncanny. Acknowledging these qualities, Greil Marcus characterizes Smith's anthology as depicting "That Old, Weird America," while Rothenberg invokes Bronislaw Malinowski's expression "the coefficient of weirdness" (*Technicians*, 21–22) to describe the poems that appeal to him.[21] Both Smith and Rothenberg see their anthologies as provocations that break the professional decorum of the fields of literature or folklore by presenting rough, unpolished, vernacular works with harsh, erotic, or shocking subject matter—trying to make something happen.

From Rothenberg's perspective, the act of juxtaposition central to collage also governs much "primitive" and archaic poetry. One of the first pieces in *Technicians*, titled "Bantu Combinations," juxtaposes pairs of disparate statements:

1. I am still carving an ironwood stick.
   I am still thinking about it.

2. The lake dries up at the edges.
   The elephant is killed by a small arrow.

3. The little hut falls down.
   Tomorrow, debts. (16)

In the commentary Rothenberg calls these couplets "examples of plot-thickening in the area of 'image': a conscious placing of image against image as though to see-what-happens." He likens these "combinations" to the haiku and the sonnet, contending that "in all these the interest increases as the connection between the images becomes more & more strained, barely definable." Citing a statement from *Life of a South African Tribe* (the source for the poems), "sometimes the imagination is so subtle that the result is almost incoherent," Rothenberg counters, "Not subtlety, though, but *energy*: the power of the word and image." The energy released by strong juxtapositions generates, he contends, a mysterious "light"—not "the light of logic & simile" but a more profound one "to which (for the first time) the word 'vision' might be said to apply" (*Technicians*, 455).

Erotic Poetics

Assemblage operates for Rothenberg and Duncan not just as a formal principle but also as a means for gathering unaffiliated energies and tying them into a new whole governed by the erotic. When Duncan speaks of the grand collage as "a poetry of all poetries," he does so within the context of a discussion of the erotic as the central node of life energy. The discussion occurs in a section of the introduction to *Bending the Bow* titled "*IT*," which begins:

"Where you are *he* or I am *he*, the trouble of an Eros shakes the household in which we work to contain our feeling in our extending our feeling into time and space."[22] Eros participates in this troubling paradox of containment and extension, of concentration upon the love object (the beloved *he*) and expansion of the power of love endlessly outward. Duncan speaks of this primal Eros as *It*, invoking thereby Freud's term for life energy, the id. From Duncan's perspective, poetry is the erotic art par excellence in which the id shines forth through the words of the poem and through its structure as a collage: "In the poem this very lighted room is dark, and the dark alight with love's intentions. *It* is striving to come into existence in these things, or, all striving to come into existence is It—in this realm of men's languages a poetry of all poetries, *grand collage*, I name It, having only the immediate event of words to speak for It. In the room we, aware or unaware, are the event of ourselves in It."[23] In this dense passage, many things are intertwined: poetry, love, selfhood, grand collage, and the energy of life. For Duncan, the poetic form that he chooses, the grand collage of created images from across time and space, mirrors or participates in the erotic energy underlying the experience of love and ultimately of all life. In other words, grand collage is inherently erotic; it creates new wholes that move inward to concentrate upon a central node—or seed or egg, as he often calls it—and that move outward to encompass the largest range imaginable.

The erotic comprises the core of Rothenberg's poetics as well, and his invocation of the "symposium of the whole" likewise participates in a vision of erotic expansion. He views the erotic as guiding the expression of bodily, ritual (communal), and mystical states in tribal and archaic poetries, operating at each of these levels to intensify experience and to break through rigid forms of control. Ultimately, this erotic poetics constitutes what Rothenberg calls, on the masthead of the ethnopoetics journals he edited, *Alcheringa* and *New Wilderness Letter*, the "*mainstream* of poetry that goes back to the old tribes & has been carried forward by the great subterranean culture."[24] Like Duncan, Rothenberg believes that there is a countercultural, "shamanistic" impulse that arose during the Paleolithic era, that can be found in the erotic, visionary, and gnostic impulses woven into all of the great archaic civilizations, and that continues into the modern era in more or less isolated tribal cultures and in the mystical countercultures of the world's major religions during the past thousand years. This tradition attracts Duncan and Rothenberg by its transgressive quality—its ability to break open restrictive social and mental constructs through provocation and vision, and through eruptions of an uncontrollable id.

For both poets, ethnographic accounts of Australian Aboriginal mythology and ritual mark a highly imaginative and explicit upsurge of the erotic into human society. In "Rites of Participation" Duncan gives an extended discussion of Aboriginal mythology based upon the works of the Freudian anthropologist Géza Róheim. Duncan cites Róheim's lengthy etymological treatment of the term *alcherina*, ultimately rendered as "dream time," and the term also becomes key to Rothenberg's ethnopoetics.[25] According to Róheim, the dream time represents in Freudian terms the mythical time of the libido, in which the parts and effluents of the human body are cathected upon the landscape. Duncan notes how, in both Freudian psychology and Aboriginal mythology and ritual, "the body of man and the body of creation" are brought together "by a 'sexual obsession' (as Jung calls it)": "The 'b[r]east, anus, semen, urine, leg, foot' in the Australian song, chant or enchantment, that is also hill, hole, se[a], stream, tree, or rock, where 'in the Toara ceremony the men dance around the ring shouting the names of male and female genital organs, shady trees, hills, and some of the totems of their tribe,' are most familiar to the Freudian convert Roheim."[26] Duncan insists that the erotic, the psychological, the ritual, and the mystical cannot be separated, contending that "the 'blood' of the Aranda, the 'libido' of the Freudian, may also be the 'light' of our Kabbalistic text."[27] At every level, he maintains, the erotic underlies and intensifies the lived experience.

In *Technicians* Rothenberg extends Duncan's erotic poetics by reworking translations of Aboriginal performance poems to emphasize the nakedly erotic imagery at the basis of a visionary mythology. Near the outset of the anthology, for instance, in the section "Origins & Namings," he titles a selection from the *Djanggawul Cycle* "Genesis II." The selection begins:

> [Song 159]
> Go, take that hot stone, and heat it near her clitoris:

For the severed part is a sacred *djuda rangga*. Covering up the clitoris
within the mat, within its transverse fibre, within its mouth,
its inner peak . . .
Go, the people are dancing there, like *djuda* roots, like spray, moving
their bodies, shaking their hair!
Carefully they beat their clapping sticks on the *mauwulan* point . . .
Go, stand up! See the clansfolk beyond the transverse fibre of the
mat!
They come from the Sister's womb, lifting aside the clitoris, coming
out like *djuda* roots . . . (*Technicians*, 9, ellipses in original)

In the commentary Rothenberg emphasizes the sexuality of the songs from the *Djanggawul Cycle*: "A heavy ripeness, the swelling & bursting of a teeming life-source, colors Australian views of the creation." This streaming libidinal energy stands revealed in the Aboriginal songs as the erotic basis for human culture: "The *Djanggawul Cycle* is the best example the present editor knows, of the celebration of human sexuality & birth in the work of genesis." Rothenberg contrasts the Aboriginal display of sexuality as the recognized basis for culture to the occlusion of that recognition in normative Western culture: "The body of the sacred sister, heat around the clitoris, the budding tree roots, spray & blood, a swarming sense of life emerging—not two-by-two, in pairs, but *swarming*—was turned-from in the West, reduced to images of evil" (*Technicians*, 447).

For Rothenberg, the phenomenon of shamanism provides the clearest model for an erotic poetics based in a conviction of the sacredness of all things: "Here is the central image of shamanism & of all 'primitive' thought, the intuition (whether fictive or not doesn't yet matter) of a connected & fluid universe, as alive as a man is—just that much alive" (*Technicians*, 487). With Duncan, Rothenberg shares an enduring fascination with the figure of the shaman, especially in the role of protopoet. Duncan's interest in shamanism goes back to some of his earliest writing: during the period 1939–41, in particular, he undertook an ambitious project in prose poetry that he called "Toward the Shaman."[28] Over time, he came to conceive of the shamanic ascent to other worlds as an image for entering the writing of other people (e.g., in *Ground Work*: Dante, the Metaphysical poets, Rumi, and Baudelaire) in order to compose his "derivative" poetry. In more literal terms, Rothenberg values the shaman as a primary figure for poetry: "The shaman can be seen as protopoet, for almost always his technique hinges on the creation of special linguistic circumstances, i.e., of song and invocation" (485). The term "technique" alludes to the title *Technicians of the Sacred*, which "itself is a take-off from Eliade's 'specialist of the sacred' who masters the 'techniques of ecstasy.'"[29] Rothenberg found the two phrases in Eliade's *Shamanism: Archaic Techniques of Ecstasy* (translated in 1964), which became one of the most influential texts for ethnopoetics. In their mutual interest in shamanism, Duncan and Rothenberg emphasize several qualities they see as defining a universal erotic poetics of the sacred: the shaman as a lone figure who visits other worlds in order to bring back poetry addressed to the ills of society; the shaman as healer who unstops the flow of erotic energy and provokes sexual display; the shaman as able to move through a variety of life forms, tying him or her to an underlying sense of the interconnectedness of all beings; and the shaman as confronting death, darkness, and disease without flinching, recognizing that "negative" forces cannot be avoided but must be encountered.

The Avant-Garde and the Vernacular

The figure of the shaman also appeals to Duncan and Rothenberg because it represents for them the integrity of individual experience against the forces of statehood, organized religion, and even artistic conformity. The poets share an anarchist preference for the powers of the creative individual over those of institutions and an anarchist belief that communalism (or tribalism) preserves the fullest potential for human experience. The preference for community over institutions also manifests in a respect for the vernacular, which for Rothenberg in particular is a central feature of his avant-garde poetics. The avant-garde has been faulted in some quarters for being an elitist enterprise, but Rothenberg insists on its vernacular quality and its embeddedness in everyday life. *Technicians* takes a huge step in this direction by demonstrating how the most innovative and challenging works of the avant-garde can be seen as analogous to works by tribal peoples. Rothenberg begins the 1967 "Pre-Face" with the heading "PRIMITIVE MEANS COM-

PLEX," arguing that just as from the perspective of linguistics there are no primitive languages, so there are no primitive poetries given the imaginative and intellectual sophistication evident in every culture: "No people has sat in sloth for the thousands of years of its history. Measure everything by the Titan rocket & the transistor radio, & the world is full of primitive peoples. But once change the unit of value to the poem or the dance-event or the dream (all clearly artifactual situations) & it becomes apparent what all those people have been doing all those years with all that time on their hands" (*Technicians*, xxv). The intelligence and sophistication Rothenberg appreciates in tribal poets reflect their care in infusing the visionary and the aesthetic into the conduct of everyday life. In this sense, they can stand as models for an avant-garde bent upon promoting a fruitful interpenetration of art and life.

As a work of the late sixties, *Technicians* owes much to its era, drawing upon the emergent aesthetic and cultural strands of concrete poetry and sound poetry, minimalism, conceptualism, performance art, multiculturalism, and investigations of the interplay of orality and literacy. Likewise, it rests upon a tradition of the vernacular in American poetry, which Rothenberg traces back to Whitman, Pound, Stein, and Williams and which he sees continuing in Olson, Duncan, Creeley, Blackburn, Snyder, and Antin, among others. Drawing together the vernacular innovations of these poets, *Technicians* also presages a more recent movement in American literary studies intent on opening "American" literature out from the geographical boundaries of the United States and from the self-conscious attempt to close itself off from the other literatures and cultures of the world in pursuit of an illusory essence of "Americanness." Rothenberg's unique contribution to this latter movement can be seen in his persistent posing of American poetry face-to-face not only with the European avant-garde but also with the most far-flung poetries of the world in time and space. If we imagine *Technicians* as imparting an image of a "world poetry," then it would be one characterized not by a set of formal qualities or by national traditions but as a series of imaginative approaches to the issues of human life—such as birth, death, love, war, food, shelter, disease, and cosmology—through a poetics that is erotic (in the broadest senses) and vernacular.

Looking back at earlier forms of the avant-garde, Rothenberg notices that not all of them value as highly as *Technicians* does "the grubbiness of contingency," which, he says, "has, in my view of it, kept us more honestly human."[30] Although Duncan makes the vernacular a key part of his poetics, his complex notion of it is governed particularly by the literary examples of Dante and Whitman. With respect to attitudes toward "grubbiness," Rothenberg finds Duncan's sense of the vernacular somewhat too aestheticized. Anecdotally, Rothenberg tells of attending a poetry reading with Duncan, who denounced in a stage whisper as "pure ugliness" the imagery of a poem that was read: "The comment stuck with me, bothered me a great deal in fact." It "came rushing back at me," Rothenberg says, when he visited Auschwitz. With the concentration camp as a reference point, he argues that ugliness is "poetry's real voice" that cannot be overlooked.[31] Duncan sensed this difference between them. In notes he wrote in 1969 when he first read *Technicians*, he questions Rothenberg's assertion that "the great fanged statue of Coatlicue or the multi-breasted Diana of Ephesus" is "more interesting and probably more truthful than the Venus de Milo or Michelangelo's Pietà" (*Technicians*, 524). Duncan worries that "Coatlicue and Diana of Ephesus are more interesting and true, as Auschwitz seems to be the truth of what our world is (or the atom bomb at Hiroshima)—these are the grand, the truly sacred shows of our time that leave the spirit shaking; and all expressions of dignity seem fronts of a lie."[32]

Their disagreements over the "truth" of Auschwitz aside, Rothenberg's more encompassing view of the vernacular brings him to conceive of poetry from a perspective of radical equality: "We're now able to draw from predecessors confronted by the same necessities. These include earlier modernists & 'primitives,' along with a range of other human beings, poets of all times & places, who remind us that we're neither the first poets nor will we be the last" (*Technicians*, 47). The emphasis in *Technicians* on the centrality of the vernacular for understanding what it means to be human has its own ethical dimension. A vernacular approach to living takes into account the immediate situation and the means for confronting it developed by oneself and those around one, and it involves recognizing that across the world there are other vernacular solutions to living that also might address the present situation. In recent years, writers in a variety of fields have approached such a vernacular ethics. In poetry, Rothenberg acknowledges the examples of Olson and Snyder as vernacularists who have looked across many cultures for clues as to how to become fully human. Likewise, Harry Smith dedicated his life to seeking vernacular patterns that support creativity and social interaction, amassing collections not only of folk songs but also of string figures (and their attendant stories) from around the world, paper airplanes from New York City, Ukrainian painted eggs, and Seminole clothing patterns.

Taking cognizance of the necessity for cross-cultural conversation, the critic Wai Chee Dimock has recently proposed a new definition of American literature as a permeable phenomenon, a definition also implicit in *Technicians* and Rothenberg's other anthologies:

> Rather than being a discrete entity, [American literature] is better seen as a crisscrossing set of pathways, open-ended and ever multiplying, weaving in and out of other geographies, other languages and cultures. These are input channels, kinship networks, routes of transit, and forms of attachment—connective tissues binding America to the rest of the world. Active on both ends, they thread American texts into the topical events of other cultures, while also threading the long durations of those cultures into the short chronology of the United States. This double threading thickens time, lengthens it, shadowing in its midst the abiding traces of the planet's multitudinous life.[33]

Dimock calls the temporal embedding of American literature within cultures of much longer duration "deep time." Like Rothenberg's assembling of "technicians of the sacred" from many times and places to address present exigencies, Dimock seeks to open up "alternate measures—African, Asian, and European" for conceiving of an American literature capacious enough to include all the "connective tissues binding America to the rest of the world."[34] For Rothenberg, a sense of deep time allows us to reclaim vernacular energies at the far margins of modern culture. He contends, for instance, that where science and religion have sought for five thousand years to supersede the past and annihilate the "*old* man," ethnopoetics wants to invite the old man (and woman) back in—while retaining what Olson calls "the will to change."[35] By invoking deep time, Rothenberg calls forth a multifarious tradition that "takes vision & conflict as the essential characteristics of poetry," ties them "to the structure of the poem & the dynamics of actual speech," and constructs a lineage from the present avant-garde back through earlier innovators all the way to Paleolithic shamans.[36] Or, as Dimock puts it, "Scale enlargement . . . enlarges our sense of complex kinship."[37]

Conclusion

There are many ways to think about Robert Duncan's impact upon Jerome Rothenberg's *Technicians of the Sacred*. In the first place, Duncan provides Rothenberg with a model of an open-form and serial poetry that explores ignored facets of experience such as mythology, the body, the unconscious, the occult, and magic. Where Duncan incorporates these aspects directly into his collagist poetry, Rothenberg in *Technicians* constructs a larger-scale assemblage that gives these facets greater scope by embodying them in songs, rituals, and other artifacts. Ezra Pound and Charles Olson also offer Rothenberg important models of collage poetry addressed to recovering lost capacities in human nature, but Duncan authorizes specifically an important amalgam of romanticism and modernism to which Rothenberg commits himself and to which Pound and Olson do not subscribe. In this particular sense, Duncan is a more exact precursor for Rothenberg's poetic orientation than are Olson and Pound, both of whom, while attracted to aspects of the mythical and the mystical, are wary of what they see as the "excesses" of romanticism. Similarly, Duncan and Rothenberg lay claim to a surrealist-derived internationalism, alien to both Olson and Pound, which Kenneth Rexroth recognized and applauded: "Of all the San Francisco group Robert Duncan is the most easily recognizable as a member of the international *avant garde*. Mallarmé or Gertrude Stein, Joyce or Reverdy, there is a certain underlying homogeneity of idiom, and this idiom is, by and large, Duncan's"; "Jerome Rothenberg is one of the truly contemporary American poets who has returned U.S. poetry to the mainstream of international modern literature . . . a swinging orgy of Martin Buber, Marcel Duchamp, Gertrude Stein and Sitting Bull."[39]

Although they share an affinity for "international modernism," Duncan and Rothenberg differ in their compositional methods. With a deeper commitment to Dada and surrealism than that of Duncan, Rothenberg often trusts to the effervescent meanings produced by stark juxtapositions of imagery, while Duncan looks for hidden correspondences (or what he calls "rimes") among the disparate elements he juxtaposes. Duncan works assiduously to highlight and ultimately balance the tensions among his materials; Rothenberg is more content to let tensions remain unresolved in order to spark the reader's active participation. This desire for participation also informs Rothenberg's commitment to intermedia art and performance art as opposed to Duncan's acting as a "one-man band," himself playing the wide variety of "instruments" he incorporates into his poems. Notwithstanding their shared allegiance to anarchism, they differ in that Rothenberg imagines the possibility of a positive politics in which people learn to speak to one another not through relations of power but based upon individual and communal experience, while Duncan brands all hopeful positions as naive and believes that politics can best be seen as a psychomachia or demonology. Likewise, although Rothenberg speaks of "the sacred" as an intensification of life that takes place usually outside of Western institutions, Duncan feared that Rothenberg's participation in the New York avant-garde would cause him to empty "the sacred" of its visionary content.[40] Both poets hold, though, that erotic energy underlies life, and each adumbrates an erotic poetics of remarkable elasticity. From the standpoint of erotic poetics, both adhere to a countercultural impulse that originates in shamanism and continues in gnostic and Tantric subcultures up to the present. Duncan, though, reads eroticism through a Freudian lens, while Rothenberg takes it more literally as the bodily display that can shatter the erotic occlusion of Western culture.

Duncan and Rothenberg join other American poets in stepping outside a nation-based model of literature in favor of invoking deep time. By honoring "the *old* man" (Rothenberg) and "first things" (Duncan), these poets propose an interchange across time and space that would open American literature to the world. In doing so, they participate in the Whitmanian vision of an American poetry that would incorporate the world's cultures. Seizing on Duncan's phrase "symposium of the whole" as instigation, Rothenberg assembles in *Technicians of the Sacred* "a poetry of all poetries" that speaks for the range of human experience as it occurs both in the postwar avant-garde and across the reaches of time.

Notes

1. Thanks to Robert Kaufman for e-mail conversations about Duncan's reactions in his notebooks to Rothenberg and *Technicians*. Kaufman, *Technicians of the Sacred*. Hereafter cited in the text as *Technicians*.
2. Duncan, *A Selected Prose*, 97.
3. Ibid., 98.
4. Rothenberg and Rothenberg, *Symposium of the Whole*, xii.
5. Dimock, *Through Other Continents*, 3, 23.
6. His first book publication was also a translation, with David Antin, of Martin Buber's *Tales of Angels Spirits & Demons* (1958).
7. Rothenberg speaking at the Kelly Writers House, April 29, 2008.
8. Rexroth, untitled paragraph.
9. Ibid.
10. Duncan, *Ground Work: Before the War/In the Dark*, 12.
11. See Finkelstein, *Not One of Them in Place*, 87–111; Meilicke, *Jerome Rothenberg's Experimental Poetry*; and Selinger, "Shekhinah in America," for discussions of Jewish issues in Rothenberg's work.
12. Duncan, *Featuring Robert Duncan*, 49.
13. Ibid.
14. Rothenberg, *Pre-Faces*, 119.
15. Duncan, *Bending the Bow*, vi.
16. Rexroth, untitled paragraph.
17. Duncan, *A Selected Prose*, 198.
18. Igliori, *American Magus*, 164.
19. Cantwell, *When We Were Good*, 194.
20. Smith, *Think of the Self-Speaking*, 81.
21. Marcus, *Invisible Republic*, 87–126.
22. Duncan, *Bending the Bow*, vi.
23. Ibid., vii.
24. Rothenberg, *Pre-Faces*, 31.
25. Duncan, *A Selected Prose*, 105.
26. Ibid.
27. Ibid., 106.
28. Faas titles the chapter of his Duncan biography that treats this period "The Shaman Poet" (*Young Robert Duncan*, 81–92), and Maynard discusses "Toward the Shaman" in relation to surrealism ("Architect of Excess," 102–23). Drawing on the scholarship of Mircea Eliade, O'Leary uses the figure of the shaman as a central interpretive device in his lengthy exploration of Duncan's poem "My Mother Would Be a Falconress" (*Gnostic Contagion*, 130–32, 144–51, 160–67).

29. Rothenberg, *Symposium of the Whole*, 59.
30. Rothenberg, *Pre-Faces*, 47.
31. Rothenberg, “Nokh Aushvitz,” 144–45.
32. Robert Duncan, Notebook 41, July 14, 1968–December 30, 1970, Robert Duncan Collection, Poetry Collection, State University of New York at Buffalo.
33. Dimock, *Through Other Continents*, 3.
34. Ibid., 4.
35. Rothenberg, *Pre-Faces*, 17.
36. Ibid., 33.
37. Dimock, *Through Other Continents*, 28.
39. Rexroth, “San Francisco Letter,” 10; Rexroth, untitled paragraph.
40. Duncan, Notebook 41, August 7, 1969.

CHAPTER NINE

How the Dead Prey upon Us: Robert Duncan and Susan Howe

CATHERINE MARTIN

When Robert Duncan died in 1988, Susan Howe published a short tribute to him in *American Poetry*, naming him as her "precursor father."[1] Yet little has been made of this self-confessed affiliation. Although Howe is more commonly linked to Charles Olson, sharing his preoccupation with American history, she is particularly attentive to the "other history" that she associates with Duncan: "A history outside time where first memories form. That other history 'beyond what we ever were, where we no longer are'" and "the history that always interested Robert Duncan."[2] Whether or not we take literally her tentative speculation that on the day of his death Duncan's spirit "stopped on its way to wherever it is we go; just for an instant" with her on the shores of Lake Erie, the suggestion is relevant to her poetics.[3] For, like Duncan in "A Poem Beginning with a Line by Pindar" or Olson in "As the Dead Prey upon Us," Howe is intrigued by the possibility that poetry might be a space, analogous to dreams or memory, where things can come back.

In a 1980 letter to George Butterick, the editor of Charles Olson's work, Howe cites these two poems as crucial to her writing. Both concur with her notion that the dead are waiting for us when we write: in Duncan's case, dead poets; in Olson's, his mother and her assorted friends. The atmosphere of Olson's "As the Dead Prey upon Us" is dreamlike, and the narrator's surprise when he gets home to find his dead mother asleep in her chair, as she always used to be, fits with Howe's sense that dreams resist progressive temporality, returning us to states of mind that refuse to give up the dead or to comprehend loss as we do in our waking lives.[4] This is perhaps what Howe means when she refers to a "history outside time": memory sporadically confronts us with previous experiences that do not seem past (or to have passed), while at the same time it withholds them from us when we consciously try to recover them. This history is "outside time" because, in preserving and returning the mind to its liminal regions, it ruptures linear time, causing a schism in the cohesive subject.

Yet where Olson's poem militates against memory's insistence on arresting us at some point in the past, Howe and Duncan are more inquiring about why the mind cannot break its attachment to certain scenes. The stale returns in "As the Dead Prey upon Us" are evidence of death in life in a different sense, of a failure to reach the nakedness of experience, which Olson urges us toward and in which he thinks history can be truly apprehended:

> the ghastliness
>
> of going, and forever
> coming back, returning
> to the instants which were not lived.[5]

Duncan's "A Poem Beginning with a Line by Pindar," in contrast, is built upon returns. Begun, as the title indicates, by the intrusion of a remembered line of poetry into his consciousness, the poem's movement is precipitated by his interrogation of its provenance—"Who is it that goes there?"—and the associations this throws up.[6]

Duncan's permissiveness to whatever might enter the field of the poem and his concern to trace out the significance of these unsolicited memories make the poem dreamlike in a different way from Olson's. Enthralled by the possibilities Sigmund Freud's dream analysis might have for poetry, Duncan argues in *The H.D. Book* that the poem "resembles the time of a dream, for it is highly organized along lines of association."[7] Elaborating on this comparison, he suggests elsewhere that, "like the mechanism of the dream," poetry's associative structure allows "a variety of times and places" to be kept "present and immediate" in a way that waking consciousness does not.[8] Similarly, his mode of writing, attuned to mistakes and the involuntary warps of language, permits a certain loosening of the censorship that governs conscious thought. For, as in Freud's dream logic, images or thoughts can be "linked together merely through a similarity in the sound of words," a similarity that, though apparently superficial, points to a "legitimate and deeper link . . . subject to the resistance of censorship."[9]

Howe's obituary for Duncan foregrounds this fascination with involuntary memory and, in particular, with the way past texts return to haunt us in the present. Across Duncan's career, whole poems are elaborated from such unsolicited encounters, whether they germinate, as the Pindar poem does, from a single remembered line of poetry or are generated by the increasingly complex intertextual occasions dramatized in his late *Ground Work* volumes, where clear-cut distinctions between "source" texts and the present poetic event that they disrupt become more and more untenable.[10] Howe's tribute, voiced as it is through attributed and unattributed quotation, recognizes the extent to which in Duncan's poetics the writing of others is viewed not as sacrosanct private property to be respectfully referenced and acknowledged but as a "gift" to be shared and occupied at will. When Duncan writes in the polemical opening to his 1960 collection *The Opening of the Field*: "Often I am permitted to return to a meadow / as if it were a given property of the mind" (7), it is telling that he should appropriate a phrase from the climax of Pound's first Pisan Canto:

> Serenely in the crystal jet
>   as the bright ball that the fountain tosses
> (Verlaine) as diamond clearness
>   How soft the wind under Taishan
>   where the sea is remembered
>   out of hell, the pit
>   out of the dust and glare evil
>   Zephyrus/Apeliota
> This liquid is certainly *a*
>   *property of the mind*
> nec accidens est   but an element
>   in the mind's make-up[11]

More telling still is Duncan's insertion of the word "given" into Pound's lines, pulling the already ambiguous valence of "property" (connoting both possession and a defining quality) toward his own sense of returning memory as something that is mysteriously bestowed. If the corresponding passage in Pound's Canto LXXIV is itself concerned with the "crystal jet" of memory and specifically with the propulsion of other writers' images into the poet's thought processes, so familiar and seemingly "of the mind" that he has to remind himself that they derive from someone else—"(Verlaine)"—in Duncan's poem no such qualification is made. Instead, Duncan's readiness to engage with what emerges "at the margins of thought" and to let the poem be structured around such an engagement constructs a relationship with past texts that is distinct from the kind of allusion and quotation encountered in high modernist poetry (*Opening*, 62). As Michael Davidson suggests, "texts appear within Duncan's poems not as privileged signs of cultural order . . . but as generative elements in the composing process."[12] Quotation does not serve metonymically as it frequently does in Pound's *Cantos* to summon a useful but still autonomous whole from elsewhere to meet the needs of the present. Rather, Duncan's word "given" and his passive construction "I am permitted" imply that a determination not the author's own is driving the arrival of these words in the mind whose logic it becomes the analytic work of the process poem to discover.

Duncan's investment in errancy and the productive force of misreading sets him apart, too, from his contemporaries in their handling of source texts. This is not the self-conscious display of factual discourse seen in, say, *The Maximus Poems*; nor is Duncan driven, as Olson is, by an urgent need to put new information out in the world, setting document against historically specific document within the dialogic space of the poem. Duncan's take on "COMPOSITION BY FIELD," going "by no track other than the one the poem under hand declare, for itself . . . instant by instant," ascribes a greater and more peculiar agency to the poem and the words that constitute it than Olson himself implies.[13] It is exactly this playfulness with ideas of ownership and originality—Duncan's consistent advocacy of a kind of authorship able to encompass what might be given or derived, whether from other writers or from the process of writing itself—that proves so attractive to Howe in her development of a poetics where the twin concepts of trespass and "permission" hold comparable sway (*Opening*, 7).

Yet if these concerns are no less operative in Howe's own writing, the terms of her engagement with both involuntary memory and the citational impulse she sees as central to American writing differ significantly from Duncan's terms. Not only is the practice of (submerged) quotation—if we can call it that—in her poems often covert and concealed where Duncan's is advertised and acted out, but Howe is more skeptical about poetry's ability to bring the past to presence. Rather, the potency of memory for Howe lies in its paradoxical ability to be both insistently present and recalcitrant, to withhold itself from fluent discourse. As she writes in *Pythagorean Silence*:

> only   Only
> what never stops hurting remains
>
> in memory
>
> In memory
> Errant turns to
>
> and away.[14]

If, for Howe, it is only through sound and errancy that such memory can enter the discursive realm, then it is for this reason that poetry represents a powerful alternative to contemporary modes of historical narrative.[15] Suspicious of the violent omissions necessary to render "history" as seamless narrative, memory remains for her an intractable otherness that cannot or perhaps *ought* not be cajoled into words. Therefore, although anamnesis is a recurrent feature of her writing, it is never made to work according to the principle of Freud's "talking cure," toward an endpoint where the pain or symptoms associated with a repressed event are relieved by bringing it into consciousness and articulating it in words.

Howe's obituary for Duncan provides a compelling instance of this resistance to recovering memory fully to consciousness. At the center of her tribute is not only an uncanny experience on the day of his death, later seemingly substantiated by a still more uncanny textual coincidence. (Walking along the edge of Lake Erie one winter afternoon, she sees something—a swing flapping wildly in the wind—that puts her in mind of Duncan. Returning home, she learns he had died earlier that day. She begins to wonder if what she saw by the lake may in fact have been a manifestation of his departing spirit.) It is also that the place, Buffalo, where this occurs triggers a sudden recollection of *her* past: "I spent the first five years of my life in Buffalo, but except for one night when I gave a reading, I never returned until this January. Now the old history comes back to me."[16] Although, in the way it "comes back" of its own volition and takes possession of her, this history resembles the unsolicited returns that intrude upon Duncan in the Pindar poem, Howe's "return" has a more subjective resonance. It is the "child [she] was" who is "suddenly here": "*She*, not I, called for Love's sake: 'Quick, quick, come look.'"[17]

The specific memory that overwhelms her here is of being separated from her father as a young child: "I lost my father in Buffalo. He enlisted in the army just after Pearl Harbor was attacked and was stationed in Europe until WWII was over."[18] Readers of Howe will be familiar with this incident, which has the status of a primal scene in her writing, being reworked from book to book, as if its convergence of private pain with the experience of history as felt affect can be neither satisfyingly articulated nor definitively resolved. Rather, it remains like her infantile self, uprooted, exiled, not content to lie down in a history that doesn't remember her, yet somehow "locked in" and "sealed against" her present self in the ice of Lake Erie, an unassimilated and potentially disruptive force.[19]

If Howe's writing has, then, frequently drawn analogies between poetry and dreams as spaces "outside time," counter to ordinary modes of thinking, the terms of both this analogy and her attempt to, as she puts it in *Pierce-Arrow*, find "another way of speaking," closer to those "memories, thoughts, feelings, which are extra-marginal outside of primary consciousness," have altered dramatically in her most recent work.[20] It is to that recent work—Howe's late work—that I now wish to turn in pursuing Howe's affinity with Robert Duncan. For, strangely, Howe's 1999 collection *Pierce-Arrow* represents in part the fruition of a much earlier inception of her thinking about the relationship between memory and writing, in which Duncan is implicated. *Pierce-Arrow*'s final poem, "Rückenfigur," is an urgent meditation on loss and the Orphic possibilities of lyric poetry, written in the wake of her husband, David von Schlegell's death in 1992. Following a long hiatus in her writing, this poem represents a departure both in form and, as Peter Nicholls has so persuasively argued, in the philosophical impetus it takes from the nineteenth-century American logician Charles Sanders Peirce and the aesthetics of Caspar David Friedrich's painting.[21] Yet the poem also revisits a set of mythic associations first articulated in her correspondence with Butterick in the early 1980s, where Howe explores the relationship of "projective verse" to her own.

In those letters Howe imagines writing as *nekuia*, a descent to the darkness, a meeting with the assembled shades who await her there: "The farther you go, the deeper the shadows, the more shadowy the Shades."[22] Citing Duncan's Pindar poem as an inspirational version of this experience, she goes on to distinguish it from her own. "For him it is a joyful one," she writes. "He welcomes the implications of the Cupid Psyche myth." In contrast, for her, "Psyche leads strangely to Persephone. And Persephone was dragged down to Darkness. The myth to a woman who is a writer is tied up with Violence, assault, 'rape.'"[23] Both mythic women represent different dangers for the (implicitly female) writer who "roams this threatening space": Persephone because one might get trapped down there, unable to break free from its monotonous cycles of repetition; Psyche, both the lengths one might go to get there (jumping to her death) and what such a descent might unleash (she very nearly succumbs to the deadly, drugging fumes of sleep with which Persephone sends her back to the surface). Where Duncan's Pindar poem is caught up in the rush of desire that he, like Psyche, experiences at the sight of Eros's "brown . . . slight body," Howe recognizes the risk attendant upon entering and allowing oneself to be determined by this realm of desire and unfinished attachment, which for Persephone entails not just the pleasurable, passionate relinquishment of volition to which Duncan accedes but violent coercion, seizure by force (*Opening*, 62).

It is tempting to read intertextuality into this plutonic scenario: to see the pallid shades as scraps or shards of other texts longing to be animated back to life; even to sense that their crowding demands upon the living poet might be invasive. However, the letters also alert us to a difference in Duncan's and Howe's writing practice around just this issue of derivation—how source materials manifest themselves in, or are made to radiate through, the poem. Howe contrasts her own hesitant, revisionary process with the ability of "those poets *men*," Olson and Duncan, to "let go with a fistful of words and let the energy of the words and something in their intellectual vision push them forward." "All my intensity goes into suggesting, moving, erasing, readjusting . . . to produce *little*, after endless labor," she writes.[24] The questions this letter raises about the troubling status of "source" texts in Howe's poetry resonate across her career, presenting as much of a critical challenge in her late work as in the poems under discussion in these letters.[25] What are we to make, as readers, of this material her writing incorporates, whose intimation of a prior yet somehow occluded context tempts us into scholarly exegesis yet resists its resolution? Can the diverse kinds of derivation her poems enact be adequately described as quotation, allusion, or intertextuality? Indeed, is the term "derivation" itself unduly freighted with connotations of origination and originality—concepts that Howe's poetry works to negate? Finally, what impetus, if any, does her late work continue to take from Robert Duncan?

Turning to *Pierce-Arrow*, we can see how the central mythic motif of Duncan's Pindar poem—looking leading to loss—might underpin "Rückenfigur" and the legends of Tristram and Orpheus around which it revolves (principally as found in Swinburne's 1882 poem *Tristram of Lyonesse* and Rainer Maria Rilke's *Sonnets to Orpheus*). Duncan's poem zeroes in on the moment when Psyche lights a lamp to look at her sleeping husband, Eros, for the first time. In doing so, she breaks her promise to him and must therefore lose him: awakening Eros with a drop of burning oil that spills from the lamp onto his body, she seals their separation. Just so, Howe reminds us, Orpheus sacrifices Eurydice for a second time by doing what *he* is forbidden to do and looking back at her. Likewise, looking (or, rather, not looking) proves equally fatal in the second story "Rückenfigur" invokes. Failing to verify with his own eyes the falsely relayed message—"Love's sail is black"—that announces Iseult's death, the ailing Tristram is sent by his resentful wife to a speedy end, one that his bereft but still living lover, Iseult, is swift to follow (*Pierce-Arrow*, 54). Where Duncan's poem is powered by the movement of desire as Psyche strives to recover Eros, Howe's too is driven by an overwhelming impulse to look back, to overcome the unbearable pain of separation that death imposes on Orpheus and Eurydice and that circumstance decrees for Tristram and Iseult.

As a closer examination of the aesthetics of looking foregrounded in each reveals, these two poems demonstrate at once a strikingly similar attitude toward the temporality of perception and yet a contrasting deployment of sound to relay or deflect this longing to restore the past to presence and recover what has been lost. Ultimately, I would argue, this represents a difference in these two poets' beliefs about the degree to which memory can be knowable in the poem. Where Duncan's search along lines of association becomes a foray into the American past, from the settling of the West to the "wrongness" of Poundian modernism, Howe's search is a more acute phenomenological enquiry into the nature of grief: how the mind accommodates itself to the loss of one so close and, in particular, how philosophy can account for what she calls elsewhere the "crushing hold of memory's abiding present."[26]

Having begun with the line by Pindar, Duncan's poem quickly shifts to its main focus, the historical mediation of the myth of Eros and Psyche, initially through Goya's painting *Cupid and Psyche*. Duncan's translation of Goya's "voluptuous" picture into the opulent, baroque language of his poem renders the moment when Psyche discovers Eros's beauty durational, as it is transposed from the "*all at once*" sensation of looking at a painting into the temporal experience of reading.[27] The lamp's forbidden illumination catches on Eros's naked torso, accentuating Goya's sensitivity to the dramatic effects of light and dark:

> The copper light
> falling upon the brown boy's slight body
> is carnal fate that sends the soul wailing
> up from blind innocence, ensnared
> by dimness
> into the deprivations of desiring sight. (*Opening*, 62)

More than a static moment, desire here is already colored by regret and separation: "Waves of visual pleasure / wrap them in a sorrow previous to their impatience" (*Opening*, 62).

In the subsequent stanzas the infectious "rime" of sounds with other sounds perpetuates the desire this moment arouses through language. Sounds are relayed in the lines: "A bronze of yearning, a rose that burns / the tips of their bodies, lips / ends of fingers, nipples" so that the first syllable of "yearning" is picked up by "burns," and "tips" by "lips" and "nipples" (*Opening*, 62). Duncan makes it clear that perception—looking—is already a kind of loss. His deflection to the auditory approximates the metonymic logic of memory, which struggles to compensate, offering endless replacements for the original, occluded object. Psyche's loss of Eros and the tasks she must undertake to recover him supply the thread that knits together the poem's disparate turns and allusions, as her search is allied to Duncan's efforts to trace out the significance of Pindar's line. Both the unceasing refraction as the poem sheds skin after skin of the Eros myth and the ricochet of repeated sounds are propelled by the same sliding process of substitution. Yet this desire, Eros, is also shown to be a moving force, the impulse that powers not only conquests seeking "entire possession" of bodies or continents but the poem itself. For it is through the mobility of association in words that, as Duncan writes, a "line of Pindar / moves from the area of my lamp / toward morning," as the poem this line inspires spreads across his page, filling the space left by Psyche's loss and Duncan's inability to "correctly" recollect its original context (69).

Susan Howe's "Rückenfigur" is also dominated by a yearning to recover what has been lost. Taking Orpheus as a model, it seeks to transgress death's absolute prohibition and time's relentless forward trajectory in order to have the past once more in its possession. Yet the poem, as much as Duncan's, leaves us "in the deprivations of desiring sight" (*Opening*, 62), since the object of our gaze is, like Eurydice, always turned away in what Howe terms "motif of retreating figure / arrayed beyond expression" (*Pierce-Arrow*, 144). As is clear from the last page of the poem, hoping to discover "divinity message" by following the "lure" of the poem's compulsive enjambments, we are doomed to disappointment (144). Within "Rückenfigur's" structure of deferral, even the last lines instruct us to "wait some recognition" (144).

As Peter Nicholls has shown, "Rückenfigur" takes its title—and indeed that very phrase "wait some recognition"—from Joseph Leo Koerner's book *Caspar David Friedrich and the Subject of Landscape.*[28] The name refers to the figures in Friedrich's paintings who stand with their backs to us, looking into a landscape that is now blocked from us, their earlier arrival making anything but a belated relationship to the scene impossible. The feeling of déjà vu that the *Rückenfigur* induces (since the scene has been seen before we see it) has a similarly circular, preemptive temporality to Duncan's depiction of the Goya painting. As Koerner says, "The déjà vu excites us with an anticipated return, yet leaves us in a state of exile; anticipation becomes finally nostalgia for a place I have never visited."[29] It is not that perception is simultaneous with retrospection; rather, it exists only in reconstruction, as memory. In contrast, Koerner argues, the *Rückenfiguren* occupy an impossible "locus of fulfilled" rather than deferred desire where the "past is made present" and "recognition" finally comes.[30]

Howe's textual strategies put the reader in a similar position. Her characteristic blocking devices, such as the tendency to diffract a phrase's momentum into an accumulation of nouns—"echo remnant sentence spar"—mean that, just as if we were viewers looking at Friedrich's canvases, our "progress into depth" is met by "its harsh curb estrangement" (*Pierce-Arrow*, 144, 133). This conflict—between desiring sight and its obstruction—is played out in the tension between eye and ear as we read "Rückenfigur," as the sideways push of the rhythm sends clauses over the end of lines, making them transgress their visual boundaries.

In a comparable way to Howe's, Duncan's poem never accedes to Psyche's desire by permitting us to return to the moment before her fall; rather, his translation of the temporality of Goya's painting into that of poetry relays and defers through sound association Psyche's desire for reunion and recovery. But his poem does uncover in the process connections that Duncan believes are significant and have been repressed in the dominant constructions of American mythology and national identity. The very momentum of the poem, in Duncan's willingness to "let go" with a fistful of words from Pindar and give in to wherever this associative process takes him, gives sway to a homoerotic desire that has been denied and that distorts and transforms the "source" text—Pindar's line—from which the poem germinates.[31] This is very different from the resistance Howe's syntactical maneuvers offer not just to sustained intelligibility but to allowing the "source" material to seize, coerce, or resolve the poem.

Although elsewhere Howe exhibits a similar penchant for phonic coincidences that reveal more important axes of comparison, here her attention to sound does not lead to disclosure. "Rückenfigur" instead ends in vacillation over the nature of sound—whether it must always be frustrated, "bitter" because "truth is silent," because it can't follow Eurydice and penetrate death's secrets, which are "silent as silent tomorrow":

> Day binds the wide Sound
> Bitter sound as truth is
> silent as silent tomorrow
> Motif of retreating figure
> arrayed beyond expression
> huddled unintelligible air
> Theomimesis divinity message
> I have loved come veiling
> Lyrist come veil come lure
> echo remnant sentence spar
> never never form wherfor
> Wait some recognition you
> Lyric over us love unclothe
> Never forever whoso move.
>
> (*Pierce-Arrow*, 144)

Yet the poem remains absorbed, too, in the "echo" one does get back, always promising to build in "sentence spar" toward a firmer intimation of the past (144). Echo finally is an apt figure for the equivocal role sound plays as both a block and a passageway to the elusive and longed-for past. Howe's pun on "sound" here as both noise and a narrow stretch of water connecting two larger bodies of land or water makes it clear that it is something to be trajected and traversed yet whose very materiality might pose an obstacle to such crossing. Earlier allusions to a "ghostly . . . ferryman" and to a "few persistent 'islands' / of half-inaudible whispers / jabbing the radioman Lethe"

(29, 113) support the inference that this "wide Sound" might be a geographical location *and* a zone of noise. If the "radioman" calls to mind Jean Cocteau's Orphée, scrolling the airwaves for poetic messages from the other side, then Howe's "sound" represents an intermediate space between the living and the dead and between signification and mere burble, consisting of noise, static, interference, "half-inaudible whispers" that can't quite be tuned in.

If echo also gestures to the minute residue—I hesitate to say invocation—of other texts below the smooth surface of Howe's lines, it is worth noting that the word "sound" has some precedence in the preface to Swinburne's long poem *Tristram of Lyonesse*. In introducing the dead lovers, Tristram and Iseult, Swinburne also puns on "sound," imbuing it with an unruly animacy that belies its role in closing the following lines, suggesting as it does noise and life rather than undisturbed slumbers:

> They have the night, who had like us the day;
> We whom *day binds*, shall have the night as they.
> We, from the fetters of the light unbound,
> Healed of our wound of living, shall sleep *sound*.[32]

In "Rückenfigur" the movement between what is "sound" and what is "silent" is never resolved. Something of the quality of Swinburne's mind-twisting, chiasmatic constructions infects Howe's writing here, since her Swinburnian inversion, "bitter sound as truth is," placing the adjective first and postponing the verb, makes these lines difficult to construe (*Pierce-Arrow*, 144). Should we read on over the line break and extend the proposition as the slide of enjambment propels us to? We are constantly going over the grammatical possibilities of these lines, trying to discern what is being compared to what: sound to truth, truth to silence, sound to silent tomorrow. This is a move characteristic of the poem, whose absence of punctuation, especially periods, means thought is continually being extended and pulled in new directions, looking to move around the limits the mind runs up against, rather than concede to them. If Swinburne's trance-inducing cadences and elongated analogies and equations work to evade the limits of mortal time and the restrictions of subjective experience with which "day binds" us, "Rückenfigur" too strives to keep open the space between what Charles Bernstein calls "the materially present sound" and its "absent meaning," looking to avoid closure and delay the cognition that, Howe is conscious, would diminish the sublime obscurity of the "wide Sound."[33]

For what distinguishes the opacity of Howe's writing in this late mode is its very impulse to "move"—the last word of the poem. Her almost imperceptible rendering of source texts here (Rilke, Swinburne) does not result in the strange accumulation of archaic language that we experience in an earlier poem like "Hope Atherton's Wanderings." There nouns are heaped together as if in witness to the obsolescence of particular discourses or the failure of transition between one culture and another (Puritan and Native American):

> Clog nutmeg abt noon
> scraping cano muzzell
> foot path sand and so
> gravel rubbish vandal
> horse flesh ryal tabl
> sand enemys flood sun[34]

There too sound patterning serves to obstruct our semantic processing of the words we are presented with. The effect is to turn language into something deliberately absurd and indecipherable. Static and inert, the words are made more awkward, absurd even, by their phonic resemblance to one another rather than energized as they are in "Rückenfigur" by the pull of sound and rhythm toward a promised transcendence.

The urgent imperatives of "Rückenfigur's" closing lines appeal to Orpheus the "veiling lyrist" to come and reverse fact with his song. They hold out the possibility that through the seductive alliteration and consonance of the repeated *l* and *v* sounds, "come veil come lure," we might indeed "slip through the lyric fence, transgress," as Rilke imagines in his *Sonnets to Orpheus*, and enter the past as now, without obstruction.[35] The poem never fully concedes to the Orphic hope that animates it, and we are, finally, brought no closer to its lyric object, which remains curiously distantiated by prepositions that declare it of and from something no longer there:

you
of light from that of
memory when eyelids close
so in dream sensation
Mind's trajected light. (*Pierce-Arrow*, 136)

Yet Howe finds remarkable ways in the momentum of her poem to approximate the fragile space of what she calls "Mind's trajected light," which the incursion of external reality constantly threatens to extinguish. If this is a poem that, in Duncan's terms, "resembles the time of a dream," it is one whose "dream sensation" of presentness is produced by the very mode of Howe's derivation, minutely meshing source texts together into new configurations and yet undercut by the undertow of absent meaning these "remnant[s]" carry with them (*Pierce-Arrow*, 136).[36] Like the mirrors eulogized in Rilke's sonnets as "openings worked in the fabric of time," the tantalizing surface of Howe's poem lures us with the hope of passing through its silvery surface into its illusory depths, even as we are met by its cold, glassy rebuff, realizing what we see is a reflection, memory as spectral repetition, whose original we cannot touch.[37]

Notes

1. Susan Howe, untitled tribute to Robert Duncan, *American Poetry* 6 (1988): 56.
2. Duncan, *Ground Work*, 71, 54.
3. Ibid., 56.
4. Charles Olson, "As the Dead Prey upon Us," in Olson, *The Collected Poems*, 390.
5. Ibid., 392.
6. Duncan, *The Opening of the Field*, 62. Hereafter cited in the text as *Opening*.
7. Duncan, *The H.D. Book*, 99.
8. Duncan, *A Selected Prose*, 110.
9. Freud, *The Interpretation of Dreams*, 125, 677.
10. See, for instance, "An Interlude of Winter Light," a poem inspired by Mallarmé's "Don du poème," in which a profusion of quotation marks, italics, and parentheses serves to blur rather than delineate the boundaries between the present poem and the "foreign matter" that enters it and gives it life (Duncan, *Ground Work: Before the War*, 151).
11. Ezra Pound, "Canto LXXIV," in *The Cantos*, 449. Emphases indicate the words Duncan appropriates.

12. Davidson, "Cave of Resemblances," 39.
13. Charles Olson, "Projective Verse," in Olson, *The Collected Prose*, 239–40.
14. Howe, *The Europe of Trusts*, 26.
15. In an interview with Edward Foster, Howe suggests poetry is "a different way of knowing things," one that "depends on chance, on randomness" (Howe, *The Birth-Mark*, 165).
16. Howe, untitled tribute to Robert Duncan, 54.
17. Ibid., 56.
18. Ibid., 54.
19. Ibid., 56.
20. The quote "outside time" is from ibid., 54; the other quotes are from Howe, *Pierce-Arrow*, 6. Hereafter cited in the text as *Pierce-Arrow*.
21. See Nicholls, "The Pastness of Landscape."
22. Howe to George Butterick, October 5, 1980, in Collis, *Through Words of Others*, 84.
23. Ibid.
24. Ibid., 88.
25. Namely, Howe's sequence "Pythagorean Silence."
26. Howe, "Sorting Facts," 326.
27. Bernstein, *Content's Dream*, 115.
28. Nicholls, "The Pastness of Landscape," 448.
29. Koerner, *Caspar David Friedrich*, 233.
30. Ibid., 234.
31. Howe to Butterick, October 5, 1980.
32. Swinburne, *Major Poems*, 211. Emphases indicate Howe's appropriations.
33. Bernstein, *Close Listening*, 18.
34. Howe, *Singularities*, 6.
35. Rilke, *Sonnets to Orpheus*, 23.
36. Duncan, *The H.D. Book*, 99.
37. Rilke, *Sonnets to Orpheus*, 73.

CHAPTER TEN

Divining the Derivers: Anarchism and the Practice of Derivative Poetics in Robert Duncan and John Cage

ANDY WEAVER

Well, communion is probably what a poem is.
—Robert Duncan, interview by John Tranter

I think everyone influences me.
—John Cage, interview by Henning Lohner

The similarities between Robert Duncan and John Cage are striking. Setting aside the biographical similarities, the two shared significant aesthetic and ideological positions: both were avowed anarchists who talked openly about how anarchism influenced their poetry; both appreciated Ezra Pound's aesthetics and—although both openly disagreed with Pound's politics—agreed with Pound that poetry was a didactic art form; both were associated with Black Mountain College and the accompanying literary movement; and both were influenced by religious and philosophical teachings from outside the Western canon (Cage by Zen and his work with the *I Ching*, Duncan by his upbringing in a practicing Theosophist household).[1] Most importantly, and the key aspect that I will examine, both Duncan and Cage stressed the derivative nature of their poetry, how they derived their writings directly from many different literary forerunners. Duncan and

Cage worked against the commonly held notion of the individual genius, the writing subject who brings forth great texts through solitary, unique brilliance. Instead, they created texts that show the importance of anarchic communities, texts that show the importance of nonhierarchical giving to and taking from others in a radically free exchange of ideas. Put simply, both Duncan and Cage attempted to teach their readers how to live ethically, which for each poet meant how to create and maintain an anarchic relationship between the individual and her community.

However, in spite of these similarities, Duncan and Cage created poems that differ in many ways. One of the most important differences involves the writers' use of derivation as a literary technique: Duncan's derivative poetics revolves around quotation and collage, combining elements from different writers in his own texts, resulting in poems that function as bricolage, while Cage's use of derivation focuses mostly on rewriting a generant text, reengaging with that text (Cage refers to this technique as "writing through") in such a way that a Cagean derivative poem is a palimpsest. However, examining their poetry in combination shows how their derivative poetics serves the same goal (of creating didactic poetry bent on convincing the reader of the ethics of anarchism) through different paths, and it also provides insight into why each writer used derivation as he did. In the end, the comparison shows that Duncan's poetry stresses that the individual proves the efficacy of the community, while Cagean derivative poetry illustrates that the community proves the efficacy of the individual. Consequently, Cage and Duncan provide two sides of the same derivative poetics coin. More importantly, both Duncan and Cage use their poetics of derivation to support an anarchist philosophy that calls for and attempts to enact both an ethical relationship between the individual and her community as well as a stance of active attention to the organic order that both writers believe underlies all creation.

Duncan, Cage, and Derivative Poetics

In the introduction to *Bending the Bow*, Duncan states: "I'd like to leave somewhere in this book the statement that the real 'we' is the company of the living, of all the forms of Life Itself, the primal wave of it, writing itself out in evolution, proposes. Needs, as our poetry does, all the variety of what poets have projected poetry to be."[2] More than an affirmation of life, this statement provides a key to Duncan's derivative poetics. Aesthetically and ideologically, Duncan wants the poem to reflect the vast variety of Nature, of "Life Itself," and the primary technique that Duncan uses to achieve this complexity in his poetry is derivation, specifically quotation. Duncan uses quotation, particularly in the *Passages* series, to create a poetic community into which he places his works: the first poem in the series, "Tribal Memories, *Passages 1*" (and the focus on tribal rather than individual memories is important), emphasizes this connection to community by invoking Mnemosyne ("Her-Without-Bounds"):

> And to Her-Without-Bounds I send,
> wherever She wanders,   by what
>   campfire at evening,
>
> among tribes setting each the City where
>   we Her people are
> at the end of a day's reaches   here
>   the Eternal
> lamps lit, here   the wavering human
>   sparks of heat and light
> glimmer, go out, and reappear.[3]

Mnemosyne, mother of the Muses, was the Greek personification of memory, and, as Duncan states, "memory is the author or matrix of poetries."[4] By invoking Mnemosyne rather than one of her daughters, Duncan reaches toward the cultural, communal, tribal memories that underlie all humanity, eschewing the individual makings of poets who invoke one of the Muses. Duncan's emphasis on the communal also appears in the lamps, the "human sparks" that "glimmer, go out, and reappear": these cultural memories are the work and inheritance of many people passed down to Duncan, who acts merely as one more person passing along the memories in these *Passages*. The epigraph from Emperor Julian also reinforces the derived, communal nature of the *Passages* as well as the point that the poems aren't Duncan's creations so much as they are Duncan's addition to and passing forward of a part of humanity's cultural heritage. The poems become part of what Duncan calls "It," the "Life Code" that shapes us all and with which we can, at moments of clarity, briefly reconnect: "*It* is striving to come into existence in these things, or, all striving to come into existence is It—in this realm of men's languages a poetry of all poetries, *grand collage*, I name It, having only the immediate event of words to speak for It."[5] Grand collage: the term stresses the interplay of elements, the lack of any central focus, which Duncan works to create in his poetry; his use of quotations is fundamentally important to creating this community in his work. Perhaps the best example of this is the "Notes" that bring *Bending the Bow* to a close, in which Duncan lists the sources from which he has borrowed. Not just a case of creative honesty, the "Notes" reiterate the derivative, communal, anarchic nature of Duncan's aesthetic and ideological project. This commitment to using quotation to illustrate the communal creativity of derivative poetics occurs repeatedly in Duncan's work, at least as early as the tentative communality of "Poetry, a Natural Thing" and "A Poem Beginning with a Line by Pindar" from 1960's *The Opening of the Field*, through the *Passages* poems, and into the great derivative poems in "A Seventeenth Century Suite in Homage to the Metaphysical Genius in English Poetry (1590–1690)," "Dante Études," and "To Master Baudelaire" from the 1980s *Ground Work* volumes.

Cage also uses quotation, but his usage tends toward the anecdotal, using indirect quotation rather than quoting another's written words. *Silence*, for example, offers dozens of small anecdotal stories, almost all of which either focus on Cage's interaction with a friend or else retell a story that a friend has told Cage; they tend to explain the relationship in their opening sentences: "M. C. Richards went to the Bolshoi Ballet"; "One day when I was across the hall visiting Sonya Sekula, I noticed that she was painting left-handed"; "Richard Lippold called up and said, 'Would you come to dinner and bring the *I-Ching*?' I said I would"; and so on. The anecdote usually offers an example (often humorous) of Cage's personal ideology: "Before studying Zen, men are men and mountains are mountains. While studying Zen, things become confused. After studying Zen, men are men and mountains are mountains. After telling this, Dr. Suzuki was asked, 'What is the difference between before and after?' He said, 'No difference, only the feet are a little bit off the ground.'"[6] Jann Passler argues that Cage uses derivation to invent a tradition for himself: "Cage's manner of inventing a tradition involves not so much extending others' ideas as re-presenting them, bringing them again to life in part because they have become and represent aspects of Cage himself."[7] While this point is accurate for these anecdotes, which stress community and commonality, this type of derivation is only a small part of Cagean derivative poetics.

The most important examples of Cage's derivative poetics are the writing-through poems. For these works, Cage began with a generant text (Joyce's *Finnegans Wake*, Thoreau's *Journal*, Pound's *Cantos*) and, by following specific rules, selected passages from the generant text, which Cage then edited (*only* through removing words) into a new poem. Cage completed five different writings-through of *Finnegans Wake*, so it is reasonable to view those poems as exemplary. In these texts Cage derived long strings of mesostics ("not acrostics: row down the middle, not down the edge").[8] Cage chose as his mesostic spine Joyce's name and then "began looking for a J without an A. And then for the next A without an M. Etcetera. I continued finding Joyce and James to the end of the chapter."[9] This creates a base text from which Cage removed words to make his poem. The first two stanzas of "Writing for the Second Time through *Finnegans Wake*" illustrate the results:

wroth with twone nathanJoe
A
Malt
jhEm
Shen

pftJschute
sOlid man
that the humptYhillhead of humself
is at the knoCk out
in thE park[10]

The poem continues in such a manner for a total of 295 stanzas (40 pages), with the length of the poem helping to emphasize its lack of normative meaning. Rather than Duncan's collage of quotations, the Cagean writing-through is a poetic palimpsest, where the generant text severely limits the possibility of what the text can say. Creation in Cage's writings-through is not a matter of creating a community of voices but rather of revivifying the author of the generant text so that Cage can enter into a textual conversation with him.

Moreover, this textual conversation works to renew, to breathe new life into the thoughts and beliefs of the author of the generant text. Cage comments about *Finnegans Wake*, for example, that "Due to N. O. Brown's remark that syntax is the arrangement of the army, and Thoreau's that when he heard a sentence he heard feet marching, I became devoted to nonsyntactical 'demilitarized' language. . . . But when in this spirit I picked up [*Finnegans Wake*], Joyce seemed to me to have kept the old structures ('sin-talks') in which he put the new words he had made."[11] The Cagean writing-through acts as an intervention, freeing Joyce's words from their old-fashioned syntactical structures, structures that Cage believes were out of date when Joyce wrote the book. Much more than an ideological updating, the writing-through creates a new text, one that exists through the combined efforts of Cage and Joyce; ascribing a singular authorship becomes impossible, especially since Joyce's nonce-words appear throughout the writing-through. This type of derivation places the site of creation in a liminal zone, a both/and yet neither/nor Cage/Joyce. The author of the piece perhaps is most accurately referred to as an imaginary John James Cage-Joyce.

Although Duncan's emphasis on collage, on bringing into his poetry disparate voices from the multitude, holds obvious differences from Cage's aesthetic project, both poets share a refusal to blindly continue the project of their forerunners. As a poetic apprentice of Ezra Pound, Duncan openly acknowledges his debts to his master. However, as Christopher Beach argues, Duncan did not subserviently adopt Pound's poetics; instead, "in Duncan's derivation of Pound's conceptions and poetic stance we find an influence that is not so much a direct transfer of ideas as a matter of artistic and intellectual inspiration. Duncan does not merely restate Pound's meaning; neither does he distort it. Instead, he enters into a 'field of possibility' provided by Pound's work."[12] This means that, "like Pound, Duncan is never satisfied with received notions of what constitutes acceptable poetic sources."[13] Taking to heart Pound's maxim "Make it new," Duncan remains faithful to his mentor by refusing to follow blindly even Pound's own pronouncements. Consequently, Duncan takes Pound as a personal master, but he also includes poets that Pound explicitly recused, such as Wallace Stevens, Walt Whitman, and John Milton. As Beach argues, "the inclusion of Milton in Duncan's canon is part of a self-conscious polemic against what he sees as the restricted lists of acceptable writers maintained by Pound and Olson."[14] Duncan deals with Pound's influence in the second *Passages* poem, "At the Loom," which begins:

A cat's purr
in the hwirr thkk "*thgk, thkk*"
of Kirke's loom on Pound's Cantos
"*I heard a song of that kind . . .*"

my mind a shuttle among
set strings of the music[15]

Pound appears immediately after the opening *Passages* poem, one that functions as a prolonged invocation of Mnemosyne; consequently, Duncan acknowledges Pound as the most important of his forebears, with his mind described as a shuttle on the loom of Pound's *Cantos*. However, although Duncan remains faithful to Pound's aesthetic of poetic collage, Duncan includes in his grand collage many writers whom Pound expressly forbade (Whitman, William Blake, D. H. Lawrence, Stevens) as well as a recurring emphasis on mysticism, something that Pound disliked.[16] Even Duncan's sequence "A Seventeenth Century Suite in Homage to the Metaphysical Genius in English Poetry (1590–1690)" works in opposition to Pound, as Duncan explains: "In Pound aesthetics takes the place of *humanitas*. . . . Humanism presented problems for the aesthetic. And Pound's abhorance [*sic*] of the Renaissance is, I think, the actual abhorance [*sic*] of humanism, but he never saw where he was, he skipped the 16th, 17th, 18th centuries. In many things, he's very much a person of the Enlightenment. My lines really mean a compromise all the way through, and the Renaissance is a compromise."[17] This stance of compromise leads Duncan to oppose respectfully Pound's rigid dos and don'ts. It also informs Duncan's derivative poetics, as it underlies his desire to gather together seemingly disparate or even opposing poetics and ideologies in order to create resonances that bring about fruitful new relationships. Setting these oppositions in relation to each other necessarily brings about conflict, but Duncan views such conflict as positive:

> The President of the Grand Symphony
> for the sake of a dread calm and harmony
> sets into motion a counter-point of contending elements,
> music's divine Strife.[18]

Divine strife, not reified order, underlies Duncan's grand collage, and it both supports and flows from his quotation of disparate authors in his poetry. As Beach notes, "rather than viewing ancestors as alternatives between which he must choose . . . , Duncan sees them as sources of differences that can be combined and recombined in productive endeavours."[19]

In Relation to the Masters: Differing Stances toward Source Material

Strife is also an aspect of Cage's aesthetics. Both Cage and Duncan openly acknowledge their aesthetic masters, but they also refuse to follow blindly those masters' teachings. Consequently, Cage can write through and re-create Joyce's novel to correct its shortcomings, while Duncan can take Pound's collage style and use it to broaden the field of poetic potentiality by including quotations from many authors Pound attempted to exclude. This similarity, though, again reveals significant differences, particularly in relation to notions of voice.

While Cage respects his forebears, his stance is often one of correction in the writings-through. Duncan, however, takes a stance of humility relative his masters; he constantly shows what and how he has learned from his forebears. In this sense, Duncan creates a personal "chrestomathy" through derivation:

> Down this dark corridor, "this *passage*," the poet reminds me,
> and now that Eliot is dead, Williams and H.D. dead,

Ezra alone of my old masters alive,   let me
                    acknowledge Eliot was one of them,   I was
     one of his,   whose   "History has many
          cunning passages, contrived corridors"

     comes into the chestomathy.[20]

A chrestomathy is a "collection of choice passages from an author or authors, *esp.* one compiled to assist in the acquirement of a language."[21] Literally, then, Duncan includes Eliot's passage in his own *Passages* (and Duncan intends the title of his series as a collection of choice passages to ring in resonance in the reader's mind). Perhaps more important is the notion that a chrestomathy teaches the collector how to acquire language, how to speak. In this sense, Duncan's derivative poetics creates for him a compendium of great ideas and of great writing, pieces that taught and continued to teach him how to write properly. Duncan situates himself as a student of his masters' language and ideas, collecting from them the choice bits and then using what he sees as the best from each (including those authors who seem incompatible or who disagree with each other). The result is that Duncan's use of chrestomathy blurs the usually sharp line between creative author and passive reader; instead, as Clément Oudart notes, "Duncan's radically open form is predicated upon a dual practice of reading writings and writing readings."[22] Due to his ongoing creation of a chrestomathy, Duncan's derivations work so that reading becomes a type of writing, and writing becomes a form of reading.

Cage, on the other hand, turns to his masters not to learn how to write properly—Cage determines *how* to write through the restrictive rules he decides upon before starting a writing-through—but strictly in order to learn what to say. In a Cagean writing-through, Cage controls the rules, but he does not control the language, which is determined by the generant text and so was actually determined by the master. In "Writing through the Cantos," for instance, Cage makes it clear that he determined the form: "To write the following text I followed the rule given me by Louis Mink, which I also followed in *Writing for the Third* (and *Fourth*) *Time through Finnegans Wake*, that is, I did not permit the appearance of either letter between two of the name. As in *Writing for the Fourth Time through Finnegans Wake*, I kept an index of the syllables used to present a given letter of the name and I did not permit repetition of these syllables."[23] Formally, Cage controls the text. However, Pound necessarily determines the language, and the first few lines of the poem show that Pound's language and themes shine through the palimpsest:

> and thEn with bronZe lance heads beaRing yet Arms
> sheeP slain Of plUto stroNg praiseD
> thE narrow glaZes the uptuRned nipple As
> sPeak tO rUy oN his gooDs[24]

Pound's themes of martial conflict and ancient rites of sacrifice to Greek gods (both of which Pound borrowed from *The Odyssey*), his interest in classical literature and in commerce, as well as specific phrases such as "the upturned nipple" and the reference to Ruy Díaz remain.[25] By entering into this textual conversation with Pound, however, Cage provides his master with new things to say, shaping and re-presenting Pound's words to make them more appropriate (in Cage's opinion) to Cage's audience, since Pound's overt didacticism, his anti-Semitism, and his Fascist sympathies—in short, Pound's politics—are excised from "Writing through the Cantos," resulting in a text that luxuriates in Pound's language and general themes but removes Pound's hierarchical ideology.

Consequently, Duncan and Cage hold very different authorial positions in relation to their masters. Whereas Duncan learns how to "speak" via his interaction with the masters, Cage provides the masters with new comments and ideas. In terms of voice, Duncan's derivative poetics teaches him to actively speak—he gains his own voice by interacting with his masters and with the community as a whole: "The man individualizes himself, deriving his individuality from the ideas and possibilities at large of manhood in a community that includes all that we know of what man is."[26] Cage, however, remains silent, merely revising his masters' speech in order to correct and update it for a new audience. Duncan's derivative poetics creates an active voice, while Cage's derivative poetics leaves him silent, unable or unwilling to speak for himself; this silence arises, as Michael J. O'Driscoll explains, because Cage's "auditory and verbal catalogs are without intention . . .

[and] therefore without meaning."[27] The result is that "if ambient sounds are called silence only because they do not form part of a musical intention, then Cage's poetic assemblages . . . are silent texts, texts without intention."[28] Emptied of intended meaning, Cagean writings-through leave Cage relatively passive and silent in "his" derivative texts. Although Cage does not completely avoid authorial agency (he determines the form, puts the rules in place, chooses the generant text and which words to edit out), this agency is severely limited; he cannot speak his own ideas because he is limited to using the themes, ideas, and words of the generant text. Like all Cagean aleatoric creations, both literary and musical, the writings-through limit the author's ego in favor of collaboration with the external world of possibilities: "Chance operations are not mysterious sources of 'the right answers.' They are a means of locating a single one among a multiplicity of answers, and, at the same time, of freeing the ego of its taste and memory, its concern for profit and power, of silencing the ego so that the rest of the world has a chance to enter into the ego's own experience whether that lie outside or inside."[29] Rather than excising authorial agency, the writings-through lessen Cage's agency in order to allow this collaboration; rather than effacing the individual, Cage wishes to open the individual to multiple possibilities. Diminishing authorial agency allows for the attentive listening that Cage demands, a point I will work through in the next section.

Anarchism, Organic Form, and Derivative Poetics

The relationship of individual to community that plays out in the different voices that both poets create is deeply connected to the poets' anarchism.[30] Indeed, Duncan and Cage treat derivation as an anarchic action, one designed to reorient society along what they see as the ethical imperative of anarchism. Both poets use derivation to highlight that creativity is, in their opinion, necessarily communal. Duncan implicitly stresses this anarchic communal creativity through his use of chrestomathy, but he also explicitly states his belief in anarchic communalism in many of his poems; for example, in "The First" (from "The Regulators") he emphasizes the anarchic, nonhierarchical nature of a transhistorical, just society: "The people of this nation thruout time are not one but a multitude each from his one / heart/ mind coming forward masst / so you cannot strike down our leader for no *one* leads us."[31] Likewise, "The Multiversity, *Passages* 21" ends with an anarchic affirmation of individual rights, "there being no common good, no commune, / no communion, outside the freedom of / individual volition."[32] His belief in anarchism leads Duncan, in the introduction to *Bending the Bow*, to declare that "the commune of Poetry becomes so real that [the poet] sounds each particle in relation to parts of a great story that he knows will never be completed."[33] Poetry, as the work of many hands (echoed in the loom image in "At the Loom, *Passages* 2," the collage image in "The Collage, *Passages* 6," etc.), necessarily exceeds the work of any one contributing individual, though each individual's contribution helps to shape the whole. This anarchic stance explains Duncan's humility toward his acknowledged masters: the chrestomathy shows Duncan's willingness to place himself in the masters' textual hands, emphasizing both Duncan's individual agency as well as his certainty that he is but one part of a much greater whole.

Although expressed differently, anarchism also underpins Cage's use of derivation. As Cage states in *Anarchy*, a book-length writing-through of quotations drawn from numerous anarchist philosophers and apologists, "Buckminster Fuller believed, and I follow him, that politicians are of no good use. They could be sent as he used to say to outer space and left there without matters getting worse for humanity here on earth. We don't need government."[34] Cage wants both himself and his readers "Not just to say anarchy / but to Do it," and he exhorts his readers "tO find new forms / of liVing / nEw / foRms of living together" that will "overcome / the Patriarchal thinking / the aUthoritarian structures."[35] Derivation supports Cage's anarchism by allowing him an individual relationship with his forebears while, in silencing his voice, letting those forebears speak again. This technique, accomplished by the writing-through method, goes hand in hand with another aspect of Cage's anarchism: listening. Cage believed that only by listening can the individual locate her place in the universe. This last point is best illustrated by briefly discussing one of Cage's best-known musical compositions, *4′33″*, a piece in which the performer sits at a piano for four minutes and thirty-three seconds without playing. As Austin Clarkson points out, critics who focus on the piece as containing the ambient sounds in the performance space "miss Cage's requirement that the act of listening is paramount, and that the minimal condition of the musical fact is the reflexive relationship between sound and the listener."[36] Moreover, because *4′33″* demands attentive, active listening, the "distinction between the self and the other, the listener and the music is minimized."[37] In other words, the listener must pay attention to the world, listening to all sounds equally, becoming simultaneously both a listener and a performer. I would argue that all Cagean writings-through that require such attention to detail provide Cage with similar listening experiences in relation to his forebears. By not speaking, by not writing his own words, he can focus on what his forebears said and are now saying again (in response to Cage's formal choices) for the first time. Cagean nonsensical writings-through clear the reader's mind of the expectation of knowledge one often anticipates receiving from the Great Author and, much like Duncan's humility in relation to his masters, also declare that "the price of enlightenment is the surrender of one's intellectual pretensions, and the acceptance of one's vulnerability in the face of new experience."[38] The individual, whether the reader or the Cagean reader/writer, must constantly understand and negotiate her place in relation to the communal whole. There are no hierarchies with Duncan or Cage, no times when the individual can passively accept a subordinate position; as Cage puts it,

Anarchy
really does have The future
people are talkIng
abOut
it is creative coNduct
As opposed to
subordiNate
conDuct it is positive
individuAlism to follow a way of thinking
that pRoposes you can assume
for your own acTs
respOnsibility
Visibly
rEsponsible
fiRst to yourself and then to society[39]

Cage and Duncan both commit to spreading anarchic principles throughout society and attempt to actively portray those principles in their writing in order to teach their readers a more ethically sound relationship between individuals and between individuals and their communities.

Part of the two poets' commitment to anarchism is a belief that an organic order underlies all of creation. Anarchism is the best ethical situation when one believes that nature has always already determined the best relationship between its elements, including human beings. As Duncan puts it, "central to and defining the poetics I am trying to suggest here is the conviction that the order man may contrive or impose upon the things about him or upon his own language is trivial beside the divine order or natural order *he may discover in them*."[40] Duncan argues that the individual must remain constantly attentive to his surroundings, both natural and textual, and must obey the order found in those surroundings. This is derivation at its most broad, not just in poetry but in ethical living in general. The individual must trust the larger whole (the community of individuals or the whole of poetry), even though the order contained in that wholeness is too large for any individual to understand: "Our engagement with knowing, with craft and lore, our demand for truth is not to reach a conclusion, but to keep our exposure to what we do not know, to confront our wish and our need beyond habit and capability, beyond what we can take for granted."[41] The individual may not understand the larger whole, but, by remaining attentive, she can engage with that whole, which remains fluid, noncontainable, and never-ending. Consequently, the individual cannot dismiss anything out of hand, since for Duncan "nothing is trivial" and "meaning and the potential for feeling permeate or saturate everything, no matter how apparently insignificant."[42] It also means that our world exists in a state of constant change, that "what is complete but rests in the momentary illusion," and that "no one / nor poet / nor writer of words // can contrive to do justice to the beauty of that / design he designs from."[43] No *one* can do the whole justice; only the communal entity can, and only then when the communal entity follows the organic rules of anarchism.

Cage also believes there is an organic order underlying all of creation; it is this belief that allows him to embrace aleatory compositional methods. Specifically, Cage's Zen studies fuel his belief that, as Gudrun M. Grabher says, "order is no longer the network of the human mind cast on the world but, rather, a structure that is inherent in reality."[44] For Cage, this belief means that chance is not chance, since everything is always already naturally ordered. As with Duncan, perceiving this natural order requires for Cage the individual's attention; Cage comments in the introduction to his lecture "Indeterminacy" (comprised of ninety stories, paratactically combined):

> The continuity of the stories as recorded was not planned. I simply made a list of all the stories I could think of and checked them off as I wrote them. . . . My intention in putting the stories together in an unplanned way was to suggest that all things—stories, incidental sounds from the environment, and, by extensions, beings—are related, and that this complexity is more evident when it is not oversimplified by an idea of relationship in one person's mind.[45]

Cage believes, like Duncan, that the organic order underlying creation exceeds any individual's comprehension. All one can do is let go of the belief in individual order and instead "give up the desire to control sound . . . and set about discovering means to let sounds be themselves rather than vehicles for man-made theories or expressions of human sentiments."[46] Although this last comment pertains to music, it applies equally well to Cage's writing-through poems, such as "Empty Words," which attempts to "transition" Henry David Thoreau's writings "from language to music."[47] When both Duncan and Cage engage in derivative poetics, they implicitly place their faith in an anarchic, organic order—Duncan quotes from his diverse sources to show an unforeseen commonality in these sources, while Cage writes through his forebears to show that any text contains a myriad of other possible texts. Neither poet relies on chance in these actions, precisely because they both believe that organic order denies the possibility of random chance.

The poets offer two complementary versions of anarchic derivative ethics: Duncan's work focuses on the role the community plays in shaping the individual, while Cage's focuses on the individual who helps shape the community.

Areas of Influence

For Duncan, influence mostly flows from the communal to the individual, as with a chrestomathy. The community must be in place in order to show the individual how to act ethically. For example, in "The Architecture, *Passages* 9" Duncan shows that the structure (literally of the house but figuratively of the community) comes from the communal whole. The poem begins with the first of several lengthy quotations from Gustave Stickley's 1909 book *Craftsman Homes*: "It must have recesses. There is a great charm in a room broken up in plan, where that slight feeling of mystery is given to it which arises when you cannot see the whole room from any one place . . . when there is always something around the corner."[48] A didactic tag, Stickley's pronouncement applies to the method of writing the poem, as Duncan darts between subjects, references, and quotations, never completely finishing one before beginning the next. Duncan, the adopted son of an architect, openly derives his structural form from Stickley, quoting from *Craftsman Homes* several times throughout the poem, including a passage that makes explicit the link between community and individual: "The staircase, instead of being hidden away in a small hall or treated as a necessary evil, made one of the most beautiful and prominent features of the room because it forms a link between the social part of the house and the upper regions."[49] The upper regions are the place of private, individual space; one enters that space by going through the "social part of the house," and Stickley and Duncan can prize the staircase as the link between the two regions. This emphasis on the connection between the regions illustrates Duncan's belief that "we ourselves can know no good apart / from the good of all men."[50] Moreover, as Thomas Gardner suggests, the metaphor of the architect involves combining separate elements into one unit: "The act of creating a household is, in fact, the act of bringing together, into an expanding but coherent structure, things that had been separate and distant."[51]

Although Duncan usually focuses on how influence flows from the communal to the individual, he also recognizes that, having learned from society one's ethical place *in* society, the individual then becomes a part of the society that influences other individuals. As he states in "Of Empire" (from "Dante Études"),

The individual man   having his own nature and truth
    and appropriate thereto   his household
outlined   in relation to groups   he finds
    himself in   freely attending, changing,
    electing,   or joining to carry forward
        the idea, the insistent phrase,
        the needed resonance   into action,

seeks to realize harmonies in his district[52]

However, one should note that Duncan believes that even after the individual begins influencing others (by becoming a "master"), that individual still must respect the needs of the community. As Stephen Collis states, "Duncan envisions a poetic anarchism that checks the ego . . . without giving authority over to some centre. Authority is thus given to the centreless commons—all of past poetry echoing in Duncan's own, the entire field of language over which many 'masters' stand and are in turn 'servants' of the commons once again."[53] In other words, becoming a master does not mean that the individual attains dominance over others; masters must maintain their ethical responsibilities as individual members of the group.

This duty of the individual to her society is what Cage focuses on in his derivative work. As he says in "The Future of Music," "less anarchic kinds of music give examples of less anarchic states of society. The masterpieces of Western music exemplify monarchies and dictatorships. . . . By making musical situations which are analogies to desirable social circumstances which we do not have yet, we make music suggestive and relevant to the serious questions which face Mankind."[54] In choosing to write through two of the dominant and dominating texts of modernism, Pound's *Cantos* and Joyce's *Finnegans Wake*, Cage does more than enter into a textual conversation with Pound or Joyce, and he does more than remove what he sees as the Fascist holdovers of syntax from Joyce's novel or the obvious Fascism of Pound's poetry; by creating a text that literally anyone could create, given the time or interest, Cage removes the aura of artistic virtuosity from the generant texts. Cage moves the emphasis from masterpieces created by great individuals who stood above the crowd to texts that emphasize the individual who refuses to pronounce or claim authority. Cage's writings-through are not *his* writings but rather his recycling of another writer's words. Rather than art, Cage wishes to create objects that engage with everyday life:

> WHEN WE SEPARATE MUSIC FROM LIFE WHAT WE GET IS ART (A COMPENDIUM OF MASTERPIECES). WITH CONTEMPORARY MUSIC, WHEN IT IS ACTUALLY CONTEMPORARY, WE HAVE NO TIME TO MAKE THAT SEPARATION (WHICH PROTECTS US FROM LIVING), AND SO CONTEMPORARY MUSIC IS NOT SO MUCH ART AS IT IS LIFE AND ANY ONE MAKING IT NO SOONER FINISHES ONE OF IT THAN HE BEGINS MAKING ANOTHER JUST AS PEOPLE KEEP ON WASHING DISHES, BRUSHING THEIR TEETH, GETTING SLEEPY, AND SO ON.[55]

Cage writes through these texts both to correct the egoism of Pound and Joyce as well as to silence himself. He presents in the nonsensical derived texts examples of how to avoid setting oneself above or aside from the community. Written in concert with another author, these writings-through show the reader how to ethically remove her ego from her actions and thus open herself to others' influence. Because the writings-through silence Cage, they allow someone or something else to speak. Consequently, "having nothing to say," Christopher Schultis explains, "allows [the] environment the opportunity to speak."[56] This move toward silencing the self so that the environment (including all contiguous communities) can speak completes, in a sense, the ethical circle Duncan began: for Duncan, the community must influence the individual, who eventually learns how to become part of the ethical community; for Cage, the individual must first act ethically toward the community, refusing to set herself above or apart, thus showing that community how its individuals should act ethically, and then the community can ethically engage with the individual without seeking to dominate or overwhelm the individual. Rather than contradictory, these two forms of influence combine into a complete whole, a cycle of influence that is only partly drawn in either Duncan's or Cage's work.

Derivation is central to both Duncan's and Cage's ethical and aesthetic programs. Although they present their derivations in different ways, both share a deeply held belief that derivative poetics will help bring about anarchism. Consequently, both poets write didactically, trying to teach their readers through form and content that anarchism provides an ethical solution to many of the contemporary world's problems. Duncan uses an emphasis on chrestomathy to teach the reader how to enact a personal anarchism. Cage, in the writings-through, shows the reader how to anarchically silence the self, thus deprivileging the Western world's emphasis on the individual and opening the reader up to the anarchic community. Therefore, though Duncan focuses on the community's influence on the individual while Cage emphasizes the individual's proper relationship with the community, both use derivative poetics to further their anarchistic ethics. They write quite differently, but, as Duncan acknowledges, their shared belief in an organic form underlying all of creation implicitly aligns their derivative poetics:

> As for Music—to know this is to know the order of all things
> set together in a key of diversities
>
> is a sweet harmony.
> [. . .]
> "By Him, the Holy Spirit, all intercourse and converse
> awake and asleep.
>
> "His intermediate powers are many,
> and this one is Eros"
>
> John Cage's open scales
>
> "who will be faced with the entire field of sound."[57]

Notes

1. Both were white males born into educated middle-class households and raised in California in the 1910s, both were homosexual (though both had short-lived heterosexual marriages as younger men), both had lifelong relationships with important artists who worked in nonliterary disciplines (Cage's relationship with the dancer/choreographer Merce Cunningham began in 1945 and lasted until Cage's death in 1992; Duncan's relationship with the visual artist Jess Collins began in 1950 and lasted until Duncan's death in 1988).
2. Duncan, introduction to *Bending the Bow*, v–vi.

3. Ibid., 9.
4. Robert Duncan, "The Delirium of Meaning: Edmond Jabès," in Duncan, *A Selected Prose*, 206.
5. Duncan, introduction to *Bending the Bow*, vii
6. Ibid., 88.
7. Passler, "Inventing a Tradition," 133.
8. John Cage, "Writing for the Second Time through *Finnegans Wake*," in Cage, *Empty Words*, 134.
9. Ibid.
10. Ibid., 137.
11. John Cage, "Writing through the Cantos," in Cage, *X*, 109.
12. Beach, *ABC of Influence*, 137.
13. Ibid.
14. Ibid., 138.
15. Duncan, *Bending the Bow*, 11–13.
16. For Lawrence, see ibid., 40–45, 70–73, 81–83; for Stevens, see Duncan, *Ground Work: Before the War*, 10.
17. Robert Duncan, interview with Michael André Bernstein and Burton Hatlen, 95.
18. Duncan, *Bending the Bow*, 126.
19. Beach, *ABC of Influence*, 141.
20. Duncan, *Bending the Bow*, 78.
21. *Oxford English Dictionary*, 3rd ed., s.v. "chrestomathy," http://dictionary.oed.com.
22. Oudart, "Genreading and Underwriting."
23. Cage, "Writing through the Cantos," 109.
24. Ibid.
25. Ezra Pound, "Canto III," in Pound, *Cantos*, 11, line 16.
26. Duncan, *The H.D. Book*, 363–64.
27. O'Driscoll, "Silent Texts and Empty Words," 631.
28. Ibid., 632.
29. John Cage, preface to "Lecture on the Weather," in Cage, *Empty Words*, 5.
30. Both poets wrote and spoke openly about their belief in anarchism, which meant for them not chaos but an ethical society without government. In his introduction to *Anarchy*, Cage supports Henry David Thoreau's comment that "that government is best which governs not at all" (v). Robert J. Bertholf summarizes Duncan's anarchism thusly: "The individual is free to act as long as his actions do not impinge on the freedom to act of other people. . . . Essential freedom means living in a society without government" ("Decision at the Apo-

gee," 4–5). For both poets, and for anarchists generally, the absence of government will bring about greater individual freedom, but it will also require from everyone a high level of personal responsibility.

31. Duncan, *Ground Work: In the Dark*, 61.
32. Duncan, *Bending the Bow*, 73.
33. Ibid., vi.
34. Cage, *Anarchy*, v.
35. Cage, "Overpopulation and Art," 19, 23.
36. Clarkson, "The Intent of the Musical Moment," 70.
37. Ibid.
38. Junkerman, "nEw / foRms of living together," 52.
39. Cage, "Overpopulation and Art," 37.
40. Robert Duncan, "Towards an Open Universe," in Duncan, *A Selected Prose*, 6, emphasis mine.
41. Ibid., 12.
42. Nathaniel Mackey, "Gassire's Lute: Robert Duncan's Vietnam War Poems," in Mackey, *Paracritical Hinge*, 101.
43. Duncan, *Ground Work: In the Dark*, 70; Duncan, *Ground Work: Before the War*, 21.
44. Grabher, "Playing Hide and Seek," 74.
45. John Cage, "Indeterminacy," in Cage, *Silence*, 260.
46. John Cage, "Experimental Music," in ibid., 10.
47. John Cage, "Empty Words," in Cage, *Empty Words*, 65.
48. Duncan, *Bending the Bow*, 26.
49. Ibid., 27.
50. Ibid., 66.
51. Gardner, "Where We Are," 303.
52. Duncan, *Ground Work: Before the War*, 105.
53. Collis, "A Duncan Etude."
54. John Cage, "The Future of Music," in Cage, *Empty Words*, 183.
55. John Cage, "Composition as Process," in Cage, *Silence*, 44.
56. Schultis, "Silencing the Sounded Self," 316.
57. Duncan, *Bending the Bow*, 62.

CHAPTER ELEVEN

The Poets' War: Inflation, Complicity, and the Daimonic

J. P. CRAIG

Robert Duncan had an early and continuing impact on Nathaniel Mackey's poetry. Mackey's dissertation, "Call Me Tantra: Open Field Poetics as Muse," is primarily a study of Duncan's work. Mackey admits to a "scared" awe of Duncan prior to meeting him in the late 1970s; after their first meeting, Mackey frequently spent time with Duncan when he visited San Francisco.[1] Mackey's ideas about inspiration and opposition have a great deal in common with Duncan's, particularly in that both emphasize the role of what Robin Blaser calls the "outside" in the poem's ethical and political engagements.[2] Both Duncan and Mackey believe the poet shouldn't try to "push" his poems in a certain direction but should instead let the organic development of his materials determine the form and theme of his poems. Yet these two poets see the production of their poems as an ethical activity engaging the political sphere. Both Mackey and Duncan attempt to explain and understand this paradox through figures of daimonic inspiration that suggest the benefits and dangers accruing from claiming to be inhabited by the other.

To begin with, this anachronistic appeal to a daimon-muse captures something of the self lost in our contemporary rush to condemn what Mackey characterizes in an interview with Ed Foster as the oversimplifications of "inflated transcendentalism" (*PH*, 273). In his discussion with Foster of the possibility for lyric poetry to transcend "ethnic, gender, racial and other forms of collective identity" (272), Mackey points out that, though such transcendence is surely suspect, it is equally an oversimplification to suggest that it takes "some kind of naiveté or presumption to even bother to aspire to something beyond [one's particular identity], something that troubles those boundaries" (273). The lyric, Mackey claims, works the ground between these two extremes and works that ground "with a certain hesitation and tentativeness that has to do with being in that complicated liminal area in which there are no easy assurances" (273). A great deal of that hesitation emerges from an attitude toward poesis and language that Mackey figures through Lorca's notion of *duende*, which in its simplest figurations is a "gremlin or spirit" that "raises and articulates trouble."[3] In the moment of, or under the influence of, duende, Mackey says in "Cante Moro," an essay on duende's cross-cultural impact on the New American Poetry, "one has worked beyond oneself. It is as if the language itself takes over. Something beyond the will, the conscious design or desire of the poet, is active, something that goes beyond univocal, unequivocal control" (199). Mackey's use here of duende to figure the ways in which "language itself takes over" resonates with Duncan's use of Lorca's notion of duende in his collection *Caesar's Gate* as a figure for the simultaneously autocratic and heretical force of poesis in which it appears to the poet as a "fairy power, the visitation from the Hill of Dreams or the gypsy camp of the Dead, freed from reality."[4] For both poets, duende represents, as Duncan puts it, "the speaking more than one knew what" or, as Mackey puts it, the "taking over of one's voice by another voice" (*CG*, xxii; *PH*, 186).

This daimonic attitude toward poesis emerges in Mackey's poetry as an ongoing appeal to otherness. But this is not the otherness of alienation; it is instead a passionate "reaching for another voice" (*PH*, 192). For Mackey, duende serves as an acknowledgment of the alien and different as they impinge upon the self. And, as in Whitman's "every atom belonging to me as good belongs to you," this rupture of the self is seen not as a dissipation or weakening of the self but as a widening of the self.[5] Relinquishing the desire for some certainties provides an intimate and certain acquaintance with what we cannot or do not know or attain. From this perspective, we know ourselves as individual leaves of the collective grass; we are neither leaf nor grass but a tension between countable and uncountable states of being. Paul Naylor accurately describes this tendency of Mackey in his essay "Some Ecstatic Elsewhere," the title of which is taken from the opening poem of Mackey's collection *Whatsaid Serif*:

> An advocacy of ecstasy runs throughout Mackey's book [*Whatsaid Serif*], and many of the poems narrate a series of journeys toward an "elsewhere" that seems to recede upon arrival. But what is the nature of the "elsewhere" ecstatic experience promises? The English word *ecstasy* derives from the Greek word *ekstasis*, which refers to a being put out of its place or standing outside of itself as the result of a trance or a dreamlike state. The "elsewhere" of ecstasy is that which is outside of the everyday subjectivity of those having such an experience. In other words, ecstatic experience is a means of getting outside the self.[6]

In ecstasy one's self becomes other; ecstasy as poetic figure or poetic practice speaks to a desire to be among the alien and different, to be alien and different to one's own self. Mackey figures this emphasis on difference as a "forking of the voice," a "splitting" or "breaking" of the voice (*PH*, 193). In reaching for this other voice, in striving for a dialogical quality within itself, the voice of the poem forks and doubles, admitting imperfection in its passionate effort to attain the voice of the other. The ecstatic effort Naylor describes is a passionate effort toward a sort of union with the other. This effort to be one with the other, to speak with the other's voice, will always fail; as Mackey puts it, in the grip of duende, "something beyond your grasp of it grabs you" (191). Though you try to possess the other, you find yourself possessed, and the other proves itself impossible to know completely.

What Mackey says for language, for poetry—this "fugitivity" of the other—has implications for poetry's ability to do political work. Mackey himself makes no bones about the difficulty he finds in moving from poesis to cultural action, as is clear in his address to the 1989 Poetry for the Next Society symposium of the Poetry Project at Saint Mark's Church, "Poetry for the Next Society: Design for Continuing Investigation." From this address we learn that he sees a clear fracture between poetry and the present, perhaps even the future. The goal of this conference was to anticipate what future poetry might be like. Instead—as is so often the case among poets—many presentations offered a lament for the poverty of poetry's current station. Mackey begins his address with a critique of both the conference's intended project and the side effect of lamentation. He suggests that the unacknowledged goal of such a project is "a new kind of prominence or even centrality for poetry, a greater salience for poetry in the society's cultural consumption patterns."[7] He suggests that the "anxiety" and "impatience" of the laments about poetry's status emerge from this buried goal. He further claims that conferees' suggestions that poetry take up "pornography" or "billboards" for a medium emerge from this unacknowledged goal. He ends his list of conferees' proposals for ways that "poetry might get closer to the mainstream" on a sour note: "Houston Baker put in his vote for Rap, and Marjorie Perloff seemed to think that some kind of Wittgensteinian Canadian poetry would be the poetry of the future. Allen Ginsberg spoke for a poetry of grief, which of the three is the one I'd bet on." Mackey's skeptical appreciation of these suggestions springs from his belief that such suggestions emerge from "a recognition of the peripherality of poetry to the society's concerns." He asks, do we *really* want poetry to become another one of "society's cultural consumption patterns"? Instead he says, "My sense of it is that for quite a while poetry will continue to be *against* the society and we would need to talk about what kinds of changes would have to take place for that to not be the case."[8]

In essence, society may not yet be worthy of its poetry. If here we have echoes of Stein's notion that art must await its contemporaries, we can hear more clearly Duncan: "So, what kind of society will the next society be? And what are the implications of that for poetics? . . . We have to ask will there be a society that we can be for and, if so, what kind of society that would be. I kept thinking of Robert Duncan's line 'would-be shaman of no tribe I know.' I wonder what kind of tribe we're going to bring about in the next society."[9] Nested in Duncan's proposed role of "would-be shaman of no tribe" is Ezra Pound's desire to lead his tribe by telling its tale, a desire that could be seen as one avenue to his advocacy of Fascism.[10] Duncan acknowledges in *Caesar's Gate* that his poetry aspires to a godlike "autocracy" (xvii). Like Pound, who could not tolerate the "errors and wrecks" of his Cantos, Duncan finds that his own structures will not cohere.[11] Rather, he is continually "betrayed by his Poetry," which taunts him with "critical voices" of its own (*CG*, xvii). Given such an unruly poetry, the poet must displace his aspirations for it, and for the real that it would govern, into the ever-receding future. Nonetheless, the subjunctive, wistful mood of Duncan's "would-be shaman" and would-be tribe voices dissatisfaction with the present. In Mackey's citation, this dissatisfaction expands to include suggestions that poetry change to accommodate the coming society. Mackey's separation of the goals of poetry and the present state of society in his "Poetry for the Next Society" address clearly derives from Duncan's own belief that the poet is, like the God of the Gnostics, "*guilty* of his creation" (*CG*, xvii). In considering Duncan's break with Denise Levertov over how a poet should oppose war, Mackey finds that the "gremlin" of inspiration can monkey-wrench the poet's communication with the other, effectively short-circuiting the poem's ability to derive itself from that interplay.

THE REASON FOR Duncan's concern about Levertov's increasingly harsh opposition to the Vietnam War can be found in passages such as the one below from her introduction to *To Stay Alive* (1971). After first observing that "Gandhi himself" said it was better to "cultivate the art of killing and being killed rather than in a cowardly manner to flee from danger," she goes on to say, somewhat paradoxically, that "in the later sections of [this book] the sense of who the guardians of life, of integrity, are, is extended to include not only those who 'disdain to kill' but all who struggle, violently if need be, to pull down this obscene system before it destroys all life on earth."[12] As both anarchist and pacifist, Duncan was especially troubled by his friend's advocacy of violence for the sake of peace. He wrote to Levertov: "If we were to read the *content* of the statement at the same level as we do in dream analysis, the American general's 'In order to save the village it was necessary to destroy it' is identical" to Levertov's own appeal for a violent pacifism.[13] Levertov resented such presumption and seeming misunderstanding from her longtime friend.

However, it was not a misunderstanding on Duncan's part but rather a different understanding of the poet's role in wartime, an understanding akin to Mackey's suggestion that poetry is against society rather than for it. By 1970, when he started to criticize Levertov as a Kali figure, Duncan already had developed in *The H.D. Book* the idea that the artist and the pacifist inhabit a separate reality, one continually under attack by more pragmatic people. There is no room in this belief for compromise; there is no way to accommodate poetry to the Next Society, for poetry is already the Next Society. And Duncan was no doubt also troubled by Levertov's casual equation of life and integrity (in her words, "the guardians of life, of integrity"), for he demands integrities rather than integrity. He insists that humanity not be integrated and homogenized. For him to be an integral part of a Communist or capitalist society is to be compelled to subscribe to one unchanging value. In political terms, Duncan is ever ready to be a heretic or a traitor, but he is reluctant to be a member; he prefers to be a "would-be shaman of no tribe"—the role both he and Mackey see as proper to the poet. From Duncan's perspective, Levertov's solution had made her a part of the problem.

Mackey, however, sees a similar tendency in Duncan's own poetry. In an essay titled "Gassire's Lute: Robert Duncan's Vietnam War Poems," Mackey addresses the ways in which the "would-be shaman" courts a hubris that invites complicity with the evils he would oppose. Working from a reading of Duncan's antiwar poems, Mackey suggests that the opposing poet is already a species of devil, puffed up at times with demons of inspiration. "Gassire's Lute" is an attempt to reconcile poetry's accounts of confidence and error, accounts that quickly get out of balance when a poet strives against war. In particular, Mackey considers Duncan's essay "Man's Fulfillment in Order and Strife" (1969), in which Duncan banishes Lyndon Johnson and warmongers like him from the human race, writing that "such men have dehumanized themselves, removed themselves from the human consequences of their acts and from the disorders that underlie their ratiocinations" (*PH*, 139).

The problem with Johnson for Duncan is that he is closed off to the world and to history. If, he argues, Johnson and men like him did not "benefit" (these are Mackey's words) from "official identity and idealism," they would "come into the full obsessional sickness of soul of their human state" (*PH*,

139). Idealism and office mask the symptoms of a deeper complaint. Mackey notes that, for Duncan, not only are Johnson and his ilk numb, but they are also clumsy. Addressing war in terms of inspiration in his poem "The Soldiers," Duncan writes that Johnson was "no inspired poet but making it badly, / amassing his own history in murder and sacrifice" in Vietnam.[14] Mackey's response to Duncan's claim is to ask, in a contrarian fashion Duncan might well appreciate, "But what if Johnson *were* inspired?" (83). His inspiration might, after all, share duende's darker tendencies. Mackey goes on to link the poet's dark inspiration with the West African myth of Gassire's lute.

The isolation, inspiration, and bloodshed in many of Duncan's own poems resonate for Mackey with the myth of Gassire's lute, in which the warrior-prince Gassire sacrifices his eight sons and his kingdom for eloquence. In this myth, first recorded for Europeans by Leo Frobenius in the early 1900s, Gassire is the eldest son of the king of Wagadu, a king whose reign and life go on long enough to frustrate his son's ambition.[15] But Gassire's aspirations are altered when, out hunting, he hears a quail singing a song to her chicks. This song fills his heart, and, pursuing it, he learns from a griot that it is called the "Dausi" and that he can acquire the power to sing it too—but at a cost. The griot tells Gassire that he will never become king but that he will become a griot and that this transformation will be the downfall of Wagadu. Gassire haughtily replies, "Wagadu can go to blazes!"

A time of war then comes for Wagadu. In each battle Gassire fights like a *damo*, a creature Frobenius's informant could not identify but that he described to Frobenius as "a terrifying creature." And in each battle Gassire loses a son, and as he carries his sons home each day, their blood drips onto the lute Gassire carries slung over his back. On the eighth day of war, Gassire is banished from Wagadu with his remaining family. In a later night of his exile, Gassire awakens to a song. When he realizes it is his bloodstained lute, untouched in the corner, singing the "Dausi," he collapses in tears. At that instant, his father dies, and Wagadu disappears (*PH*, 71–73).

In this myth of a would-be artist driven by ambition into a terrifying, bestial rage that feeds his art with blood and a kingdom, Mackey sees an analogue to Duncan's rage against war and sees in Duncan a dehumanization like that which Duncan himself imputes to Johnson. What if this is inspiration? What if a damo is the poet's daimon? If it is, Mackey suggests that "our inspiration is also our peril, a risk of inflation whose would-be rise can take us down into Hell. The singer of the tale is caught between cosmology (the claim that for better and for worse this is how it is) and morality (the claim that were it not for human vices things would turn out well)" (*PH*, 74). This dilemma of cosmology or morality reveals to Mackey something of the nature of being that manifests itself in the daimonic as a figure for inspiration. We are all sometimes caught in contradictions between "cosmology" and "morality," just as we can catch Duncan in contradiction when we read him telling Levertov in an all-caps shout that war is human nature and in the same year claiming in "Man's Fulfillment in Order and Strife" that Johnson's inhumanity leads him to war.[16] In placing himself at a remove and allowing these judgments, Duncan arrogates to himself much the same distance for which he damns Johnson. But Mackey reminds us that this is the nature of inspiration:

> The age-old sense of inspiration as an inspiriting, an invasion of a human vessel by a non-human daimon or spirit, carries the danger of a loss of touch with human realities and feelings. Taken seriously, the notion complicates and unsettles what we mean by "human," since if we're subject to such invasions our susceptibility has to be a factor of what being human means. Ideology and morality tend to posit fixed notions of what is properly to be regarded as human, notions to which the otherness of inspiration may pose a threat. We see Duncan caught in this complication. (*PH*, 83)

What if, he is asking, the damo does enter the poet who welcomes it? If an inspired poet-prince becomes inhabited by a monster, then Johnson's monstrosity evidences inspiration of a similar order—disorder as *Dis*-order. For Gassire, for Johnson, and even for Duncan, inspiration, being filled with the spirit, invites a single-mindedness. Fixed upon a single creative goal, these makers feed their lutes with blood, sacrifice love to inspiration. They cease to respond and instead go to war, sacrificing brothers, fathers, and the kingdom itself.

In *The H.D. Book* Duncan acknowledges that war is congenial to the poet's needs.[17] Mackey believes that Duncan's diagnosis of "disorders that underlie" the thought of men like Johnson is indebted to the idea of war as a revelatory symptom.[18]

> But the war is also, [Duncan] points out, an event to be gloated over, if not celebrated, an event which bodies forth on a blatant scale what was suspected of the dominant order all along. The war provides H.D. with an opportunity, in *Trilogy*, to respond to that order's dismissal of poetry, to take the offensive with an "I told you so." The manifestly destructive, homicidal imperative of the reigning sense of things elevates the outcast to a privileged position. The relegation of the poet to the absolute fringes of the dominant order allows her to dissociate herself from the war, from the suicidal values it brings to light. "This," she can say, "is not our field, / we have not sown this." (*PH*, 96–97)

The war's attack on poetic value provides these poets, Duncan and H.D., an opportunity to counterattack with a defense of poetic value. It is, after all, Levertov's abandonment of the cause of poetry to instead deploy the poem as what Michael Davidson calls "a record of personal positions and responses to historical events," in essence her abandonment of poetry as a next society, that so rankled Duncan.[19] Duncan would have it, much as H.D. would, that the distance that dehumanizes Johnson humanizes themselves. Both are invested fully in a vision of the poet as conduit of a more human(e) value, but this vatic stance partakes of a distance from which these poets can say with Gassire that "Wagadu can go to blazes!"

The damning of the present society in the myth of Gassire's lute appealed to and was cited by Pound, H.D., Duncan, and Olson. In part this is an artifact of the moderation of modernist nihilism coming after the shock and loss of the First World War. In the myth the warrior-poet shouts, "Wagadu can go to blazes!" In the cycle of myths that is sung in the "Dausi," Wagadu goes to blazes again and again, only to reappear and be destroyed again a total of four times, one for each cardinal direction. Each apocalypse presages rebirth, as if each instance of the city were a rough draft of the next: "Every time that the guilt of man caused Wagadu to disappear," Frobenius's *African*

Genesis reads, "she won a new beauty which made the splendor of her next appearance still more glorious."[20] Like H.D. in her *Trilogy*, Pound, Olson, and Duncan claim to see what "our" schematizing, synoptic, Gorgon-great eye cannot—at some cost to themselves. Mackey suggests that this is one of the dangerous double edges of poetry. As he says in an interview with Paul Naylor, poetry not only has the ability to "console suffering or to compensate or sublimate trouble," but it also can "in fact instigate trouble" through this very capacity to console (*PH*, 347). Part of the particular appeal of the myth of Gassire's lute for him at the time he wrote "Gassire's Lute: Robert Duncan's Vietnam War Poems" was that Gassire's tale stood "for idealization itself, idealizing memory or expectation and the trouble in mind and outside the mind it can create" (348).

This greater emphasis on trouble and danger distinguishes Mackey somewhat from Duncan. This divergence appears in their appeals to different myths of autochthonous peoples. Duncan both subscribes to and questions the idea of perfectibility in his recourse to the "Golden Ones" of Greek myth, the *epichthonoi* in "Before the Judgment, *Passages* 35." The epichthonoi appear in Duncan's poem as a sort of omnipresent conscience, "ancestral spirits of whatever good we know" who know "what the heart secretly knows."[21] To the ancient Greeks, the epichthonoi were the ghosts from a prior perfect, peaceful, and productive golden age, but they are inaudible and invisible to the present. Their only role is to hang around and observe our comparatively poor showing. In his essay "Prophetic Frustrations," Peter O'Leary reads this inaccessibility as a moderation of the desire for perfection: "Duncan's 'Golden Ones' serve as emblems of the lost covenant, of the speech vanished with their assumption into a ghostlier existence. They exist on the one hand as proof of the certainty of his prophecy but on the other as reproof of its inherent failure, because they are mute to the world which cannot hear them or understand their wisdom. Their swarming in the honeycomb of memory is as vital as it is entombed, only faint buzzings in our unconscious."[22] Existing now only as "faint buzzings," the epichthonoi serve well as an emblem of Mackey's interpretation of Duncan's poesis, which demands that the poet attend to language as revelatory and intoxicating, informing and misleading.

Unlike Duncan, who offers the image of a failed prior perfection in the

Golden Ones, Mackey looks to a myth of original imperfection told by the North African Dogon people. For Mackey, the Dogon's mythic ancestors, the Andoumboulou, are "rough drafts" of humanity. The Andoumboulou appear often in Mackey's creative and critical work, most notably as the namesake of his long poetic sequence "Song of the Andoumboulou," which, like Duncan's *Passages* series, is an ongoing, discontinuous sequence of poems that reveal the originary, fundamental fissures and tensions in language and culture through parataxis and soundplay. Similarly, in Dogon myth the Andoumboulou were "flawed, failed precursors of humans."[23] The Andoumboulou were flawed because they had sprung from the creator-god Yurugu's incestuous coupling with his own placenta; their mother was only an aspect of a male god who had already lost the feminine half of his soul in his rush to be born.[24] Rather than declining from a lost perfection, as in Duncan's cosmology, humanity is only a continuation of past imperfection and incompletion.

For Paul Naylor, the reconciliation of the "lost twinness" passed to the Andoumboulou by their father, Yurugu, is a "central preoccupation" of Mackey's poetry.[25] As ghostly ancestral spirits, the Andoumboulou "raise important questions concerning our access to history and tradition," but their implications for the future differ from that of Duncan's epichthonoi.[26] As invisible, mute, and perfect witnesses, the Golden Ones serve as somewhat of a reproof, as a reminder of what we have lost. Already imperfect, the Andoumboulou suggest what we have to gain. But in both cases the idea of a flaw as a possibility—as warning or warrant—is central. In reminding the poet that he or she is flawed, both the Andoumboulou and the Golden Ones, in the context of Mackey's interests, serve as a reminder that the poet's daimon may be a damo, that he or she may be bloodthirsty in a desire to damn the other or to use conflict as an occasion for poetry. Mackey applies the idea of duende as a corrective model for the poet's inspiration because its impish, gremlin nature is a reminder of the possibility that the poet may do harm. At the same time, duende encourages the poet to accept the flaw that comes with the "forking of the voice" that seeks to admit the other into his song as an ethically necessary but always unsuccessful effort to reconcile the "lost twinness" of humanity suggested by the Andoumboulou (*PH*, 193).

In his reading of Duncan's "A Lammas Tiding" and "My Mother Would Be a Falconress," Mackey demonstrates how notions of flaw and failure serve to warn against or correct Duncan's tendencies toward violence, and this reading illustrates how duende informs Mackey's own poetics as he develops them in relation to Duncan's. Coming just before "My Mother Would Be a Falconress" in *Bending the Bow*, "A Lammas Tiding" gives the circumstances of the arrival in a dream of the first lines of "My Mother Would Be a Falconress." In it he writes:

> Searching out the poetic lore of what America is, I had been reading Blake's *Vision of the Daughters of Albion* these last few nights just before going to sleep. "*With what sense is it that the chicken shuns the ravenous hawk?*" I had read, and I said to myself, yes, there are bloody men, and I am not one of them but of chicken-kind, for I would never draw blood. Which goes to show one should be careful of vain self-delusions entertaind at bedtime. For now my dream would have me a hawk. And, hearing my account, Jess comments: "Especially since chickens do draw blood." Whereupon, I recall those horrible cannibalistic hens I tended at Treesbank, that needed only the first sign of blood that might be left after egg-laying to tear at each other, bloody not from hunger but from malice, like so many poets furious in their pecking order.[27]

"A Lammas Tiding" is analogous to Mackey's recitation of the myth of Gassire's lute. Like the myth, which begins with a quail singing to her chicks, Duncan's "A Lammas Tiding" situates "My Mother Would Be a Falconress" in a personal and domestic setting. And, just as Gassire's quest for the ability to sing the "Dausi" has implications for his kingdom, Duncan applies the revelation figured in "My Mother Would Be a Falconress" more globally to poetic communities—those "pecking orders"—and to national identity—to "what America is." Ruminating that "dreams ever betray our minds," Duncan also observes "a curious displacement upward."[28] The comment of his domestic partner, Jess, serves to remind Duncan that his chicken aspiration has a hawkish appetite, much as Gassire's quest for poetry transforms him into a bloodthirsty damo. In Mackey's reading, Duncan's vision of himself as a falcon moderates this upward displacement: "Here Duncan practices what he elsewhere preaches. The idea that the war puts us all on trial, not just as a nation but as individuals, that it brings us to the revelation of a personal 'burden of original sin,' works to erode presumptions of exemption and righteousness, eat away at the vanity of a self-congratulatory image. The chicken sees himself to be a hawk underneath it all" (*PH*, 173–74). In acknowledging the imperfection of his revelation, or his interpretation of it, in admitting he is both chicken *and* hawk, Duncan gains a more perfect vision of himself, thanks to the intercession of Jess, his beloved other and the gremlin that sabotages his self-congratulation. To seek greater perfection than this knowledge of imperfection and fallibility, to demand certainty of himself, is to deny the part of himself that is like Gassire and, as he writes in the last line of "My Mother Would Be a Falconress," "would draw blood."[29] As in duende, the poet is himself and is what he would disclaim as other.

This vision of human imperfection is something Mackey continually works at in his essay "Gassire's Lute." For Mackey, the idea that the poet's self is, like the Andoumboulou, incomplete is an inducement to accept conflict as a revelation of a larger whole, as a manifestation of what he calls the double-jointedness of reality: "Crucial to what one means by double-jointed is that things bend contrary to their customary courses, even to the point of appearing out of joint. The mystery of the seeming defect that paradoxically fits, of a destiny time works to fulfill through being out of joint, is something whose praises Duncan repeatedly sings. The points where things appear disturbed or disjointed, where 'divergences appear,' body forth and bear the brunt of a claim the eternal makes upon time" (*PH*, 113). For Mackey, this means the poet is "privy to the distempers as well as the dictates of the spirit" and sees himself to be a hawk beneath his chicken pretense (114). To return to a previous example, what is true for Duncan is true for Levertov: her warlike peace activism reveals her to be a hawkish chicken. But Mackey's Duncan is also a chicken committed to a surrender or openness to language, as he claims we can see in Duncan's most explicitly antiwar poem, "An Essay at War":

> This is what [Duncan] aims for and claims to be doing throughout ["An Essay at War"], surrendering, for example, to the multiple meanings of words rather than wielding them as though he could diminish and

> thus master their meanings. In the first chapter of "The H.D. Book" as well, he articulates a poetics of surrender, speaking of a willingness "not only to use things but to be used by them" on his way to asserting that "instead of having ideas or feelings, the poet lets ideas or feelings 'have' him." (*PH*, 108)

Though as Richard Deming observes, "Duncan's inspiration as well as his importance as an antiwar poet is dependent on war itself," Mackey sees Duncan's poetry as "a warlike alternative to war" in which "inconclusiveness removes the lure of victory" (*PH*, 108).[30] That is, Duncan and Levertov are in some ways identical in their mixed approach to war, but Levertov is unwilling to realize or accept the implication or imputation that her motives are mixed, nor is she willing to accept the threat to agency and self implicit in allowing "ideas or feelings" to have their own violent way with her.

In Mackey's and Duncan's view, the poet gains by surrendering to imperfection and permeability and by accepting the fugitivity, the otherness, of that which possesses him. From this perspective, the poet's belief that the "ordeals of Hell give birth to a vision of Heaven" is a way of keeping faith (*PH*, 142). Tempered by the acceptance of imperfection, Duncan's "godly transformative glance"—though it is flawed and arrogant—becomes a source of hope and possibility, a "rising up though conditions counsel despair" (156). This "rising up" has several implications. The first of these is that accepting imperfection has epistemological consequences because it allows the poet to cope with the multiplicity of experience. When critics complain of a poem's obscurity, Mackey argues, their frustration arises not from "lack of meaning" but from "the variousness of meaning," from an acknowledgment of "the world's refusal to submit to a conclusive interpretation" (102). Second, accepting imperfection—the impossibility of closure—also gives the poet a sense of significance despite society's perceived lack of need for poets. Mackey writes of Duncan's refusal of "socially sanctioned goals" and "socially sponsored motivations" that "to embrace the worthlessness of poetry, to rejoice in being useless, is to take a stand against what commonly passes for value" (94).

Finally, the notion of permeability that accompanies this idea of imperfection also gains the poet a great deal of poetic capital. As Andrew Mossin notes, by claiming inauthenticity and foregrounding derivation, Duncan converts a "defect" to a virtue and to a "working principle of his practice," a permission to borrow, experiment with, and rework materials originating outside himself.[31] This syncretizing license allows Duncan to, as Mackey claims in "Gassire's Lute," do healing work, where healing "at its very root, has to do with making whole. 'The writing triumphs,' Duncan remarks, 'for it most approximates the total configuration.' . . . We recall him saying elsewhere that 'the very heightened sense of the relatedness of everything sets poets apart.' Throughout his writings he takes issue with any stance which would outlaw this feeling for connectedness" (*PH*, 101). It is Duncan's desire to make whole that Mackey sees as the reason for Duncan's attacks in *The H.D. Book* on the New Critics. He continues from the passage above:

> The once fashionable notion of "pathetic fallacy" comes under repeated attack in "The H.D. Book" as an example of the assault on poetic vigor by a rationalist, convention-ridden, product-oriented sense of the world. The vested interest such a sense of the world has in the deficit of meaning from which it suffers leads it to be protective of its predicament, as in the New Criticism. It wants to confine all thought to an acceptable despair, to harass, ridicule, or simply ignore any departure from acceptable containments of a poet's feeling for rapport. (*PH*, 101)

Mackey's affinity with Duncan's approach is clear in his use of "poetic vigor" to describe the inconclusiveness some others—Harold Bloom, the New Critics—would likely see as weakness. The poem as well-wrought urn, in its refusal to acknowledge its multiplicity, isolates itself from the world around it. In proposing itself as its own measure, the "autotelic" poem becomes unhinged from the world's syntax.

Mackey and Duncan would rather have the poem be a hinge between the world and its syntax. Such a hinge must necessarily, as Mackey has it, *creak*.[32] In Mackey's work, language strains with the burden of meaning, the "creaking and erosion to which words are prone"; this creakiness makes "a certain amount of play inescapable." As in Duncan's work, this play emerges from an apostasy in the face of certainty:

A first unfallen
church it might have been. Let
run its course it would have gone
otherwise, time's ulterior bequest . . .
This they had a way of imagining,
this
they so wished it to be. Abstract he
at the back of her mind, she at the
back of his, each the other's Nub
constituent, ghost of an alternative
life . . .
They were we before we were, ancestral,
we
who'd never not be ill at ease.[33]

In this passage, the rapidly shifting, conditional meanings of words struggle to both break free from and remain faithful to the "claim the eternal makes upon time" (*PH*, 113). The first line break signals a break with tradition: it is not this primal man and woman who have fallen but the church and its *doxa* that have always-already fallen. And the desire itself fluctuates. Is this "unfallen / church" they imagine? Or is it this pair have a way of imagining? Did "this / they" wish for it to be that the unfallen church had come to be, or do they wish for it to be as it is, that such a church only might have been? Even the man and woman themselves exist abstractly for one another as a notion, an abstraction, drawn away, abstracted, from real presence. They are the constituents of Nub, which, for Mackey, is "a place name and a diagnosis" of and for a place of "failed extension and falling short" that is "chronically resided in, repeatedly arrived at." Yet for all the straining toward that never reaches, Mackey demands a critique, for Nub is also "the flailing republic . . . the United States has become" in its own War on Terror.[34] As in Duncan's *Passages*, the poetry can only be against the present, cannot offer solutions, can only "never not be ill at ease" with an inevitably fallen, imperfect state.

MACKEY'S READING OF Duncan in "Gassire's Lute" describes his own poetic practice. As Richard Deming notes, Duncan's more open mode is the poetic practice Mackey uses in his own healing work:

> On a larger scale, then, we see in Mackey's thinking the recurring assertion that the cross-talk of cultures and languages need not lead to assimilation or to normalized cultural codes but to an unsettled space or network of ideals and practices continually in the process of recontextualizing itself. For Mackey, this seeking out of alternative worldviews is part of an artist's aesthetic duty and perhaps moral obligation. "As a writer," he tells us, "one has to find one's tradition, create one's tradition, and in doing that one creates lines of affinity and kinship that can cut across national boundaries, ethnic boundaries, and so forth" (*PH*, 190). He prefaces this entreaty to self-fashioned genealogy by saying "Call it influence without anxiety."[35]

In such a poetics, the other is a hermeneutic opportunity rather than an enemy to be overcome, as in Harold Bloom's model of influence, in which the inspiring mentor and the present poet play out a zero-sum game in an Oedipal drama. The absence of the possibility for victory does not eliminate the possibility of action. This sort of openness to the possibilities of language and response takes on an ethical, exhortatory tone when the times demand it. But this openness also demands an ongoing acknowledgment of the other as inspiration, even when that other is bloodthirsty. Speaking of recent engagements with the Bush administration's wars in his poetry, Mackey says: "Even if we're not over there, we're inside the war and the war's inside us. As a writer, you register or inscribe both what's inside and what's outside, and the conversation, often antiphonal, between the inside and the outside. . . . For me, this comes with writing over a long period of time, with the fact that writing is a long-distance run."[36] Much like Duncan, Mackey sees his own attacks on current evil as an open and ongoing engagement with What Is. For both, that evil inhabits the poet's body as a portion of What Is. The poet's efforts to both acknowledge and reject this presence lead to poems calling in a forking, creaking voice for a more perfect Next Society. In Mackey's reading of and lesson from Duncan, engagement of the other relies heavily on the ability to sound an antiphonal music in which poesis and obscurity reveal fissures and futures, problems and possibility.

Notes

1. Mackey, *Paracritical Hinge*, 288. Hereafter cited in the text as *PH*.
2. Blaser, "The Practice of Outside."
3. Naylor, "Some Ecstatic Elsewhere," 596.
4. Duncan, *Caesar's Gate*, xvi. Hereafter cited in the text as *CG*.
5. Whitman, "Song of Myself," 63.
6. Naylor, "Some Ecstatic Elsewhere," 593.
7. Mackey, "Poetry for the Next Society," 1–3.
8. Ibid., 1–2.
9. Ibid., 3.
10. Robert Duncan, "Structure of Rime: Of the Five Songs," in Duncan, *Ground Work: In the Dark*, 78.
11. Ezra Pound, "Canto CXVI," in Pound, *Cantos*, 796. Originally published in *Drafts and Fragments of Cantos CX–CXVII* (New York: New Directions, 1969).
12. Denise Levertov, *To Stay Alive* (1971), collected in Levertov, *Poems 1968–1972*, 107.
13. Duncan and Levertov, *Letters*, 663. The "American general's" remark first appears as spoken by an anonymous "United States major" in an article by Peter Arnett on the destruction of the Vietnamese city of Ban Tre (population 35,000). The remark quoted by Arnett differs slightly from Duncan's version; it reads: "It became necessary to destroy the town in order to save it" ("Major Describes Move," *New York Times*, March 15, 1968, A3).
14. Duncan, *Bending the Bow*, 113.
15. "Gassire's Lute" is a Soninke myth first collected by Frobenius in volume 9 of his 1921 collection *Atlantis: Volksmärchen und Volksdichtung Afrikas*. It is available in English in a collection authored by Frobenius and translated by Fox, *African Genesis*.
16. "THERE HAS BEEN NO TIME IN HUMAN HISTORY THAT WAS NOT A TIME OF WAR" (Duncan and Levertov, *Letters*, 661).
17. In *The H.D. Book* Duncan argues that, in H.D.'s *Trilogy*, "the actual War, the incendiary attacks, the deprivations, come to illustrate or manifest another war the lover and poet knew under attack, to reactivate the violence felt in the critical and social rejection of her person and her art that H.D. had known. But these voices that accuse have been brought over into the authority of the poem; they are voices of the poetic consciousness itself. The adversary is heart-felt" (334).

18. "Disorders that underlie" is from Duncan, "Man's Fulfillment in Order & Strife," 139. Duncan is defending his "dehumanizing" of Johnson in the poem "Up Rising."
19. Davidson, "Review," 547.
20. Leo Frobenius, "Gassire's Lute," in Frobenius, *African Genesis*, 98.
21. Duncan, *Ground Work: Before the War*, 29.
22. O'Leary, "Prophetic Frustrations," 139.
23. Edwards, "Notes on Poetics," 573.
24. Funkhouser, "Location and Dis-ghosts."
25. Paul Naylor, "Nathaniel Mackey: The 'Mired Sublime,'" in Naylor, *Poetic Investigations*, 78.
26. Ibid.
27. Duncan, *Bending the Bow*, 51.
28. Ibid.
29. Ibid., 54.
30. Deming, "Review," 257.
31. Mossin, "Unveiling Expectancy," 552.
32. Mackey, *Djbot Baghostus's Run*, 145.
33. Mackey, *Splay Anthem*, 123.
34. Ibid., xv.
35. Deming, "Writing Dialectic," 255.
36. Mackey, interview by David Hadbawnik.

CHAPTER TWELVE

Talking Cosmos: Robert Duncan and Ronald Johnson

PETER O'LEARY

1

Curiously, the source for one of Robert Duncan's most influential statements about his poetry is the jacket copy for the first New Directions printing in 1969 of his book *Roots and Branches*, published originally by Scribner in 1964. "I am not an experimentalist or an inventor," intones Duncan, "but a derivative poet, drawing my art from the resources given by a generation of masters—Stein, Williams, Pound; back of that by generations of poets that have likewise been dreamers of the Cosmos as Creation and Man as Creative Spirit; and by the work of contemporaries: Zukofsky, Olson, Creeley and Denise Levertov."

This statement resonates with the pronouncements found in Duncan's "Pages from a Notebook," first published in 1953 but placed famously after Olson's "Projective Verse" in *The New American Poetry* from 1960, in which Duncan asserts his work to be a "composite indecisive literature, attempting the rhapsodic, the austere, the mysterious, the sophisticated, the spontaneous," further claiming, "where I am ambitious only to emulate, imitate, reconstrue, approximate, duplicate: Ezra Pound, Gertrude Stein, Joyce, Virginia Woolf, Dorothy Richardson, Wallace Stevens, D. H. Lawrence, Edith Sitwell, Cocteau, Mallarmé, Marlowe, St. John of the Cross, Yeats, Jonathan Swift, Jack Spicer, Céline, Charles Henri Ford, Rilke, Lorca, Kafka, Arp,

Max Ernst, St.-John Perse, Prévert, Laura Riding, Apollinaire, Brecht, Shakespeare, Ibsen, Strindberg, Joyce Cary, Mary Butts, Freud, Dalí, Spenser, Stravinsky, William Carlos Williams, and John Gay," adding H.D. in a subsequent paragraph.[1]

2

Derive, from the Latin *derivare*, "to turn a stream from its channel," from *de-*, "from," and *rive*, "river; or, from a river." Its cognate in literary thought is *influence*, from the Late Latin, *influentia*, "a flowing in," from the Late Latin *influere*, "to flow in," from *in-* plus *fluere*, "to flow." From a river flowing in. Or flowing in from a river.

But there's a pun coursing through Duncan's notion of the derivative. He claims derivation in contradistinction to experimentation and innovation. One of the definitions of *derive* is "to originate." As in one chemical deriving from another. It's also suggestive of the descent of one organism from another in a process that involves structural changes, namely, evolution. In claiming derivation, Duncan is suggesting that he originates from the figures he lists—"dreamers of the Cosmos as Creation and Man as Creative Spirit"—and that he is the evolved organism of this process.

And what is flowing into Duncan? Not only poetry but *tradition*. From the Latin *traditio*, from *traditus*, which is the past participle of *tradere*, "to deliver." As in delivering something into the hands. As part of a trust, as a part of a legally binding covenant. Duncan is claiming to be carrying the tradition delivered into his own hands by poetry itself.

Here, a recitation from Eliot's "Tradition and the Individual Talent" is useful. "Tradition," writes Eliot, "is a matter of much wider significance [than following the ways of the generations immediately before us]. It cannot be inherited, and if you want it you must obtain it by great labour." For the poet willing to undertake this great effort, Eliot assures us that "we shall often find that not only the best, but the most individual parts of his work may be those in which the dead poets, his ancestors, assert their immortality most vigorously."[2] Though this labor is great, its potentials are boundless. Tradition serves as a vast, renewable resource. Nathaniel Mackey, writing of Duncan's derivative poetics, suggests that Duncan "shows tradition to be porous rather than impermeable, to be fissured and incomplete rather than comprehensive and monolithic."[3] Furthermore, Mackey insists, "Duncan's repeated recourse to the work of predecessor poets as sources for his own work attests to limits dialectically related to a theme of unboundedness found in his and their work. *His having to do with sources leads to the idea of a transcendent Source*."[4] Duncan himself reads tradition as astrology, the sublunary influences of destiny and fate: "In the constellation of Poetry there are thousands of distant stars and more immediate planets, lighting the night sky of those who delite in that art with a plenitude of brilliancies, and in time each new poet in his vocation comes to realize that he has a kind of horoscope or constellation of his own in which particular poets in the past appear as influencing spirits in his shaping of his poetic destiny."[5]

What do I know of the old lore? Duncan asks this question as the title to the second poem in *Roots and Branches*. "A young editor wants me to write on Kabbalah for his magazine."[6] "'Kabbalah,'" writes Harold Bloom, "has been, since the year 1200, the popularly accepted word for Jewish esoteric teachings concerning God and everything God created. The word 'Kaballah' means 'tradition,' in the particular sense of 'reception,' and at first referred to the whole of Oral Law."[7] In other places, Kaballah is defined as "the received." To receive poetry is to participate in the esoteric transmission of lore/wisdom/knowledge carried by its forebears. To feel its influence pouring down from the stars.

Duncan claims to draw his art from the resources given by a generation of masters. *Resource*, from an old French verb whose past participle is *resourse*, to arise anew. *Re-*, "again," plus *sourdre*, "to spring up as water." From the Latin *surgere*, "to arise, to surge." The focus of all this flowing power of tradition is on the action of its reception: that it is given, that it is received. *Give*, which comes from itself—it's an original word. It means "to surrender into the power of another."

Literature is given; it is not an acquisition but a gift. "That art that matters to us," says Lewis Hyde, "which moves the heart, or revives the soul, or delights the senses, or offers courage for living, however we choose to describe the experience—that work is received by us as a gift is received."[8]

3

There are two modes for perceiving the tradition of literature as an active participant—"a dreamer of the Cosmos"—in that tradition: the first is political and economic. Its terms tend to be legalistic, ambitious, affiliative, and oriented toward individual survival. The second is religious and erotic. Its terms tend to be theosophical, vocational, amative, and oriented toward the preservation of lineage. The political-economic mode, which operates in a poetry marketplace, can be seen in the contest/prize structure that dominates American poetry publishing, in the influence of prestigious creative writing programs in the universities, in the leadership of poet/financiers in arts organizations, and even in the material critiques of poetry by various Language poets. The religious-erotic mode, which functions as an initiatic process, can be seen in a handful of poetry publishers committed to the book arts, in workshops modeled on the activities of various New American poets, in the cultivation of Internet archives, and even in the work of some Language poets. (All of these examples represent instances; they don't exhaust the possibilities of these categories.) The friendship of Robert Duncan, born in 1919, and Ronald Johnson, born in 1935, who overlapped in San Francisco for nearly twenty years, is an example of the second mode of perception, involving what Hyde calls "an erotic commerce, joining self and other, so the gifted state is an erotic state: in it we are sensible of, and participate in, the underlying unity of things."[9] Undoubtedly, most poets experience an overlapping perception where both modes are active. All poets want survival and preservation in some form. Nevertheless, it's my sense that American poetry is presently dominated by the first mode of perception, where economic and political matters drive the commerce.[10]

A return to the religious and erotic model, which I'd like to argue for here, might begin to suggest a link between *affiliation* and *affinity*, bringing them into viable contact, useful congress. This model, in my sense of it, more vigorously and deliberately engages derivation and tradition in Duncan's sense of these terms than does the economic and political model. Affiliation, in the political-economic sense, is valuable because it tends to reinforce an institutional connection: for instance, it answers the question, where did you go to school? As often as not, that becomes a crucial biographical datum in a poet's story, especially as far as publishing and legacy are concerned. In the religious-erotic notion, affiliation is replaced with lineage, which tends not to be institutional so much as an affinity: a poet finds himself or herself drawn to certain work; that poet find himself or herself drawn to other writers drawn themselves to that work; that poet then commits himself or herself to examining, serving, preserving, and propagating that work. The difference and the link between affiliation and affinity are that affiliation has a legalistic element; affinity, as in Ronald Johnson's notion that "affinities are all," has a self-selected, self-determined element, one that elides legal or even rational understandings of connections, adhering instead to the passional, vocational convictions that drive poets to believe one kind of work over another.

4

In the first letter I wrote to Ronald Johnson, during the summer of 1992, seeking his advice on what to do with my life, I mentioned my interest in Duncan's poetry. He took my petition for aid seriously, replying to it honestly:

> At 24? Who knows—by then I was already on my way to "follow my bliss" as Mr. Campbell, of Myth fame, insists. But then I'd been steeled by an absolute conviction that I should come out of a small Kansas town to find a world of excitement in ideas. There, I went as you say to the Masters. In those days that was easy—there were the academics, then those with new ideas: Olson, Duncan, Creeley, Zukofsky, Bunting, etc., a clear tradition of attention to the language itself as a conductor for the lightning of the soul. We were lucky, too, to discover new and electric musics there. These days, I'm afraid, with hundreds and hundreds of poeticules thronging the academies, the prospect of finding one's way as a poet—a poet, say, of any worth to change and charge the language anew—must daunt the best.

A clear tradition of attention to the language itself . . . He warned me, "Peers are necessary, always, but I wouldn't recommend much contact with the mediocre," having already observed that Duncan was more a poet to learn ideas from than technique, allowing himself nevertheless to sigh, "Ah, how

I miss Robert. I see Thom Gunn, but he's not really a friend like the Dunc who was always available to bounce ideas off and talk Cosmos."[11]

To talk Cosmos is to share the prospect of language as conductor and lightning of the soul. (In "Man's Fulfillment in Order and Strife," Duncan proposes, "Back of Dante's idea of himself as poet and of the meaning of his visionary recital was his idea of God as poet or creator, of God's Art which is Nature, and of the cosmos as poetry or creation.")[12] Though Johnson pays more explicit debts in his poetry to the examples and works of Louis Zukofsky and Charles Olson, Duncan received the dedication of four of his most important works: "The Different Musics," written in the late 1960s, published in *Valley of the Many-Colored Grasses*; "BEAM 17, *The Book of Orpheus*," written in the mid-1970s, published in *ARK: The Foundations*; "ARK 71, Arches V," his elegy for Duncan after he died in 1988, from the Ramparts of *ARK*; and, most importantly, in 1977, *Radi os*, Johnson's rewriting through excision of *Paradise Lost*, arguably his most enduringly popular and innovative work. The dedication to Duncan in that work reads, "I would like particularly to thank Robert Duncan for his encouragement through my solitary quest in the cloud chamber—that place, he assured me, 'The Authors are in Eternity.'"[13]

Duncan's "Variations on Two Dicta of William Blake," from *Roots and Branches*, begins:

> The Authors are in eternity.
> Our eyes reflect
> prospects of the whole radiance
> between you and me
>
> where we have lookd up
>   each from his being.
> And I am the word "each."
> And you are the word "his."[14]

Blake's dictum comes from a letter to his close friend and patron Thomas Butts from 1803. Elsewhere, Blake says of Eternity, "Whatever can be Created can be Annihilated Forms cannot / The Oak is cut down by the Ax, the Lamb falls by the Knife / But their Forms Eternal Exist, For-ever. Amen Halle[l]ujah."[15] Johnson called *Radi os* "the book Blake gave me." It's carved directly out of the enduring forms of Milton's language and Blake's thought.

The authors in eternity. Milton and Blake. Dickinson and Whitman. Dante. "BEAM 17" ends: "That clockwise, counterclockwise, as blue bindweed to honeysuckle, the cosmos is an organism spirally open on itself, into the pull of existence. In the beginning there was the Word—for each man, magnetized by onrush, is Adam to his Tyger." Johnson's poem articulates what might be called the "derivative imperative," namely, that each poet, pulled open by existence, is both the universe's original being and its revelatory beast, articulated in the sound and sight of the poem itself.

5

Johnson met Duncan through Jonathan Williams, who himself had met Duncan when he was a guest instructor at Black Mountain College in 1956, invited there by Olson, rector of the college at that time, to replace Robert Creeley, who was departing for the West Coast.[16] Johnson met Williams in Washington, DC, in 1958, when both were spending the summer there, Williams on a Guggenheim, and Johnson waiting to move to Columbia to finish his bachelor's degree, having completed a stint in the army, where he earned tuition money through the GI Bill. They were smitten with each other and soon moved together to New York City, Johnson going to college and Williams working at Eighth Street Bookshop, spending their evenings at the Cedar Tavern. Because of Williams's Black Mountain connections in New York and elsewhere, Johnson thought himself to have unofficially attended that school. He met and associated regularly with many of Williams's fellow Black Mountain students as well as with its teachers, poets, and painters alike. Johnson and Williams lived together on and off through the late fifties. In 1961 they hiked the length of the Appalachian Trail; then in 1962 they headed to England to hike the countryside, on and off, for another two years, staying with poets and artists, and in 1966 they made a Grand Tour–style visit to Europe as well.

During these years, Williams was actively assembling the Jargon Society, his publishing venture and arts nexus. Many, if not most, of Johnson's contacts during these years were Jargon contacts, or those with poets from affiliated, sympathetic projects, such as the Scottish poet Ian Hamilton Finlay and his publication *Poor. Old. Tired. Horse.* In 1964, when Johnson was twenty-eight years old, Williams published his first book, *A Line of Poetry, a Row of Trees*, in a beautiful edition, printed by the Auerhahn Press in San Francisco. It arrived six years after the Jargon Society published Duncan's *Letters* in a similarly handsome edition. At the Jargon Society, to give a sense of context and company, between *Letters* (Jargon 14) and *A Line of Poetry, a Row of Trees* (Jargon 42), there were Olson's *Maximus Poems*, Levertov's *Overland to the Islands*, Loy's *Lunar Baedeker & Time-Tables*, Creeley's *A Form of Women*, and many others.

Arriving in San Francisco immediately following the Summer of Love, having split with Williams, Johnson numbered Duncan among his contacts. They had been corresponding through the 1960s, more often than not to share news with each other, though once when Johnson was soliciting work for a project of one-word poems he was collaborating on with Finlay. Johnson regularly sent Duncan and Jess postcards, Christmas cards, and updates of his and Williams's whereabouts. When he arrived in San Francisco in the fall of 1968, he tried repeatedly to telephone Duncan and Jess to see them. It's clear from the letters that survive that he and Duncan would see each other around from time to time, but never as often as Johnson would have liked. In December 1969 Johnson sent a postcard with this typed message to Duncan:

> Dear Robert: I never seem to be able to reach you via BULLPUP [which letters spelled Duncan's and Jess's telephone number] so I shall relate a dream I had of you several months ago. You were a blind bard seated at a large table. We were, several of us, gathered around the table. In front of you was a magic typewriter which had its keys covered with gold art-nouveau tendrils, and when inspired you touched the glass over the keys and a poem was inscribed from its mystic connections onto a kind of tapestry on the wall. The poem I saw was interwoven with curious lilies to the edge. Jess would read the poem for you and tell you whether or not what was inspired had really appeared there or not. That you had a magic typewriter I knew—but lilies! Lilies as well![17]

Typewriters facilitate correspondence as well as poems. I've argued—in relation to the prodigious exchange between Duncan and Denise Levertov—that the era beginning in 1950 (with "Projective Verse," the great manifesto of the virtue of the typewriter) through the end of the 1970s (before the advent of the word processor) be called the "Age of Correspondences."[18] The typewriter is its agent of transmission. Johnson's first letter to me begins:

> Thank you for confiding your hopes and fears, and in such arresting script! I write a fine hand, but give out after a paragraph the typewriter has me such in thrall. I am of that brief period, now computers hold sway, of that blessed machine which first became necessary for Henry James via dictation, then creative equipment for Pound, Williams, Olson, well—you name them. I can *think* only on the typewriter, with my fingers. A similar age would be that of Impressionism, when tubes of paint became available to work out of doors. I seem to be the last of these dinosaurs.

Duncan, famously, as a result of ongoing frustrations with the publishers of his books, insisted on completely controlling the appearance of his fourth book with New Directions, *Ground Work: Before the War*, published in 1984. In "Some Notes on Notation," which appears at the beginning of the book, he relates the visual presentation of the book to his physiological experience of his poems: "The cadence of the verse, and, in turn, the interpenetration of cadences in sequence is, for me, related to the dance of my physical body. My hands keep time and know more than my brain does of measure." Following the edicts of "Projective Verse," Duncan later in these "Notes" instructs: "All 'typographical' features are notations for the performance of the reading. Margins signify."[19]

6

On February 24, 1974, Johnson wrote to Williams: "Meant to get this out earlier, but finishing IVES & G. DAVENPORT essays, plus a Wor(l)ds section for Rbt. Dunc. For Jn. Tgt., *plus* the last week or so finally getting the end of Wor(l)ds Book I DONE. !!!"[20] In 1974 John Taggart devoted an issue of his journal *Maps* to Duncan. It begins with a long editorial essay by Duncan rehearsing his frustrations with John Martin, the publisher of Black Sparrow Press, who had issued an edition of Duncan's *Tribunals*, a suite of later inclusions in his series *Passages*, that had, for various reasons, infuriated Duncan. But it also includes the entire text to one of Duncan's most steadfastly derivative poems whose full title runs, "A Seventeenth Century Suite in Homage to the Metaphysical Genius in English Poetry (1590–1690): Being Imitations, Derivations & Variations upon Certain Conceits and Findings Made among Strong Lines." The beginning to the coda of the "Suite" channels cosmic energies into a mediumistic ventriloquism:

> Yes, darkness. Out of darkness.
>
> They have fed themselves into their lives.
> Wholly, it seemd, they fed their burning into mine.
> Dim fires of old loves linger on.
> It is the darkness into which they consume themselves
> that makes of it all for me a music of no return, of long
> the darkness, the dark fuel feeding forth the flame,
> of long lingering flaring up and flaming
> illuminations and dyings down, the ember-life of a
> persistent love

Having found these voices and spirits in the Avernal darkness of the poem, Duncan flings them forth into the heavens:

> O starry Net of Lives
> outflung! And our little lives at last
> among them realized! Elohim-Cloud of bright
> expectancies, quickening hunger for worlds
> out of boundless Source seeking its bounds[21]

Out of boundless Source seeking its bounds—this paraphrases tradition, perceived as an "Elohim-Cloud," a cosmos. (Whitman, in "Democratic Vistas," calls for a poetry of "the whole orb, with its geological history, the cosmos, carrying fire and snow, that rolls through the illimitable areas, light as a feature, though weighing billions of tons.")[22] The same issue of *Maps* includes Johnson's homage to Duncan, titled, "WOR(L)DS 24, for Robert Duncan." It's an early version of BEAM 17. *Wor(l)ds*, with the *l* nested inside of "Words," was Johnson's working title for *ARK* nearly until its first installment was published in 1980 as *ARK: The Foundations* by North Point Press. In this draft, Johnson rehearses the story of Orpheus, beginning with the unpacking of a concrete poetic pun: moving from tri-part to trip-art, he unravels the meanings of trip to suggest the journey of transformation Orpheus undergoes: "The means the action of the universe is metamorphosis —its articulation, metaphor. And its ultimate form is rayed like a star that is never quite stilled." To this he adds an abbreviation of the dream he had of Duncan:

> (but the dream came that Duncan was
> a blind seer: see-er.   And that he sat
> at a typewriter to write a screen before
> us—a page "illuminated" to the last
> morning-glory whorled bird's nest, in-
> sect-in-tendril, antennaed edge)[23]

Duncan is Orpheus at the typewriter for Johnson. He was one of the guiding figures for *ARK*, which Johnson described on September 11, 1974, to Williams as "a picture of the new cosmos inside out":

> [Everything] is being stuffed in the interstices of WOR(L)DS and RADI OS, and I begin to think sometimes I should give up the task of making up The Seventies out of the shambles of the pre-literate Sixties, and retire—preferably with an oversexed lover—to the country. But if *someone* doesn't start em reading again what will ever happen to our books. The last book languishes, as it is, somewhere in the desk, and sometimes even if WOR(L)DS is a picture of the new cosmos inside and out, black holes in space and all, it seems written against Windmills.[24]

If someone *doesn't start em reading again*. This is the vocational urge (and urgency) of the religious and erotic tradition of literature. "ARK 71," Johnson's elegy for Duncan, includes the lines:

Intact as effigy,
windmill stood face plain
tablets applaud far climbs of man

to elevate the status quo unite
Replenish yr land,
nor diminish dimension

new thought won bannered ledge,
green shoots through ashes
escarpment plunge

self to persist, pretend
Time abut Font
watchword accumulated attention[25]

The poem suggests monumental striving as much as it portends replenishment, renewal, and the value of persistence. Much as these possibilities signify a clichéd sense of accomplishment ("self to persist" could appear as a self-help mantra), they also provide watchwords for the accumulated attention Johnson had been paying to Duncan through the course of their friendship.

7

In his essay on the Duncan-Johnson connection, Norman Finkelstein includes a quotation from a letter he received from Johnson shortly after the publication of Finkelstein's book *The Utopian Moment in Contemporary American Poetry*, which, presumably, Finkelstein had sent to Johnson. (It was one of the first scholarly books to deal with Johnson's poetry.) Finkelstein writes that the interest in cosmology that Duncan and Johnson shared "had led me to assume, while writing *The Utopian Moment*, that Duncan had influenced the younger Johnson, both in terms of what Duncan calls the 'Grand Collage' of form and the equally grand content of the two poets' projects."[26] Johnson wrote to Finkelstein to challenge his assertion of influence: "As to Dunc, I can remember well Jonathan Williams' publication of his 'Letters,' which somehow 'gave me permission,' young as I was, to be romantick in the face of Olson, etc. But living in S.F., Robert and I were always buddys, respecting each others' territories. Our common ground was on the central childhood myth engendered by the Oz books—*he always accepted me as an equal, not an acolyte.*"[27] When he was writing his essay, Finkelstein contacted me to confirm this correction, which I did, insofar as my knowledge of their friendship—gleaned entirely through conversation and letters with Johnson—allowed me. About the Duncanian sense of permission Johnson mentions in his corrective letter, Finkelstein astutely conjectures: "The 'permission' from older to younger poet to which Johnson alludes may be the single most important aspect of that uncanny phenomenon we call influence."[28] My sense at present is to challenge Johnson's claims of equality with Duncan and to distress the sense of influence at work in their friendship. Duncan may, in fact, have accepted Johnson as an equal, but Johnson came to him as a petitioner.

Asymmetries. Except under unusual circumstances, there is really no equality in friendships between two poets from different generations or cohorts. Despite Johnson's claims to Finkelstein, he was certainly petitioning Duncan for his blessing on, for his interest in, and for his care about Johnson's work. Put another way, Johnson, like Eliot's poet obtaining a tradition by great labor, was *deriving* himself from Duncan. Consider the following three petitions as evidence.

The first is Johnson's dream of Duncan at the mediumistic typewriter, recounted above. Consider the circumstances: Johnson has been in San Francisco for over a year but begins the postcard, "I never seem to be able to reach you . . . " He's been trying to call Duncan to "reach him" but has failed. In the absence of that contact, he is permitted a dream, one of decidedly Duncanian shape and form: a mystical typewriter, the atmosphere of a séance or artistic salon, Art Nouveau ornamentations and tapestries filling out the details. As a dream, it's in kind with Duncan's dream of grand permission, the one recounted in "Often I Am Permitted to Return to a Meadow":

> It is only a dream of the grass blowing
> east against the source of the sun
> in an hour before the sun's going down
>
> whose secret we see in a children's game
> of ring a round of roses told.[29]

As I mentioned above, the religious-erotic mode of perceiving tradition functions through a poetic initiation. Johnson's dream of Duncan serves as a petition for initiation to become an acolyte of the theosophical secrets the dream portends.

The second text is "A Fairy Tale for Robert Duncan," written by Johnson in the mid-1970s and published in *Parnassus* in 1976. It's a work unique in Johnson's oeuvre: he wrote no other such fairy tales, no other work so blatantly adulatory, no other work that—like Duncan's prose in *The H.D. Book*—crossed between fable, poetry, and commentary with such hybrid ease. The fairy tale begins, "Once upon a time, in a country where the clocks no longer went round like the sun (and our clocks), there lived a Magus who could see things both far and near—and both at once." Duncan's self-presentation was rendered archetypal in "The Ballad of the Enamord Mage" from *The Opening of the Field* (and given visual dimension by Jess in "Enamord Mage: Translation #6" from 1965). Johnson is essentially presenting Duncan's archetype back to him, embellished in Baumian prose. He continues:

> From childhood The Magus had been taught the lore of The Old Ones. He had been found and adopted when an infant because his future parents could read the stars, and this particular child held a constellation about him of a pattern different from all the rest. He learned of Swords and Cups, and numbers' meaning, and what the fire said in the grate when it crackled, but best of all he liked to return and return again to the imaginary lands men before him had forged from the quicksilver of the lore: the crystal labyrinth in the center of the brain of earth, and a city of emerald to which all the roads of gold led.[30]

Not only does the acolyte (which means "follower") receive the myth of the Master's tradition, he incorporates his master into that myth, thus, in the words Mackey uses to describe Duncan's own derivative imperative, "completing an Uroboroslike circuit of justification" so that "the poetry and its poetics are one."[31] I'd add "the poets," so that "the poets, the poetry, and their poetics are one."

Johnson's fairy tale ends with an equally telling passage in which Johnson fancifully quotes from a tome recounting the magical history of this Magus:

> Later, in a book, it was written "The two poets of our time whose passion it has been to limn the anima, The White Goddess, are Robert Graves and Robert Duncan. Graves rewove all Myth to clothe her, and Duncan's quest has been to find her multiple face in the equally multiple-eyed psyche. His style is *Art Nouveau*—the molten skew of his lines 'most rich, most glittering, most strange,' as Gustav Moreau advised his followers. It is from this period, too we find the ideal of courtly love brought to its most obsessive gesture: Moreau's hieratic Salome, Klimt's women in a stasis of gold and poppies, the lily ladies as vases, Millais' Ophelia, Ozma, the bronze Medusas. No man of words is without his ancestors to language, and Robert's branch through Lorca, Shelley, to Dante addressing Beatrice." *Affinities are all.*[32]

The two pages of the fairy tale prior to this paragraph, which is marked off by an asterisk, are consistent with the opening: Brothers Grimm with a dash of Tolkien. Here, in the guise of a quotation from a book, Johnson provides an astute encapsulation of Duncan's poetic art as well as a perceptive sense of his lineage. This paragraph resembles the infrequent critical prose Johnson produced in the seventies, mostly reviews, most of it published in *Parnassus*. He wasn't a gifted critic, but he was an engaged reader, and he had a great eye for comparisons. It's as if, having paid tribute to the Wizard in Duncan's Oz, Johnson was free, at last, to begin to be himself.

He follows this paragraph with a quotation from "My Mother Would Be a Falconress," the stanza in which the "gay falcon treading her wrist" retrieves for his mother a mutilated sparrow. Johnson follows this quotation with the statement "*The world wrote back*," followed by lines from a seeming poem:

> The scientific work involved many people
> and approaches. It is symbolized by the tools that
> were employed: microscopes, mass spectrometers,
> nuclear reactors, magnetometers and seismometers
> (the last left forever with their ear pressed
> against the surface of the moon, listening to
> its internal rumblings).

These lines are a quote from an article in *Scientific American* from 1975, and they reflect a technique standard to Johnson's poetic composition: bricolage by quotation.[33] A few sentences later, Johnson finishes his fairy tale with these words: "*And they lived in co-existence ever after.*"[34] This appears to be what Johnson was attempting with this bizarre piece: not to live in the world as Duncan's (or the Master's) equal but to co-exist in that world through his own techniques, less deliberately incantatory than Duncan's, since derived from a collage poetics, but magical, in their own way, nevertheless.

The third petition is actually a pair of texts: a Christmas card from Duncan and Jess to Johnson from 1969–70 and the text of an introduction to a reading by Duncan at the Poetry Center in San Francisco in 1984 by Johnson. Separated by fifteen years, marking effectively the time Johnson had been in San Francisco and working on *ARK*, these texts shed light on the love and respect that informed their friendship, particularly in Johnson's own sense of it.

On the back of the Christmas card, Duncan wrote, "Dear Ron, / Thank you for the Different Musics [and] the Valley of the Many-Colored Grasses. You are one of the few poets where a dedication is in tune."[35] Johnson had recently sent Duncan a copy of *Valley of the Many-Colored Grasses*, which includes the poem "The Different Musics," dedicated to Duncan. The poem, among other things, is a precognition of things to come in *ARK*; in many ways it permits *ARK* to come into being only a few short months later. (Johnson began *ARK* in 1970, at the age of thirty-five.) Duncan goes on to wish Johnson a Happy New Year, sending on his love.

Johnson's introduction to Duncan is a moving, sweet tribute, delivered on September 22, 1984, at the Poetry Center.

> The first I heard of him, I remember seeing Jonathan Williams finish an early book of Duncan's, arrived that day in the mail, and Jonathan saying: "Ah, Robert—he always comes through!" And true, I was always to find Robert coming through, book after blooming book.
>
> Like no one else, he ever, too, left room on the page for my own inspiration to grow and flourish. The title poem of my third book, The Different Musics, was not only dedicated to him, it used his tools to break new ground for my own poetic.

> He is also one of the two friends I have on this earth who knows everything I want to know, and always gives me more than I imagined.
>
> Robert Duncan indeed needs no introduction to you—or the world for that matter, which pokes him now and again as if he were Walt Whitman. They are right: he is larger than life, and ours. Lucky we are to have him in the sparkling flesh.[36]

To break new ground for my own poetic. Like Duncan's, Johnson's own poetic is a tradition not to be inherited but to be obtained by great labor. "BEAM 17, *The Book of Orpheus*," recall, ends with the proclamation "In the beginning there was the Word—for each man, magnetized by onrush, is Adam to his Tyger." Think of this statement, dedicated to Duncan as Johnson was in the midst of figuring the typology that would project into his poetry to come, as the transformation, at last, of Duncan's derivative poetic imperative into his own.

8

Lineage as a polemical concept came brightly to light in the development of the Ch'an school of Buddhism in the late seventh and early eighth centuries. "Arising out of intra-Buddhist sectarian arguments, Ch'an embodied a reaction against dualistic doctrinal formulations—especially regarding enlightenment and nonenlightenment."[37] When Ch'an was imported into Japan, it was called Zen.

The core of Ch'an teaching was a rejection of traditional textual, institutional, and ethical guides for attaining Buddhahood. Instead, the purity of one's own mind was favored. Spiritual breakthrough was accomplished through a variety of techniques and interventions, including meditation, the use of silence, deliberate irrationalizations of thought and reality, and even acts of violence. Nevertheless, it produced seminal texts to describe, commemorate, and coax these breakthroughs, each of which reinforced the value of the lineage that had brought these understandings to light, originating when Bodhidharma brought the concept of *dhyana*, or "mindful absorption" in Sanskrit, from India into China in the late fifth century.

Necessarily, such breakthroughs of consciousness are overseen by enlightened masters. One's experience is authenticated only by a master, no matter the emphasis on the purity of one's own mind. In this sense, Ch'an religious practices mirror mystical and shamanistic practices from religious traditions the world over. To devote yourself to a tradition—to write against windmills—is to connect yourself with a master and to study the lineage from which he or she descends. "The shaman and the inspired poet," writes Duncan, "who take the universe to be alive, are brothers germane of the mystic and the paranoiac. We at once seek a meaningful life and dread *psychosis*, 'the principle of life.'"[38] When North Point Press published *ARK: The Foundations* in 1980 as one of its first poetry titles, the inside flap of the dust jacket included an endorsement, one of the few he ever wrote, by Duncan, meant to indicate the recognition Duncan made in the work that the universe portrayed there was suitably alive, in keeping with the fraternity of mystics, paranoids, and poets. "For the consciousness [Johnson] writes from not only springs from the revelation present in the creative imagination we draw from the realms of science and of poetry, but . . . that consciousness goes forward: it 'launches' thought and feeling upon the arc of an apprehension of vision beyond its own vision."[39]

Thought and feeling upon the arc of an apprehension of vision beyond its own vision = derivation. That is, the work that arises from it connects with a tradition it both receives and passes on but does not entirely control. What is the value of this erotic commerce, the joining of the self with other? Is a derivative poetics truly more worthwhile than an individually asserted one? Is the religious and erotic perception of tradition, as opposed to the political and economic one I invoked earlier, truly better than writing against the windmills of other energies?

Poetry is made as much from correspondences and connections as it is from dialogues with masters past and present. For whatever energy is spent by a poet in the commerce of the economic concerns of ambition and survival, there is a portion spared to be donated to the preservation of a tradition, to the expression of a cosmos. *Donate*, from the Latin *donum*, "gift." At the center of *ARK: The Foundations*, "BEAMS 21, 22, 23, *The Song of Orpheus*" brings the opening of *Radi os*, carved from the opening of *Paradise Lost* ("O / Tree / into the World, / Man / the chosen / Rose out of Chaos: / Song") into *ARK*. The excisional technique of *Radi os* is repeated pointedly in this

Song of Orpheus, which serves as the answer to a question posed by a mercurial *angelos* portrayed in the *Three Tracts*, a thirteenth-century Kabbalistic treatise, of Eleazar of Worms, who says,

> *When one sees the fire flaming*
> *up from the distance*
> *one is only seeing the smoke that*
> *surrounds it.*
> *Moreover the angel asks:*
> What do you see?

Initially, quoting Eleazar, Johnson writes, "I have seen the Eternal / *interior, / not ocular, vision*," at which point the poem commands: "Reply."[40] This invocation begins "PALMS," a fifteen-page visionary re-creation of the Psalms, in which Johnson selects at least one word from each of the 150 Psalms in the King James version of the Bible. It begins:

> Be
> the man that walk in the way of day and night
> like a tree of water, leaf
> chaff which the wind
> stand in
> imagine the earth set against sun,
> uttermost parts like a potter's O: trembling sands round about
> Arise, and ray.
>
> Stand in
> your own heart,
> and be still.
> the light upon us
> in time to the voice of ice:
> no throat out in the multitude of ions belled But shout
> for joy.[41]

Notes

1. Duncan, "Pages from a Notebook," 406–7.
2. Eliot, "Tradition," 100.
3. Nathaniel Mackey, "Uroboros: Robert Duncan's *Dante* and *Seventeenth Century Suite*," in Mackey, *Discrepant Engagement*, 98, emphasis added.
4. Ibid., 92.
5. Robert Duncan, "The Sweetness and Greatness of Dante's *Divine Comedy*," in Duncan, *Fictive Certainties*, 142.
6. Duncan, *Roots and Branches*, 3.
7. Bloom, *Kabbalah and Criticism*, 15.
8. Hyde, *The Gift*, xii.
9. Ibid., 163.
10. Recently, poet Dale Smith has begun a discussion of what he calls "Slow Poetry," which emphasizes community, local production of poetry and poetry publication, and lineage. What's interesting about Slow Poetry as a concept is that, like the Slow Food movement it derives from, it is a critique of the economic and political model of poetry, poetic tradition, and poetic production that uses the terms of economics and politics to level its criticisms. See, for instance, Smith's July 2008 column, "Slow Down," at Bookslut (http://www.bookslut.com/marsupial_inquirer/2008_07_013233.php) or the numerous entries at his blog, "Possum Ego," beginning with the post on June 24, 2008 (http://possumego.blogspot.com/2008/06/slow-poetry.html).
11. Ronald Johnson to the author, June 30, 1992.
12. Duncan, "Man's Fulfillment in Order and Strife," 123.
13. Johnson, *Radi os*, iii.
14. Duncan, *Roots and Branches*, 48.
15. William Blake, "Milton," 32:36–38, in Blake, *The Complete Poems*, 586.
16. In Clark, *Charles Olson*, 252.
17. Ronald Johnson to Robert Duncan, December 21, 1969, Robert Duncan Collection, Poetry Collection, State University of New York at Buffalo (hereafter cited as RDC).
18. O'Leary, "Duncan, Levertov, and the Age of Correspondences."
19. Duncan, *Ground Work: Before the War*, n. pag.
20. Ronald Johnson to Jonathan Williams, February 24, 1974, RDC.
21. Duncan, *Ground Work: Before the War*, 91.
22. Walt Whitman, "Democratic Vistas," in Whitman, *The Complete Poetry & Prose*, 984.
23. Johnson, "WOR(L)DS 24, for Robert Duncan."
24. Ronald Johnson to Jonathan Williams, September 11, 1974(?), RDC.

25. Johnson, *ARK*, n. pag.
26. Finkelstein, "Exploring the Johnson-Duncan Connection," 47.
27. Ibid., emphasis added.
28. Ibid., 48.
29. Duncan, *The Opening of the Field*, 7.
30. Johnson, "A Fairy Tale for Robert Duncan," 260.
31. Mackey, *Discrepant Engagement*, 89.
32. Johnson, "A Fairy Tale," 262.
33. This information was gleaned through Google Books, which provided the source but not the access to the actual article; Johnson was a dedicated reader of *Scientific American* when he could manage it.
34. Johnson, "A Fairy Tale," 262.
35. Robert Duncan to Ronald Johnson, December 1969, box 1, folder 44, Ronald Johnson Collection, Special Collections, Kenneth Spencer Research Library, University of Kansas Libraries. See Ross Hair's essay in this collection for further consideration of this dedication.
36. Ronald Johnson, introduction to Robert Duncan's poetry reading, from the Ronald Johnson Archive, courtesy of the Ronald Johnson Literary Estate.
37. Smith, *The HarperCollins Dictionary of Religion*, 193.
38. Robert Duncan, "The Truth and Life of Myth," in Duncan, *Fictive Certainties*, 2.
39. Robert Duncan, endorsement for Johnson, *ARK: The Foundations*.
40. The writings of Eleazar of Worms are found in *Three Tracts*. (Johnson was quoting from the first page of the first of the three tracts, "The Book of Prophecy.")
41. Johnson, *ARK: The Foundations*, n. pag.

BIBLIOGRAPHY

Adorno, Theodor W. *Notes to Literature I & II.* Translated by Shierry Weber Nicholson. New York: Columbia UP, 1992.

Alpert, Barry. "Ronald Johnson: An Interview." In *Ronald Johnson: Life and Works.* Edited by Joel Bettridge and Eric Murphy, 545–59. Orono, ME: National Poetry Foundation, 2008.

Aristotle. *On Poetry and Style.* Translated by G. M. A. Grube. New York: Bobbs-Merrill, 1958.

Baudelaire, Charles. *Oeuvres complètes.* Vol. 1. Edited by Claude Pichois. Paris: Gallimard, 1975.

Beach, Christopher. *ABC of Influence: Ezra Pound and the Remaking of American Poetic Tradition.* Berkeley: U of California P, 1992.

Benjamin, Walter. "On Some Motifs in Baudelaire." In *Illuminations.* Translated by Harry Zohn, 155–200. New York: Schocken, 1969.

Bernstein, Charles. *Close Listening: Poetry and the Performed Word.* New York: Oxford UP, 1998.

———. *Content's Dream.* Los Angeles: Sun & Moon, 1986.

Bernstein, Michael André. "Bringing It All Back Home: Derivations and Quotations in Robert Duncan and the Poundian Tradition." *Sagetrieb* 1.2 (1982): 176–89.

———. "Robert Duncan: Talent and the Individual Tradition." *Sagetrieb* 4.2/3 (1985): 177–90.

Bertholf, Robert J. "Decision at the Apogee: Robert Duncan's Anarchist Critique of Denise Levertov." In *Robert Duncan and Denise Levertov: The Poetry of Politics, the Politics of Poetry.* Edited by Albert Gelpi and Robert J. Bertholf, 1–17. Stanford, CA: Stanford UP, 2006.

———. *Robert Duncan: A Descriptive Bibliography.* Santa Rosa, CA: Black Sparrow, 1986.

———. "Robert Duncan: Blake's Contemporary Voice." In *William Blake and the Moderns.* Edited by Robert J. Bertholf and Annette Levitt, 92–110. Albany: SUNY P, 1982.

Birnbaum, Henry. "Orizons." *Poetry* 94.3 (1959): 156–63.

Blake, William. *The Complete Poems*. Edited by Alicia Ostriker. New York: Penguin Classics, 1977.

Blaser, Robin. "The Practice of Outside." In *The Collected Books of Jack Spicer*. Edited by Robin Blaser, 271–326. Santa Rosa, CA: Black Sparrow Press, 1996.

Bloom, Harold. *Kabbalah and Criticism*. New York: Continuum, 1993.

Breton, André. "Full Margin." Translated by Edouard Roditi. *View* 4.1 (1944): 132–33.

———. *Manifestoes of Surrealism*. Translated by Richard Seaver and Helen R. Lane. Ann Arbor: U of Michigan P, 1969.

Buber, Martin. *Tales of Angels, Spirits & Demons*. Translated by Jerome Rothenberg and David Antin. New York: Hawk's Well, 1958.

Burkholder, J. Peter. *All Made of Tunes: Charles Ives and the Uses of Musical Borrowing*. New Haven, CT: Yale UP, 1995.

Cage, John. *Anarchy*. Middletown, CT: Wesleyan UP, 2001.

———. *Empty Words: Writings '73–'78*. Middletown, CT: Wesleyan UP, 1981.

———. Interview by Henning Lohner, July 31, 1990. In *Writings through John Cage's Music, Poetry and Art*. Edited by David W. Bernstein and Christopher Hatch, 260–97. Chicago: U of Chicago P, 2000.

———. "Overpopulation and Art." In *John Cage: Composed in America*. Edited by Marjorie Perloff and Charles Junkerman, 14–38. Chicago: U of Chicago P, 1994.

———. *Silence: Lectures and Writings*. Middletown, CT: Wesleyan UP, 1973.

———. *X: Writings '79–'82*. Middletown, CT: Wesleyan UP, 1983.

Cantwell, Robert. *When We Were Good: The Folk Revival*. Cambridge, MA: Harvard UP, 1996.

Chace, William. *The Political Identities of Ezra Pound and T. S. Eliot*. Stanford, CA: Stanford UP, 1973.

Clark, Tom. *Charles Olson: The Allegory of a Poet's Life*. New York: Norton, 1991.

Clarkson, Austin. "The Intent of the Musical Moment: Cage and the Transpersonal." In *Writings through John Cage's Music, Poetry and Art*. Edited by David W. Bernstein and Christopher Hatch, 62–112. Chicago: U of Chicago P, 2000.

Collis, Stephen. "A Duncan Etude: Dante and Responsibility." *Jacket*, October 2004. http://jacketmagazine.com/26/dunc-coll.html (accessed August 9, 2008).

———. *Through Words of Others: Susan Howe and Anarcho-Scholasticism*. Victoria, BC: ELS Editions, 2006.

Corman, Cid. "Meeting in Firenze." *Sagetrieb* 1 (1982): 120–24.

Cowell, Sidney, and Henry Cowell. *Charles Ives and His Music*. New York: Oxford UP, 1969.

Creeley, Robert. "For L.Z." *New Directions* 39 (1979): 151–53.

Davidson, Michael. "A Book of First Things: *The Opening of the Field*." In *Robert Duncan: Scales of the Marvelous*. Edited by Robert J. Bertholf and Ian W. Reid, 56–84. New York: New Directions, 1979.

———. "Cave of Resemblances, Caves of Rimes: Tradition and Repetition in Robert Duncan." In *Robert Duncan: A Special Issue*. Edited by Michael Cuddity. *Ironwood* 22 11.2 (1983): 33–44.

———. *Ghostlier Demarcations: Modern Poetry and the Material World*. Berkeley: U of California P, 1997.

———. "Marginality at the Margins: Robert Duncan's Textual Politics." *Contemporary Literature* 33.2 (1992): 275–301.

———. "Review: A Cold War Correspondence: The Letters of Robert Duncan and Denise Levertov." *Contemporary Literature* 42.3 (2004): 538–56.

Deming, Richard. "Review: Writing Dialectic." *Twentieth Century Literature: A Scholarly and Critical Journal* 51.2 (2005): 249–58.

Derrida, Jacques. *The Gift of Death*. Translated by David Wills. Chicago: U of Chicago P, 1995.

Dimock, Wai Chee. *Through Other Continents: American Literature across Deep Time*. Princeton, NJ: Princeton UP, 2006.

Duncan, Robert. "The Adventure of Whitman's Line." In *Fictive Certainties: Essays by Robert Duncan*, 194–210. New York: New Directions, 1985.

———. "As Testimony: Reading Zukofsky These Forty Years." *Paideuma* 7 (1978): 421–27.

———. *Bending the Bow*. New York: New Directions, 1968.

———. *Caesar's Gate*. Berkeley, CA: Sand Dollar, 1972.

———. *Featuring Robert Duncan*. Spec. issue of *Audit/Poetry* 4.3 (1967).

———. *Fictive Certainties: Essays by Robert Duncan*. New York: New Directions, 1985.

———. "The Fire." *Poetry* 106 (April 1965): 32.

———. *Ground Work: Before the War*. New York: New Directions, 1984.

———. *Ground Work: Before the War/In the Dark*. Edited by Robert J. Bertholf and James Maynard. Rpt. New York: New Directions, 2006.

———. *Ground Work: In the Dark*. New York: New Directions, 1987.

———. *The H.D. Book*. Edited by Michael Boughn and Victor Coleman. Berkeley: U of California P, 2011.

———. Interview by John Tranter, May 4, 1985. Rpt. online in *Jacket*, October 2004. http://jacketmagazine.com/26/dunc-tran-iv.html.

———. Interview with Michael André Bernstein and Burton Hatlen. *Sagetrieb* 4.2/3 (1985): 87–135.

———. "An Interview with Robert Duncan." Jack R. Cohn and Thomas J. O'Donnell. *Contemporary Literature* 21.4 (1980): 513–48.

———. *Le récit et sa représentation: Colloque de Saint-Hubert, 5-8 mai 1977*. Edited by Roger Dadoun. Paris: Payot, 1978.

———. *Letters: Poems 1953–56*. Rpt. Chicago: Flood Editions, 2003.

———. "Letters to Robin Blaser & Jack Spicer." Edited by Gary Burnett. In *Robert Duncan: A Special Issue*. Edited by Michael Cuddity. *Ironwood 22* 11.2 (1983): 96–133.

———. *a little endarkenment and in my poetry you find me: The Naropa Institute Interview with Robert Duncan, 1978*. Buffalo, NY: Poetry/Rare Books Collection; Chicago: Rodent P; Boulder: Erudite Fangs Editions (joint publication), 1997.

———. "Man's Fulfillment in Order and Strife." In *Fictive Certainties: Essays by Robert Duncan*, 111–41. New York: New Directions, 1985.

———. *The Opening of the Field*. New York: Grove, 1960.

———. "Pages from a Notebook." *Artist's View* 5 (July 1953). Rpt. in *The New American Poetry*. Edited by Donald Allen, 400–407. New York: Grove, 1960.

———. "Pages from a Notebook." 1954. In Robert Duncan, *A Selected Prose*. Edited by Robert J. Bertholf, 13–22. New York: New Directions, 1995.

———. "Preface to a Reading of Passages 1–22." *Maps* 6 (1974): 53–55.

———. "Reviewing *View*, an Attack." *ARK* 1 (1947): 62–67.

———. *Robert Duncan: An Interview by George Bowering and Robert Hogg, April 19, 1969*. Toronto: Printed at the Coach House, 1971.

———. *Roots and Branches*. New York: New Directions, 1964.

———. *A Selected Prose*. Edited by Robert J. Bertholf. New York: New Directions, 1995.

———. "The Truth and Life of Myth." In *Fictive Certainties: Essays by Robert Duncan*, 1–59. New York: New Directions, 1985.

———. "Wind and Sea, Fire and Night." *Opening the Dreamway: In the Psyche of Robert Duncan. Spring* 59 (1996): 48–77.

———. *The Years as Catches: First Poems, 1939–46*. Berkeley, CA: Oyez, 1966.

Duncan, Robert, and Denise Levertov. *The Letters of Robert Duncan and Denise Levertov*. Edited by Robert J. Bertholf and Albert Gelpi. Stanford, CA: Stanford UP, 2004.

Edwards, Brent Hayes. "Notes on Poetics Regarding Mackey's *Song*." *Callaloo: A Journal of African-American and African Arts and Letters* 23.2 (2000): 572–91.

Eleazar of Worms. *Three Tracts*. Translated by Jack Hirschman and Alexander Altmann. Berkeley, CA: Tree Books, 1975.

Eliot, T. S. "A Note on Ezra Pound." *To-day* (September 1918): 5–6.

———. "A Note on the Verse of John Milton." In *Milton: A Collection of Critical*

Essays. Edited by Louis L. Martz, 12–18. Englewood Cliffs, NJ: Prentice Hall, 1966.

———. *The Sacred Wood: Essays on Poetry and Criticism*. London: Methuen, 1945.

———. "Tradition and the Individual Talent." In *The Waste Land and Other Writings*, 99–108. New York: Modern Library, 2001.

Faas, Ekbert. "An Interview with Robert Duncan." *boundary 2* 8.2 (1980): 1–19.

———. *Towards a New American Poetics: Essays & Interviews*. Santa Barbara, CA: Black Sparrow, 1979.

———. *Young Robert Duncan: Portrait of the Poet as Homosexual in Society*. Santa Barbara, CA: Black Sparrow, 1983.

Ferguson, Priscilla Parkhurst. "The Flâneur on and off the Streets of Paris." In *The Flâneur*. Edited by Keith Tester, 22–42. London: Routledge, 1994.

Ficino, Marsilio. *The Book of Life*. Translated by Charles Boer. Woodstock, CT: Spring Publications, 1996.

———. *Meditations on the Soul: Selected Letters*. Translated by the Language Department of the School of Economic Science, London. Rochester, VT: Inner Traditions International, 1996.

Fink, Bruce. *The Lacanian Subject: Between Language and Jouissance*. Princeton, NJ: Princeton UP, 1995.

Finkelstein, Norman. "Exploring the Johnson-Duncan Connection." In *Ronald Johnson: Life and Works*. Edited by Joel Bettridge and Eric Murphy Selinger, 47–71. Orono, ME: National Poetry Foundation, 2008.

———. "Late Duncan: From Poetry to Scripture." *Twentieth Century Literature* 51.3 (2005): 341–72.

———. *Not One of Them in Place: Modern Poetry and Jewish American Identity*. Albany: State U of New York P, 2001.

Freud, Sigmund. *The Interpretation of Dreams: The Penguin Freud Library Volume 4*. Translated by James Strachey. Edited by Angela Richards. London: Penguin, 1991.

Frobenius, Leo. *African Genesis: Folk Tales and Myths of Africa*. Translated by Douglas C. Fox. 1937. New York: Benjamin Blom, 1966.

Funkhouser, Christopher. "Location and Dis-ghosts: Nathaniel Mackey's Recent Work." *RIF/T: An Electronic Space for Poetry, Prose and Poetics*. Edited by Kenneth Sherwood and Loss Pequeño Glazier. 1994. http://wings.buffalo.edu/epc/rift/rift02/revi0201.html (accessed July 13, 2011).

Gardner, Thomas. "Where We Are: A Reading of Passages 1–12." *Sagetrieb* 4.2/3 (1985): 285–306.

Gelpi, Albert. "Poetic Language and Language Poetry: Levertov, Duncan, Creeley." In *Robert Duncan and Denise Levertov: The Poetry of Politics, the Politics of*

Poetry. Edited by Albert Gelpi and Robert J. Bertholf, 180–98. Stanford, CA: Stanford UP, 2006.

———. *Robert Duncan and Denise Levertov: The Poetry of Politics, the Politics of Poetry*. Edited by Albert Gelpi and Robert J. Bertholf. Stanford, CA: Stanford UP, 2006.

Grabher, Gudrun M. "Playing Hide and Seek in the Nothing that Is: Silent Meaning and Order in the Poetry and Aesthetics of John Cage." In *Ideas of Order in Contemporary American Poetry*. Edited by Diana von Finck and Oliver Scheiding, 63–80. Würzburg, Ger.: Königshausen & Neumann, 2007.

Graff, Gerald, and James Phelan, eds. *The Tempest: A Case Study in Critical Controversy*. Boston: Bedford/St. Martin's, 2000.

Gunn, Thom. "Homosexuality in Robert Duncan's Poetry." In *Scales of the Marvelous*. Edited by Robert J. Bertholf and Ian W. Reid, 143–60. New York: New Directions, 1979.

Hamilton, Jeff. "Drawing the Line: Laura Riding, Robert Duncan and the Poetic Legacy of Crisis in the New Humanism." PhD diss., U of Washington, 2001.

Hatlen, Burton. "Stalin and/or Zukofsky: A Note." *Paideuma* 8 (1979): 149–51.

H.D. *Collected Poems 1912–1944*. New York: New Directions, 1983.

Helgerson, Richard. *Self-Crowned Laureates: Spenser, Jonson, Milton, and the Literary System*. Berkeley: U of California P, 1983.

Herron, Carolivia. "Milton and Afro-American Literature." In *Re-membering Milton: Essays on the Texts and Traditions*. Edited by Mary Nyquist and Margaret W. Ferguson, 278–300. New York: Taylor and Francis, 1987.

Hertz, David Michael. *Angels of Reality: Emersonian Unfoldings in Wright, Stevens, and Ives*. Carbondale: Southern Illinois UP, 1993.

Howe, Susan. *The Birth-Mark: Unsettling the Wilderness in American Literary History*. Hanover, NH: Wesleyan UP, 1993.

———. *The Europe of Trusts*. New York: New Directions, 1990.

———. *Pierce-Arrow*. New York: New Directions, 1999.

———. *Singularities*. Middletown, CT: Wesleyan UP, 1990.

———. "Sorting Facts; or, Nineteen Ways of Looking at Matter." In *Beyond Document: Essays on Non-Fiction Film*. Edited by Charles Warren, 295–344. London: Wesleyan UP, 1996.

Hyde, Lewis. *The Gift: Imagination and the Erotic Life of Property*. New York: Vintage, 1983.

Igliori, Paola. *American Magus: Harry Smith—a Modern Alchemist*. New York: Inanout, 1996.

Ives, Charles E. *Essays before a Sonata and Other Writings*. Edited by Howard Boatwright. London: Calder & Boyars, 1969.

———. *Memos*. Edited by John Kirkpatrick. London: Calder & Boyars, 1973.

Jaszi, Peter. "On the Author Effect: Contemporary Copyright and Collective Creativity." In *The Construction of Authorship: Textual Appropriation in Law and Literature*. Edited by Martha Woodmansee and Peter Jaszi, 29–56. Durham, NC: Duke UP, 1994.

Jenkins, G. Matthew. *Poetic Obligation: Ethics in Experimental American Poetry after 1945*. Iowa City: U of Iowa P, 2008.

Johnson, Mark Andrew. "*Passages*: A Cross-section of the Universe." In *Robert Duncan: A Special Issue*. Edited by Michael Cuddity. *Ironwood 22* 11.2 (1983): 183–91.

———. *Robert Duncan*. Boston: Twayne, 1988.

Johnson, Ronald. *ARK*. Albuquerque, NM: Living Batch, 1996.

———. *ARK: The Foundations*. San Francisco: North Point, 1980.

———. "ARK: The Ramparts (Arches I–XVIII)." *Conjunctions* 15 (1990): 148–89.

———. "A Fairy Tale for Robert Duncan." *Parnassus* 5.1 (1976): 260–62.

———. "Persistent Light on the Inviolably Forever Other." *Margins* 13 (August–September 1974): 13.

———. *Radi os*. Rpt. Chicago: Flood Editions, 2005.

———. *The Valley of the Many-Colored Grasses*. New York: W. W. Norton, 1969.

———. "WOR(L)DS 24, for Robert Duncan." *Maps* 6 (1974): 68–69.

Junkerman, Charles. "nEw / foRms of Living Together: The Model of the Musicircus." In *John Cage: Composed in America*. Edited by Marjorie Perloff and Charles Junkerman, 39–64. Chicago: U of Chicago P, 1994.

Kahn, Charles H. *The Art and Thought of Heraclitus: An Edition of the Fragments with Translation and Commentary*. Cambridge: Cambridge UP, 1979.

Kamenetz, Rodger. "Realms of Being: An Interview with Robert Duncan." *Southern Review* 21 (1985): 5–25.

Kaufman, Robert. *Technicians of the Sacred: A Range of Poetries from Africa, America, Asia, Europe & Oceania*. Edited by Jerome Rothenberg. 1968. Garden City, NY: Doubleday, 1985.

Keenaghan, Eric. "Vulnerable Households: Cold War Containment and Robert Duncan's Queered Nation." *Journal of Modern Literature* 28.4 (2005): 57–90.

Koerner, Joseph Leo. *Caspar David Friedrich and the Subject of Landscape*. London: Reaktion Books, 1990.

Lacan, Jacques. *Écrits*. Translated by Bruce Fink. New York: Norton, 2002.

Lambert, Philip. *The Music of Charles Ives*. New Haven, CT: Yale UP, 1997.

Leavis, F. R. *Revaluation: Tradition and Development in English Poetry*. New York: George W. Stewart, 1947.

Levertov, Denise. *Poems 1968–1972*. New York: New Directions, 1987.

Lohner, Henning. "The Making of Cage's One." In *Writings through John Cage's Music, Poetry and Art*. Edited by David W. Bernstein and Christopher Hatch, 260–97. Chicago: U of Chicago P, 2000.

Longenbach, James. "Mature Poets Steal: Eliot's Allusive Practice." In *The Cambridge Companion to T. S. Eliot*. Edited by A. David Moody, 176–88. Cambridge: Cambridge UP, 1994.

Lyotard, Jean-François. *Discours, figure*. Paris: Klincksieck, 1971.

Mackey, Nathaniel. *Discrepant Engagement: Dissonance, Cross-Culturality, and Experimental Writing*. Cambridge: Cambridge UP, 1993.

———. *Djbot Baghostus's Run*. Los Angeles: Sun & Moon, 1993.

———. Interview by David Hadbawnik. *Front Porch* 4 (2007): n. pag.

———. *Paracritical Hinge: Essays, Talks, Notes, Interviews*. Madison: U of Wisconsin P, 2005.

———. "Poetry for the Next Society: Design for Continuing Investigation." *Project Papers of the Poetry Project of St. Mark's Church* 2 (1990): 1–3.

———. *Splay Anthem*. New York: New Directions, 2006.

Mallarmé. *Oeuvres complètes*. Vol. 2. Edited and annotated by Henri Mondor and G. Jean-Aubry. Paris: Gallimard, 1945.

Marchand, Jean José. *Sur "Mon Cœur mis à nu" de Baudelaire*. Paris: L'Herne, 1970.

Marcus, Greil. *Invisible Republic: Bob Dylan's Basement Tapes*. New York: Holt, 1997.

Marcuse, Herbert. *Eros and Civilization*. Boston: Beacon, 1974.

Marx, Karl. "Economic and Philosophical Manuscripts of 1844." In *Vol. 3, Collected Works*, 229–346. New York: International Publishers, 1975.

———. *Grundrisse*. Translated by Martin Nicolaus. London: Penguin Books, 1973.

Maynard, James. "Architect of Excess: Robert Duncan and the American Pragmatist Sublime." PhD diss., State U of New York at Buffalo, 2006.

McGann, Jerome. "Laura (Riding) Jackson and the Literal Truth." *Critical Inquiry* 18.3 (1992): 454–73.

Mead, G. R. S. *Thrice Greatest Hermes: Studies in Hellenistic Theosophy and Gnosis*. York Beach, ME: Samuel Weiser, 2001.

Meilicke, Christine A. *Jerome Rothenberg's Experimental Poetry and Jewish Tradition*. Bethlehem, PA: Lehigh UP, 2005.

Michelson, Peter. "A Materialist Critique of Robert Duncan's Grand Collage." *boundary* 8.2 (1980): 21–43.

Milton, John. *Complete Prose Works of John Milton*. Edited by Don Wolfe et al. New Haven, CT: Yale UP, 1953.

———. *Paradise Lost: A Norton Critical Edition*. Edited by Gordon Teskey. New York: Norton, 2005.

Mossin, Andrew. "Unveiling Expectancy: Nathaniel Mackey, Robert Duncan, and the Formation of Discrepant Subjectivity." *Callaloo: A Journal of African-American and African Arts and Letters* 23.2 (2000): 538–62.

Nancy, Jean-Luc. *Being Singular Plural.* Translated by Robert D. Richardson and Anne E. O'Byrne. Stanford, CA: Stanford UP, 2000.

———. *The Inoperative Community.* Minneapolis: U of Minnesota P, 1991.

Naylor, Paul. *Poetic Investigations: Singing the Holes in History.* Evanston, IL: Northwestern UP, 1999.

———. "Some Ecstatic Elsewhere: Nathaniel Mackey's *Whatsaid Serif.*" *Callaloo: A Journal of African-American and African Arts and Letters* 23.2 (2000): 592–605.

Nicholls, Peter. "The Pastness of Landscape: Susan Howe's *Pierce-Arrow.*" *Contemporary Literature* 43.3 (2002): 441–60.

O'Driscoll, Michael J. "Silent Texts and Empty Words: Structure and Intention in the Writings of John Cage." *Contemporary Literature* 38.4 (1997): 616–39.

O'Leary, Peter. "Duncan, Levertov, and the Age of Correspondences." *Chicago Review* 51.1/2 (2005): 232–39.

———. *Gnostic Contagion: Robert Duncan and the Poetry of Illness.* Middletown, CT: Wesleyan UP, 2002.

———. "Prophetic Frustrations: Robert Duncan's *Tribunals.*" In *Robert Duncan and Denise Levertov: The Poetry of Politics, the Politics of Poetry.* Edited by Albert Gelpi and Robert J. Bertholf, 126–47. Stanford, CA: Stanford UP, 2006.

Olson, Charles. *The Collected Poems of Charles Olson.* Edited by George F. Butterick. Berkeley: U of California P, 1987.

———. *The Maximus Poems.* Edited by George F. Butterick. Berkeley: U of California P, 1983.

———. "Projective Verse." In *Collected Prose.* Edited by Donald Allen and Benjamin Friedlander, 239–49. Berkeley: U of California P, 1997.

Oudart, Clément. "Genreading and Underwriting: A Few Soundings and Probes into Duncan's *Ground Work.*" *Jacket*, April 2007. http://jacketmagazine.com/32/oudart-genreading.shtml (accessed August 11, 2008).

Passler, Jann. "Inventing a Tradition: Cage's 'Composition in Retrospect.'" In *John Cage: Composed in America.* Edited by Marjorie Perloff and Charles Junkerman, 125–43. Chicago: U of Chicago P, 1994.

Polizzotti, Mark. *André Breton: Selections.* Edited by Mark Polizzotti. Berkeley: U of California P, 2003.

Pound, Ezra. *The ABC of Reading.* 1934. New York: New Directions, 1960.

———. *The Cantos of Ezra Pound.* New York: New Directions, 1970.

———. "Notes on Elizabethan Classicists." In *Literary Essays of Ezra Pound.* Edited by T. S. Eliot. 1918. New York: New Directions, 1988.

———. *The Spirit of Romance*. 1910. New York: New Directions, 1968.

Rabaté, Jean-Michel. *The Future of Theory*. London: Blackwell's, 2002.

———. *Jacques Lacan: Psychoanalysis and the Subject of Literature*. London: Palgrave, 2001.

Rees, Valery, with Martin Davies. *Marsilio Ficino: His Theology, His Philosophy, His Legacy*. Leiden: Brill, 2002.

Reid, Ian W. "The Plural Text: 'Passages.'" In *Scales of the Marvelous*. Edited by Robert J. Bertholf and Ian W. Reid, 161–79. New York: New Directions, 1979.

Rexroth, Kenneth. "San Francisco Letter." *Evergreen Review* 1.2 (1957): 10.

———. Untitled paragraph on Jerome Rothenberg. *VORT* 7 (1975).

Riding, Laura. *Anarchism Is Not Enough*. 1928. Edited by Lisa Samuels. Berkeley: U of California P, 2001.

———. *The Poems of Laura Riding*. New York: Persea, 1980.

———. *The Telling*. New York: Harper & Row, 1973.

Rilke, Rainer Maria. *Sonnets to Orpheus* with *Letters to a Young Poet*. Translated by Stephen Cohn. Manchester: Carcanet, 2000.

Rimbaud, Arthur. *Oeuvres complètes*. Edited by Pierre Brunel. Paris: Pochothèque, 1999.

Rothenberg, Jerome. "Nokh Aushwitz." In *Jewish American Poetry: Poems, Commentary, and Reflections*. Edited by Jonathan N. Barron and Eric Murphy Selinger, 137–45. Hanover, NH: Brandeis UP, 2000.

———. *Pre-Faces & Other Writings*. New York: New Directions, 1981.

Rothenberg, Jerome, and Diane Rothenberg, eds. *Symposium of the Whole: Range of Discourse toward an Ethnopoetics*. Berkeley: U of California P, 1983.

Sammons, Todd H. "A Note on the Milton Criticism of Ezra Pound and T. S. Eliot." *Paideuma* 17.1 (1988): 87–97.

Scarry, Siobhán. "Capable of Devotion: Robert Duncan, Mary Fabilli, and the Productive Agons of Friendship." *Jacket* 2. Forthcoming.

Schultis, Christopher. "Silencing the Sounded Self: John Cage and the Intentionality of Nonintention." *Musical Quarterly* 79.2 (1995): 312–50.

Scroggins, Mark. *The Poem of a Life: A Biography of Louis Zukofsky*. New York: Shoemaker & Hoard, 2007.

Selinger, Eric Murphy. "*ARK* as a Garden of Revelation." In *Ronald Johnson: Life and Works*. Edited by Joel Bettridge and Eric Murphy Selinger, 323–42. Orono, ME: National Poetry Foundation, 2008.

———. "Shekhinah in America." In *Jewish American Poetry: Poems, Commentary, and Reflections*. Edited by Jonathan N. Barron and Eric Murphy Selinger, 250–71. Hanover, NH: Brandeis UP, 2000.

Sheringham, Michael. *André Breton: A Bibliography*. London: Grant & Cutler, 1972.

Smith, Dale. "Slow Down." Bookslut. http://www.bookslut.com/marsupial_inquirer/2008_07_013233.php (accessed August 10, 2008).

Smith, Harry. *Think of the Self-Speaking: Harry Smith—Selected Interviews*. Edited by Rani Singh. Seattle: Elbow/Citiful, 1999.

Smith, J. Z., ed. *The HarperCollins Dictionary of Religion*. San Francisco: Harper San Francisco, 1995.

Steiner, George. *After Babel: Aspects of Language and Translation*. New York: Oxford UP, 1998.

Swinburne, Algernon Charles. *Major Poems and Selected Prose*. Edited by Jerome McGann and Charles L. Sligh. New Haven, CT: Yale UP, 2004.

Taylor, Thomas. *Selected Writings*. Edited by Kathleen Raine and George Mills Harper. London: Routledge and Kegan Paul, 1969.

Thoreau, Henry David. *Walden*. Edited by Stephen Fender. Oxford: Oxford UP, 1997.

Trask, Michael. *Cruising Modernism: Class and Sexuality in American Literature and Social Thought*. Ithaca, NY: Cornell UP, 2003.

Tyler, Hamilton, and Mary Tyler. "In the Beginning, or Recatching *The Years as Catches*." In *Scales of the Marvelous*. Edited by Robert J. Bertholf and Ian W. Reid, 1–13. New York: New Directions, 1979.

Van Anglen, K. P. *The New England Milton: Literary Reception and Cultural Authority in the Early Republic*. University Park, PA: Penn State UP, 2008.

Voss, Angela. "*Orpheus Redivivus*: The Musical Magic of Marsilio Ficino." In *Marsilio Ficino: His Theology, His Philosophy, His Legacy*. Edited by Valery Rees with Martin Davies, 227–41. Leiden: Brill, 2002.

Whitman, Walt. *The Complete Poetry & Prose*. New York: Library of America, 1980.

———. "Song of Myself." In *The Complete Poems*. Edited by Francis Murphy. New York: Penguin, 1975.

Wittreich, Joseph. *The Romantics on Milton: Formal Essays and Critical Asides*. Cleveland: Case Western Reserve UP, 1970.

Woodmansee, Martha. "On the Author Effect: Recovering Collectivity." In *The Construction of Authorship: Textual Appropriation in Law and Literature*. Edited by Martha Woodmansee and Peter Jaszi, 15–28. Durham, NC: Duke UP, 1994.

Woodmansee, Martha, and Peter Jaszi, eds. *The Construction of Authorship: Textual Appropriation in Law and Literature*. Durham, NC: Duke UP, 1994.

———. Introduction to *The Construction of Authorship: Textual Appropriation in Law and Literature*. Edited by Martha Woodmansee and Peter Jaszi, 1–13. Durham, NC: Duke UP, 1994.

Wordsworth, William. *Letters of William Wordsworth: A New Selection*. Edited by Alan G. Hill. Oxford: Oxford UP, 1984.

———. *Poetical Works of William Wordsworth*. Edited by Ernest de Selincourt and Helen Darbishire. Oxford: Clarendon, 1949–63.

Zukofsky, Louis. "A." Baltimore, MD: Johns Hopkins UP, 1978.

———. *Bottom: On Shakespeare*. Berkeley: U of California P, 1987.

———. *Complete Short Poetry*. Baltimore, MD: Johns Hopkins UP, 1991.

———. *Prepositions +: The Collected Critical Essays*. Foreword by Charles Bernstein. Additional prose edited by Mark Scroggins. Middletown, CT: Wesleyan UP, 2000.

CONTRIBUTOR'S NOTES

J. P. CRAIG is an assistant professor at Alabama State University. He holds a doctorate in contemporary North American poetry and poetics from the University of Iowa and an MFA in poetry from the University of Memphis.

SARAH E. EHLERS is a PhD candidate in English at the University of Michigan, specializing in modern and contemporary poetry and U.S. literary radicalism. Her dissertation is entitled "Critical Conditions: Politics and the Death of Twentieth-Century American Poetry." She has published in such journals as *Against the Current*, *Modern Language Quarterly*, and *Paideuma*.

GEORGE FRAGOPOULOS is assistant professor of English at Queensborough Community College, CUNY. His criticism, essays, and translations can be found online at *The Quarterly Conversation*, *Words without Borders*, and *The Critical Flame*. His translations of Manolis Anagnostakis's poetry are forthcoming from Fairleigh Dickinson Press.

STEPHEN FREDMAN is professor of English at the University of Notre Dame. He is the author of *Poet's Prose: The Crisis in American Verse* (1983, 1990), *The Grounding of American Poetry: Charles Olson and the Emersonian Tradition* (1993), *A Menorah for Athena: Charles Reznikoff and the Jewish Dilemmas of Objectivist Poetry* (2001), and *Contextual Practice: Assemblage and the Erotic in Postwar Poetry and Art* (2010). He has edited *A Concise Companion to Twentieth-Century American Poetry* (2005) and, with Steve McCaffery, *Form, Power, and Person in Robert Creeley's Life and Work* (2010).

ROSS HAIR is a lecturer in American studies at University of East Anglia and is the author of *Ronald Johnson's Modernist Collage Poetry* (Palgrave Macmillan, 2010) and coeditor of *Minting the Sun: A New Selection of Ted Walker's Poetry* (University of Chichester, 2010). He has also written on Lorine Niedecker, Jonathan Williams, Thomas A. Clark, and Ian Hamilton Finlay.

CATHERINE MARTIN completed a PhD at the University of Sussex on twentieth-century American poetry. Her research examines the relationship between memory and poetics, focusing in particular on the work of Ezra Pound, Robert Duncan, and Susan Howe. She has taught twentieth-century British, American, and Irish literature and literary theory at the University of Sussex and Royal Holloway, University of London.

PETER O'LEARY. Vocations to poetry and religion have committed Peter O'Leary to the pursuit of what Saint Bonaventure named an *itinerarium mentis in deum*, or the journey of the mind to God, with particular attention devoted to the mystagogical-initiatic and the mytho-poetical. *Luminous Epinoia*, published by the Cultural Society, is his most recent book. He lives in Berwyn, Illinois, and teaches at the School of the Art Institute of Chicago and for the Committee on Creative Writing at the University of Chicago.

CLÉMENT OUDART, a former Fulbright visiting scholar in the University at Buffalo's Poetry Collection (2005–6), received his PhD from the Université de la Sorbonne Nouvelle in Paris in 2009. His dissertation, "The Metamorphosis of Modernism from H.D. to Robert Duncan: Toward a Poetics of Relation," was awarded the university's Dissertation Prize (Prix de thèse) and was published in French by the Presses Sorbonne Nouvelle in 2010. He is currently an assistant professor at the Department of English of the University of Toulouse–Le Mirail, France.

SIOBHÁN SCARRY teaches modernism and twentieth-century American poetry at the University of Victoria, British Columbia. She is currently completing her PhD with SUNY Buffalo; her dissertation-in-progress explores the ways in which poetries from Whitman and Dickinson up through the mid-twentieth century have engaged with and re-envisioned notions of community. Scholarly work from this project is slated to appear in *Jacket 2* and *Sagetrieb*. Also a creative writer, Scarry has published work in *Greensboro Review*, *jubilat*, *Mid-American Review*, *New Letters*, *P-Queue*, *Sentence: A Journal of Prose Poetics*, and other journals.

JEFFREY TWITCHELL-WAAS currently lives in Malta, edits the Z-site on the works of Louis Zukofsky (www.z-site.net), and occasionally translates from contemporary Chinese poetry.

ANDY WEAVER has published or has forthcoming articles on John Cage, Fred Wah, Darren Wershler-Henry, and Steve McCaffery as well as articles on Robert Duncan. He teaches contemporary poetry and poetics at York University. He has also published several books of poetry, most recently *gangson* (NeWest, 2011).

INDEX

Abbé of Citeaux, xvii
Adorno, Theodor, 107–8, 120
Alcheringa, 161
Allen, Donald, 89, 153, 155
Alpert, Barry, 129, 131, 133–34, 141
American Poetry, 173
Antin, David, 158, 165
Apuleius, *The Golden Ass*, xvi
Aristotle, 82
The Artist's View, 130, 132
Auschwitz, 166

Bangladesh, 39
Barthes, Roland, 36
Baudelaire, Charles, xii, 45, 109, 112–13, 120, 164
Beach, Christopher, 6, 134, 194–96
Beethoven, Ludwig van, 146
Berkeley, 54
Bernstein, Charles, 186
Bernstein, Michael André, 45, 147
Bertholf, Robert J., 4, 7, 11, 18, 29
Birnbaum, Henry, 75–76
Black Mountain College, 189, 237
Black Mountain Poets, 151
Black Mountain Review, 68
Blackburn, Paul, 151, 165
Blake, William, 7, 18, 33–34, 45, 133, 195, 236–37
Blaser, Robin, 211
Bloom, Harold, 225, 227, 233
Bosch, Hieronymus, 136
Bowering, George, xi
Breton, André, 46, 59–64
Brothers Grimm, 245
Brown, Norman O., 156
Buber, Martin, 168
Burkholder, J. Peter, 134, 146
Butterick, George, 173, 179

Cage, John, 81, 189–207
Cahiers du sud, 61
Calas, Nicolas, 61
Celan, Paul, 118, 153–54
Chamberlain, John, 158
Clarkson, Austin, 200–1
Cocteau, Jean, 185
Coleridge, Samuel Taylor, xiv–xv
Colette, 109
Collis, Stephen, 205
Conner, Bruce, 158
Corman, Sid, 68
Cornell, Joseph, 158
Cosimo, Piero di, 136–39, 142
Creeley, Robert, xv, 68, 151, 165, 237

Dante, xvii, 18, 34, 164, 166, 237
Davenport, Guy, 133
Davidson, Michael, 16, 30, 46, 53, 59, 141, 176, 219

Deming, Richard, 224, 227
Derrida, Jacques, 109–10
Díaz, Ruy, 198
Dickinson, Emily, 237
Dimock, Wai Chee, 153, 167–68
DNA, xx
Duchamp, Marcel, 168
Duncan, Robert, "The Adventure of Whitman's Line," xv, xviii; "An African Elegy," 15; "After Reading *Barely and Widely*," 69–76; "Among My Friends Love Is a Great Sorrow," 13; "The Architecture, *Passages* 9," 204; "At the Loom, *Passages* 2," 195, 200; "The Ballad of the Enamored Mage," 244; "Before the Judgment, *Passages* 35," 200; *Bending the Bow*, 7, 32, 76–77, 97–100, 156, 160, 190, 192, 200, 222; *Caesar's Gate*, 212, 214–15; "The Collage, *Passages* 6," 200; 'The Currents," 99; "The Dance," 144–45; "Dante Études," 192, 204–5; "The Delirium of Meaning," 118–19; "The Dignities," 119; "A Drift," 121; "Entre les Deux," 117–18; "An Essay at War," 223–24; "Et," 114–16; "The Fire, *Passages* 13," 130, 133–42, 144, 146; "The First," 199–200; *Ground Work*, 37, 77, 80, 91, 100, 156, 164, 175, 192; *Ground Work: Before the War*, 16, 25–26, 35; *Ground Work: In the Dark*, 26, 35, 38, 108; *The H.D. Book*, xiv, xvi, 38, 64, 76, 94, 97, 113, 174, 216, 219, 225, 244; *Heavenly City, Earthly City*, 54; "The Homosexual in Society," 4–5; "In Perplexity," 55–59; "In Place of a Passage 22," 102; "In Waking," 108–9; "In Wonder," 119–21; "Jamais (*Passages*)," 79–84; "A Lammas Tiding," 222; *Letters, Poems 1953–1956*, 54, 238; "Man's Fulfillment in Order and Strife," 29, 216, 218, 236; "Moving the Moving Image, *Passages* 17," 134; "The Multiversity, *Passages* 21," 200; "My Mother Would Be a Falconress," 222–23, 245; "Night Scenes," 45–64; "Often I Am Permitted to Return to a Meadow," 98; *The Opening of the Field*, 69, 97, 134, 139, 144, 175, 192, 244; "Orders: Passages 24," xvii; "Pages of a Notebook," 96, 101, 231; *Passages*, xii, xviii, 16, 77–78, 91, 99–104, 117, 137–38, 156, 191–92, 195, 197, 221, 226, 240; "Passages 4 (Where It Appears)," 101; "Passages 28 (The Light)," 102; "Passages 31 (The Concert)," 103; "Passages 33 (Transmissions)," 103–4; "A Poem Beginning with a Line by Pindar," xv–xvi, 11, 173, 175, 178–83, 192; "Poetry, a Natural Thing," 192; "Returning to the Rhetoric of an Earlier Mode," 19; "Rites of Participation," 8, 151, 162; *Roots and Branches*, 19, 45, 48, 51, 76, 231, 233, 236; "The Self in Postmodern Poetry," 101; "A Seventeenth Century Suite," 25–28, 32–33, 35–41, 192, 195, 240; "A Song of the Structures of Rime Ringing as the Poet Paul Celan Sings," 154; "Spelling, *Passages* 15," 141; *Structure of Rime*, xii, 100, 112; "Structure of Rime I," 97–98; "To Master Baudelaire," 192; "Tribal Memories, *Passages* I," 191; *Tribunals*, 240; "The Truth and Life of Myth," xv, 17, 77; "Up Rising," 26, 31–33; "Variations

on Two Dicta of William Blake," 236; "Variations upon Phrases from Milton's *The Reason of Church Government*," 4, 9–12, 14–16; "Wind and Sea, Fire and Night," 135; *The Years as Catches*, xix, 3, 5, 7, 10, 13, 18–19; "The Years as Catches," 4, 14, 15, 18–19

Edwards, Chris, 120
Eliade, Mircea, 164
Eliot, T. S., xiv, xvii, 5–6, 10, 16, 67, 92, 132, 134, 197, 232, 243

Faas, Ekbert, 4, 60
Fabilli, Mary, 46, 53–59, 63–64
Ferguson, Priscilla, 60
Ferlinghetti, Lawrence, 153
Ficino, Marsilio, 136, 138–39, 142
Fink, Bruce, 111
Finkelstein, Norman, 26, 35–36, 146, 242–43
Finlay, Ian Hamilton, 238
Floating Bear, 48, 52
Ford, Charles Henry, 60–61
Fort Knox, 9–10
Foster, Ed, 211
Freud, Sigmund, 36, 70, 112–13, 116, 118, 161, 174–75, 177
Freudian, 119, 156, 162, 169
Friedrich, Caspar David, 179, 183
Frobenius, Leo, 217, 219–20

Gardner, Thomas, 204
Gassire's Lute, 217–20, 222–23
Gelpi, Albert, 29, 57
Genesis, 9, 120, 140
Goya, Francisco, *Cupid and Psyche*, xvi, 181, 183
Grabher, Gudrun M., 203
Gunn, Thom, 3, 47, 236

Hamilton, Jeff, 89–90
H.D., xv, 45, 73, 219–20, 232
Helgerson, Richard, 8, 15
Heraclitus, 7, 81–82, 135
Herbert, George, 26
Hermes Trismegistus, 134
Herms, George, 158
Hertz, David Michael, 134, 146
Higgins, Dick, 158
Hogg, Robert, xi
Howe, Susan, 173–87
Hyde, Lewis, 233–34

I Ching, 189
Indiana, Robert, 158
Ives, Charles, 133–34, 140, 142, 146–47
Izambard, Georges, 112

Jabès, Edmond, 110–12
Jaszi, Peter, xiv–xv, 129
Jenkins, G. Matthew, 41–42
Jess, 76, 158, 238, 244, 246
Johns, Jasper, 158
Johnson, Lyndon B., 31, 216–19
Johnson, Mark Andrew, 31, 137
Johnson, Ronald, 129–47, 234–49
Jonson, Ben, 26, 40
Joyce, James, 118, 168, 193–94, 196, 205–6
Julian, Emperor, 191

Kahn, Charles H., 135
Keenaghan, Eric, 4
Keller, Helen, xx
Kienholz, Edward, 158
Koerner, Joseph Leo, 183

Lacan, Jacques, 109, 111–12, 114, 116, 118, 121
Lawrence, D. H., 195
Leavis, F. R., 6
Levertov, Denise, 27–30, 56–57, 59, 215–16, 218–19, 223–24, 238–39
Lorca, Federico Garcia, 212
Lyotard, Jean-Francois, 121

Mabille, Pierre, 61
Mac Low, Jackson, 81, 158
Mackey, Nathaniel, 25–26, 33–35, 211–28, 232–33, 244
Mallarmé, Stéphane, xii, 80, 168
Mallorca, 68
Marcus, Greil, 159
Marcuse, Herbert, 156
Marisol, 158
Martin, John, 240
Marx, Karl, xviii–xix
Metaphysical Poetry, 16, 25–26, 164
Michelson, Peter, 26, 33–34
Milton, John, 3–20, 195, 237
Mirandola, Giovanni Pico della, 138
Mossin, Andrew, 98–99, 225
Motherwell, Robert, 158
Mozart, Wolfgang Amadeus, 19

Nancy, Jean-Luc, xviii, 27–28, 31, 34–35, 37, 41
Naylor, Paul, 212, 220–21
Nerval, Gérard de, 109
Nevelson, Louise, 158
The New American Poetry, 89, 155, 231
New Wilderness Letter, 161
New York, 46–47, 53–54, 57–58, 60–61, 64, 69, 153, 158–59, 167, 169, 237
Nicholls, Peter, 179, 183
Niedecker, Lorine, 76
Nierendorf Gallery, 61
Norris, John, 26

O'Driscoll, Michael J., 198–99
The Odyssey, 198
O'Leary, Peter, 130, 135, 220
Olson, Charles, xiii, 6, 68–71, 79, 141, 145, 151, 165, 167–68, 173–74, 176, 180, 195, 219–20, 236–37; "Projective Verse," 231, 239
Origin, 68
Osiris, 108
Oudart, Clément, 197
Owens, Rochelle, 158

Palmer, Michael, 120–21
Paris, 47, 59, 60, 62
Parnassus, 245
Passler, Jann, 193
Perse, Saint-John, 117
Pierce, Charles Sanders, 179
Plato, 9, 139, 151
Pletho, Georhios Gemistos, 138
Pound, Ezra, xiv, xvi, 5–7, 10, 25, 67, 75, 114–15, 117–18, 141, 152, 154–55, 165, 168, 175–76, 189, 193–96, 198, 205–6, 214–15, 219–20
Proclus, xvii, 136

Raleigh, Walter, 26, 37, 39
Rebaté, Jean-Michel, 114
Reich, Wilhelm, 156
Rexroth, Kenneth, 168
Riding, Laura, 89–96, 99–100, 103–5
Rilke, Rainer Maria, 107, 180, 186–87
Rimbaud, Arthur, 112–13
Roditi, Éduard, 61–62
Róheim, Géza, 162

Rothenberg, Diane, 152
Rothenberg, Jerome, 151–69
Rumi, 164
Russell, Sanders, 60

San Francisco, 68–69, 130, 153, 158, 211, 234, 238, 243, 246
Satie, Erik, 45
Scholem, Gershom, 154
Schultis, Christopher, 206
Scientific American, 246
Seitz, William, 158
Selinger, Eric Murphy, 133
Shakespeare, William, 18, 47, 62, 64, 83, 131; *The Tempest*, 46, 50–53
Simenon, Georges, 109
Sitting Bull, 168
Sitwell, Edith, 133
Smith, David, 158, 167
Smith, Harry, 158–59
Snyder, Gary, 165, 167
Southwell, Robert, 26–28
Stein, Gertrude, 54, 165, 168, 214
Steiner, George, 119
Stevens, Wallace, 195
Stickley, Gustave, 204
Swinburne, Algernon Charles, 180, 185–86

Taggart, John, 78–79, 84, 239
Tanguy, Yves, 60
Taylor, Thomas, 139
Thoreau, Henry David, 193, 203
Tolkien, J. R., 245
Trask, Michael, 58
Tyler, Hamilton, 5, 15, 19

Verlaine, Paul, 107, 176
Verne, Jules, 109
Vietnam War, xviii, 27–29, 31, 33–35, 215, 217, 220
View, 60–61
VORT, 129
Voss, Angela, 138

Whitman, Walt, xii, xv, xvi, 156, 165–66, 195, 212, 237, 240, 247
Williams, Jonathan, 68, 237–39, 242, 246
Williams, William Carlos, 83, 120, 133, 165
Woodmansee, Martha, xiii–xiv, 129
Wordsworth, William, xiv, 18

Zukofsky, Celia, 69, 83
Zukofsky, Louis, xv, 67–85, 154, 236

CONTEMPORARY NORTH AMERICAN POETRY SERIES

Industrial Poetics: Demo Tracks for a Mobile Culture
By Joe Amato

What Are Poets For? An Anthropology of Contemporary Poetry and Poetics
By Gerald L. Bruns

Reading Duncan Reading: Robert Duncan and the Poetics of Derivation
Edited by Stephen Collis and Graham Lyons

Postliterary America: From Bagel Shop Jazz to Micropoetries
By Maria Damon

Purple Passages: Pound, Eliot, Zukofsky, Olson, Creeley, and the Ends of Patriarchal Poetry
By Rachel Blau DuPlessis

On Mount Vision: Forms of the Sacred in Contemporary American Poetry
By Norman Finkelstein

Form, Power, and Person in Robert Creeley's Life and Work
Edited by Stephen Fredman and Steven McCaffery

Redstart: An Ecological Poetics
By Forrest Gander and John Kinsella

Jorie Graham: Essays on the Poetry
Edited by Thomas Gardner
University of Wisconsin Press, 2005

Gary Snyder and the Pacific Rim: Creating Countercultural Community
By Timothy Gray

Urban Pastoral: Natural Currents in the New York School
By Timothy Gray

Racial Things, Racial Forms: Objecthood in Avant-Garde Asian American Poetry
By Joseph Jonghyun Jeon

We Saw the Light: Conversations between the New American Cinema and Poetry
By Daniel Kane

History, Memory, and the Literary Left: Modern American Poetry, 1935–1968
By John Lowney

Paracritical Hinge: Essays, Talks, Notes, Interviews
By Nathaniel Mackey
University of Wisconsin Press, 2004

Behind the Lines: War Resistance Poetry on the American Homefront
By Philip Metres

Hold-Outs: The Los Angeles Poetry Renaissance, 1948–1992
By Bill Mohr

Frank O'Hara: The Poetics of Coterie
By Lytle Shaw

Renegade Poetics: Black Aesthetics and Formal Innovation in African American Poetry
By Evie Shockley

Radical Vernacular: Lorine Niedecker and the Poetics of Place
Edited by Elizabeth Willis